Ancient Mortuary Traditions of China

Ancient Mortuary Traditions of China

Papers on Chinese Ceramic Funerary Sculptures

George Kuwayama
Editor

Published by
Far Eastern Art Council
Los Angeles County Museum of Art

Distributed by
University of Hawaii Press

Published by the
Los Angeles County Museum of Art
5905 Wilshire Boulevard
Los Angeles, California 90036

Library of Congress Cataloging-in-Publication Data

Ancient Mortuary Traditions of China :
Papers on Chinese Ceramic Funerary Sculptures
George Kuwayama, editor.
p.   cm.
Includes bibliographical references.
ISBN 0-87587-157-7 (pbk.)
1. Ming ch'i—Congresses.
2. Funeral rites and ceremonies—China—History—Congresses.
I. Kuwayama, George.
II. Los Angeles County Museum of Art.
NK4165.A53 1991
732'.71'07479494—dc20

This symposium was held at the
Los Angeles County Museum of Art
on December 5 and 6, 1987,
in conjunction with the exhibition
The Quest for Eternity.

Cover: Warrior, China, Qin dynasty (221-207 B.C)
Painted earthenware, Ht. 183 cms.
Tomb of the First Emperor of Qin, Lintong,Shaanxi.

Table of Contents

Foreword

America's admiration for the cultural achievements of humankind's oldest continuous civilization has long been evident, and the Los Angeles County Museum of Art has been fortunate in being able to host several important exhibitions of Chinese art since its opening in 1965.

In 1987 the Overseas Archaeological Exhibition Corporation of the People's Republic of China and the Los Angeles County Museum of Art jointly organized a special exhibition of Chinese ceramic sculpture, *The Quest for Eternity*. One hundred and fifty-seven tomb sculptures excavated from funerary sites in China were exhibited. These works of art dating from the Neolithic period through the Ming dynasty provided a comprehensive view of Chinese funerary customs and the artistic development of Chinese ceramic sculpture over five thousand years.

An important educational component to this exhibition was a symposium held at the Los Angeles County Museum of Art to which leading scholars in the field of Chinese art, history, and archaeology were invited to participate. The papers were notably cogent, and in response to broad interest in the significant research presented at the conference, the papers are herewith being recorded in more permanent form.

This publication was made possible by the support provided by the museum's Far Eastern Art Council, and we take great pleasure in sharing current scholarship in this field with a wider audience.

Earl A. Powell III
Director
Los Angeles County Museum of Art

Acknowledgments

In recent years our perceptions of the art and culture of the ancient Chinese has changed radically with the revelations provided by the enormous number of archaeological discoveries. This is especially true of our understanding of Chinese funerary customs and of the ceramic sculptures interred in tombs.

In 1987 a comprehensive exhibition of Chinese funerary figures dating from the Neolithic period to the Ming dynasty was held at the Los Angeles County Museum of Art in collaboration with agencies of the Ministry of Culture, the People's Republic of China. The exhibition included sculptural works newly discovered from regions, periods, and in styles hitherto unknown to modern audiences. These archaeologically excavated objects of certain provenance provided an unusual opportunity to gain new insights into the art and culture of China.

To interpret the significance of these unique works of art a symposium was held at the Los Angeles County Museum of Art on December 5 and 6, 1987. Scholars addressed the issues that arose from the impact of recent archaeological excavations on existing classic texts and how these discoveries augment our knowledge about the life, customs, and material culture of ancient China. Other papers explored Chinese beliefs and practices concerning the world after death from an enhanced archaeological perspective.

I am particularly grateful to all those who have made this publication possible through subsidy or through the fruits of their labor, and I would like to thank Elly and Robert Nordskog, the Sammy Yu-kuan Lee Foundation, and the Far Eastern Art Council for their sponsorship. Many individuals, including museum staff members as well as specialists in the publishing industry, worked tirelessly to bring this volume to fruition, and I would like to express my gratitude to Jean Kissell, who assisted in this and other publications on Chinese art and archaeology. All production matters were efficiently coordinated by Joan Roche, and the readability of the papers was enhanced by the judicious editing of Chris Keledjian, while the handsome layout was designed by Michelle Gauthé. It was a pleasure to have the able and cheerful assistance provided through all phases of this project by Juliann Lanser and Rima Krisst of the Far Eastern Art Department.

George Kuwayama
Senior Curator
Far Eastern Art Department
Los Angeles County Museum of Art

The Quest for Eternity in Ancient China: The Dead, Their Gifts, Their Names

David N. Keightley

University of California, Berkeley

What does *The Quest for Eternity*, the title of the present exhibition, mean? "Eternity" is not a word that we use much in modern America. *Funk and Wagnalls* defines it as "Existence without beginning or end; endless duration." Given both our present scientific cosmography and the parlousness of our nuclear defense systems, such conceptions as "no beginning or end" and "endless duration" seem neither relevant nor realistic, but the questions I shall be asking here are the following: What did eternity mean to the ancient Chinese? Was there something particularly "Chinese" about the artistic expression of eternity in ancient China? Did the ancient Chinese conceive of eternity in terms of "endless duration"? Would they, like the English religious poet and mystic Henry Vaughn (1622-95), have envisaged eternity "like a great ring of pure and endless light"? Or would their conceptions have been radically different?

If we think about eternity, we will certainly think about death, about individual existence, and about what is likely to be preserved after death. That the Chinese have paid characteristic attention to the treatment of the dead further encourages us to seek the answers to my questions about eternity in China in the realm of ancient Chinese mortuary practice. And my search for the Chineseness of the answers also encourages me to start by looking at non-Chinese experience.

1. Eternity, Art, and the Individual

The classical scholar John Finley has referred to what he calls "the heroic mind" among the Archaic Greeks.

His account is worth quoting in full for the contrasting light it throws on Chinese expressions of eternity:

> When in the sixth book of the *Iliad* Hector briefly returns to Troy...and meets his wife and infant son at the gate and reaches out to take the boy in his arms, the child draws back frightened at his father's bronze armor and helmet with horsehair crest; whereupon Hector laughs, takes off the helmet, and lays it all-shining on the ground. In so deeply felt a scene surely no one but Homer would have paused to note that helmet still shining beside the human figures. It is as if in whatever circumstances it too keeps its particular being, which does not change because people are sad or happy but remains what it is, one of the innumerable fixed entities that comprise the world. Similarly in the heroic poems ships remain swift, bronze sharp, the sky starry, rivers eddying. Though heroes fight and die, everything in the outflung world keeps its fit and native character.[1]

I am attracted by this passage because of its reference to "innumerable fixed entities" (represented in Finley's example by Hector's shining helmet), entities that do not change in their nature to suit the emotions of the viewer. I shall not dwell on the matter here,[2] but I would suggest that there are no comparable scenes, no eternal "shining helmets," in early Chinese literature and in early Chinese art.

By this I mean two things. First, early Chinese art is more committed to the pathetic fallacy. Nature reflects and expresses man's hopes and fears. In the songs of the

Shijing, for example, where early Chinese lyricism is most prominent, trees, flowers, birds, islands, flowing waters, and so on are all pregnant with allegorical or symbolic meaning, usually moral. Second, early Chinese art tends to avoid the particular for the particular's sake. It is an art less concerned with vivifying details, such as "shining helmets," than with general meanings. It is an art more of concept than of percept.

This generalizing feature of early Chinese art is illustrated at every turn by the objects in this exhibition. If any of the objects portray a particular individual, we do not know who the individual was. Certainly many of the objects were made by particular individuals, but again, we do not know who the individual makers were. We have the art, but we do not have the artists. These were objects designated for some form of eternity—their presence in tombs encourages us to make that association—and it is therefore of interest to us that their concern was, as I have been suggesting for early Chinese art as a whole, with capturing the general rather than the particular. We have representations of what one might call "Bactrian camel-ness" (no. 51), or "hunter on horseback-ness" (no. 70), or "woman with loose chignon-ness" (no. 83), and so on, rather than of particular camels, hunters, or women. One "warrior with shield" looks much like another (no. 12). There are no Hectors here, no paintings or statues—such as we frequently have from classical Greece— that tell us the names of the figure represented and the name of the artist. Even the seven-thousand terra-cotta soldiers buried to guard the tomb of the first emperor of China, for all their seeming individualness (no. 7), appear to have involved a repertoire of standardized facial features such as moustaches and beards, used in various combinations.[3]

2. Eternity and Death

I would like to stress this lack of particularity, of individuality, even in conceptions of eternity. Heaven knows, "eternity" by its very nature may be generalized and nonindividual—Henry Vaughn certainly thought so—but to the extent that we associate eternity with death and with some form of postmortem existence and endurance, then it is no surprise to find that the early Chinese carried their love of the general, their lack of interest in particulars, into their representations of death itself. Indeed, for all the highly developed interest in ancestor worship and the care of the dead, it is a striking feature of early Chinese visual art that we have, to the best of my knowledge, no representations of death, no pictures of corpses or funeral rites; and we have no textual passages that begin to match the gory descriptions of mayhem that Homer, for example, provides. There is no early Chinese representation of death or dying to match the numerous mourners and mortal thrusts portrayed on Geometric and Archaic

Greek vases or to match the late sixth-century B.C. vase painting of Sarpedon's corpse, its wounds gushing blood.[4] Once again early Chinese art displays little interest in the particular details associated with the individual, with the body, with the material world.

I do not mean to imply by this that early Chinese culture was uninterested in details in general. I would suggest that in their search for eternity, as in their treatment of many other strategic areas of human activity, the early Chinese preferred to look for, emphasize, and record detail, not in their representations of the human figure, not in the soldiers, riders, and women whose generalized forms grace this exhibition, but in the minutiae of ritual activity. Ritual activity, to the extent that it is intended to be repeated, is by its nature generalized; we will once again find no shining helmets in our ritual texts. We will, however, find in those texts a passionate attention to dimension, quality, placement, orientation, sequential order, hierarchy, timing, and correct attitude that is surely one of the defining characteristics of early Chinese culture.

To quote one example, the section on "Laying Out the Materials for Dressing the Corpse," from the chapter "The Mourning Rites of an Officer (*Shih sang li*)," in the *Yili, The Book of Etiquette and Ceremonial*—probably a Warring States text that reflects an idealized vision of Spring and Autumn practice[5]—reads as follows:

> (a) The articles for the dressing of the corpse are laid out in the center of the east chamber, with the collars to the west, and graded from the south. They are not folded.
> (b) Cloth is used for the clean underclothing.
> (c) The pin with which the topknot is made up is of mulberry wood, four inches long, and tapered towards the center.
> (d) There is a cloth napkin, a cloth-breadth square, and not cut away in the center.
> (e) The throat-piece is of dark silk two feet broad and five long, and split at the ends.
> (f) For ear-plugs white floss silk is used.
> (g) For the eye-covering dark silk is used, one foot two inches square and lined with red, and with bands fitted to the corners.[6]

This minute account of stuffs and dimensions and sequences, which continues for a total of eighteen paragraphs, is followed by a series of equally detailed sections on "The Articles for the Bathing, Feeding, and Mouth-Filling" (five paragraphs), "The Washing of the corpse" (thirteen paragraphs), "Putting Food and Treasure Into the Mouth" (seven paragraphs), "The Putting on of the Grave-Clothes" (eight paragraphs), and so on. One clue to early Chinese conceptions of eternity must, I think, be found in this passionate concern with precisely ordered ritual acts, whose carefully defined details were repeated at death after death and structured according to the status of the deceased vis-à-vis the mourner,[7] so that the more noble received greater ritual attention than their inferiors, the more senior dead received greater respect than the recently dead. Nothing was as comforting to the early Chinese, nothing asserted so eloquently the triumph of life over death, of culture over dissolution, than the correct and enduring practice of the mortuary rituals. One begins to suspect that the Chinese conception of eternity was likely to be involved with repetitions of ritual practice.

I would note briefly that such a concern with ritual suggests two important conclusions about the nature of early Chinese culture in general. S. C. Humphrey's hypothesis that "societies in which power is personal and labile will show a more intense interaction between the living on the occasion of death...whereas those in which it is solidly anchored in corporate groups may focus their attention more on the care of the dead"[8] would seem to be supported by the Chinese case, where our textual evidence reveals an elite society that was certainly composed of corporate kin-based groups (on this point, see note 31). It will also be noted that elaborate funerary and mourning rituals are as likely to be a means for asserting status as they are for assuaging sorrow.[9] In the Chinese case, where the society laid great stress on hierarchical ritual distinctions for treating the living, as well as the dead, there can be little doubt that those who practiced the mortuary rites assiduously earned great status among the living by doing so.

3. Death in the Neolithic
3.1 Mortuary Ritual

The concern with ritual detail in mortuary context can be recognized in Neolithic burials from at least the third millennium B.C. The virtue of an object, its ability to qualify for some vision of eternal order, presumably depended, in part, on its particular material features, on its "shiningness." It also depended, however, on its function, the way in which it fitted into a context of well-ordered, precisely specified, ritual acts. One can see the genesis of such contextual ritual concerns in the care with which grave goods were placed in graves. Neolithic mourners appear to have drawn a distinction between the vessels they placed next to the corpse—which presumably had belonged to the deceased in life—and those they placed at a greater distance, as on the ledge above the corpse or outside the walls or lid of the burial chamber. One may take note, for example, of at least four fifth-millennium B.C. burials at Banpo in which an amphora was found in the earth fill a half meter or more above the grave chamber.

Unlike those amphoras, which were often standing upright, found in other graves, these four were on their side,[10] suggesting that they had been emptied in some last funeral rite, as the grave was being filled.

Equally eloquent testimony to the existence of mortuary rituals is found in the practice of collective secondary burial, which was well established in the Wei River valley as early as the first half of the fifth millennium B.C. At Yuanjunmiao, for example, 64 percent of all the people buried in the cemetery had been treated in this way.[11] Two points bear on our pursuit of eternity. First, it would seem that the bones that received secondary burial were less individualized, less personal, than the bones that received primary burial. I make this judgment on the basis of the number and distribution of grave goods. In the primary burials the goods tend to be more numerous and to be placed by particular skeletons. In the secondary burials the goods are far fewer on a per-skeleton basis, and they appear to be associated with the group, rather than with any one particular set of bones in the group. Since secondary burial is generally thought to be a rite that confirms somebody has truly died, it is interesting to observe that true death, the true passage to eternity, appears to have involved, in Neolithic China, a relinquishing of personal possessions in favor of a more collective ownership of whatever goods were placed in the grave. The treatment of death, as we have earlier observed, involved generalization.

Second, these reconstituted skeletons, laid out in the supine-extended position, provide an eloquent commentary on how one's body, at least, was to be preserved for eternity. The goal was to imitate life, the skeleton having first been ritually disarticulated, cleaned up, and reconstituted, in order to do so. Life and the *hun* (spirit-soul) might have fled the bones, but good order was still required.

By the third millennium B.C. the large number of *dou* (pedestals), tall-stemmed *bei* (goblets), or *hu* and *ping* (vases) placed on the second-level ledges of some Eastern tombs suggest the remains of a funeral banquet.[12] In the two late-period burials, M10 and M25, at Dawenkou, for example, only two *bei* (goblets) lay next to the corpse in each case, whereas eight and twenty goblets respectively lay on the ledge or outside the coffin or burial chamber.[13]

It is plausible to assume that the tall-stemmed goblets, which were characteristic East Coast vessels, may have been associated in these mortuary rituals with the disorder of intoxication, as a means of assuaging grief, perhaps, and also as a symbolic expression of vitality and disorder to counter the sterility and order of death.[14] The burial freezes in time that moment of ritualized disorder, partially revealing to us, across a span of some five thousand years, how Neolithic Chinese dispatched their dead on the voyage to eternity.

3.2 Mortuary Jades

One can see the concern with both order and eternity

in the extraordinary ritual activity associated with mortuary jades. Jade is the most obdurate of materials; its "sublime impracticality," as somebody has termed it, requires remarkable patience and pertinacity to saw, drill, and grind it. The perforation of stone tools—axes and knives in particular—with one or more holes was a characteristic technological trait of numerous Eastern and Eastern-derived cultures of the Chinese Neolithic.[15] That many of the most elegantly perforated axes are particularly finely polished, are frequently of jade, show no traces of use, and appear to be associated with high-status burials suggests that the drilling of these perforations, one of the most demanding skills known to the Neolithic, converted these objects into symbols of cultural achievement and status, representing both the craftsman's perseverance and the owner's ability to enjoy the labor of others.

These considerations, in addition to the beauty, rarity, and endurance of the material, help explain the value attached to the jade *bi* (disks) and *cong* (tubes) of the Eastern cultures of the Chinese Neolithic. Found only in burial areas, they appear to have been specifically religious, mortuary objects.[16] This strongly suggests that the most demanding, as well as the most enduring, of all Neolithic objects to manufacture were made for the dead! This is not to deny that pot fragments have endured as well as jades, but, given the physical hardness of jade, it would have been clear to the inhabitants of the Chinese Neolithic that, whereas pots could break and lose their forms, jade objects were likely to endure in their original shape. Pots were made for daily use, and their burial—frequently with their soot markings and other signs of wear and tear—seems to have expressed the belief that postmortem existence was a continuation of premortem existence. The jade disks and tubes, by contrast, were not apparently used in daily life. They served to mark the very different condition and expectations of the ritually dead.

The ritual significance of these jades is strikingly illustrated by the Liangzhu stratum tomb M3 at Sidun in Jiangsu (circa 2500 B.C.). This was the burial of a male who was about twenty years old, in which 57 of the approximately 120 grave goods were jade *bi* and *cong*. A reconstruction of the funeral rites provides an unusually vivid sense of what happened in one Lower Yangzi burial some 4,500 years ago. First, the mourners placed over ten jade *bi* on the ground, together with at least three perforated axes; these were then burnt in a fairly intense conflagration.[17] As the fire was about to go out, the corpse was placed on top of these jades. The mourners then carefully surrounded the deceased with jade *cong*: four were placed below the feet, twenty-seven were placed around the dead man, and one was placed squarely in front of his face. In addition, one sand-tempered red-ware *gui* (basin) was placed at his head, and a *hu* (vase), a high-footed *dou* (serving stand), and a *pan* (dish) were placed beyond his feet. The mourners positioned most of the fourteen jade and stone tools at the right side and by the left arm of the dead man, with one perforated ax being placed under his head; only two adzes were placed under his legs. At the end, the mourners laid the two finest jade *bi* over the chest and abdomen of the deceased and covered the entire assemblage with earth.[18]

It is not easy to determine the function (or functions) of all these jades. The later Chinese belief that jades buried with a corpse prevented physical decay[19] may have already been present in Neolithic times, for certain jade objects, such as arrow-shaped and disk-shaped *han*, were occasionally placed in a corpse's mouth.[20] Here, at least, would be one possible association between eternity, represented by physical continuity, and jade. Whether the round *bi* disk symbolized the heavens and the squared *cong* the earth— as these objects were to do in later times—is uncertain.[21] One can, however, hazard some speculations. The richness of Neolithic symbolism is at least suggested by Elizabeth Lyons's comments about the value of jade in later Chinese culture:

> Both the visual beauty of jade and the spiritual quality of virtue it was once believed to possess are reflected in the language. *Yü li*, standing like jade, i.e., pure, chaste, handsome, would probably be familiar to the ancestors of Western culture as *klos kai agathos*, good and beautiful. Or, a man whom we describe as having a heart of gold, would have a jade heart in China. Poetry's golden boys and girls are Chinese, beautiful, talented youths, and they may become adults with lofty and pure aims, said to have bones of jade.[22]

For the situation in the Neolithic I would suggest, first, that the perimeter of jade *cong* around the corpse, many of them decorated with protomonster-mask decorations at their four corners, played some kind of apotropaic function. Second, the fact that this perimeter was made with jade suggests that its defensive strength depended upon some quality in the material itself, as well as in the unique *cong* shape. Third, the hardness of jade suggests that this defense was meant to last, if not for eternity, then certainly for a long time. Fourth, the fact that many of the jades were burnt and that some were broken and buried in separate areas of the burial indicates that some ritual activity may have involved the destruction of the symbols of eternity themselves, perhaps as a symbolic representation of entering the new world of death, where what had been "killed" endured.[23] Fifth, one wonders if the *bi* disk was not in some way kindred to Vaughn's "ring of endless light." Its circularity and its generally smooth surface, unmarked by the mask faces that were placed on the *cong*, do suggest a different symbolic function for these disks. The use of *bi* made of glass paste, stone, and wood in Eastern Zhou and Han tombs, suggests that, at least in later times, the value of these disks lay in their shape more than in their material.[24]

Whatever the true symbolic values of these objects may have been, the Neolithic Chinese were right to put their hopes for some enduring mark of their existence and beliefs into jade. For in numerous cases of Neolithic burials, such as M5 itself at Sidun, the bones of the deceased have virtually disappeared with the ravages of time. It is the jades that remain to tell us of those who lived so long ago. The Neolithic quest for eternity, whose true nature we can glimpse most dimly, has had some not inconsiderable success.

4. Death in the Bronze Age

With the discovery of bronze casting the inhabitants of China in the second millennium B.C. had a new material with which to conduct their quest for eternity. The present exhibition, being focused on ceramics, contains no mortuary or any other Shang or Zhou bronzes; we cannot, however, ignore them in our attempt to understand early Chinese mortuary practice. As one would expect on the basis of what I have said so far, bronze was primarily devoted to the manufacture of ritual objects, and those objects were marked by a passionate concern with hierarchical, ordered, abstract, nonnaturalistic design. In the Shang dynasty, numerous bronzes were placed as grave goods in elite tombs. Like the jades before them, the bronzes have generally endured well. I have heard an archaeologist at Anyang assert that the chemistry of the buried bronzes assisted the corruption of the human bones, with the ironic result that the skeletons of nonelites, buried without or at a distance from bronze vessels, have often been better preserved than those of the elites. The bronzes and the bones of the lowly sacrificial victims buried without benefit of bronzes survived. Once again the symbolic, ritual object has outlasted its individual owner.

I want to turn next, however, to another aspect of the quest, that is, to what I am beginning to think of as less a quest for eternity and more a quest for eternal recognition, with the understanding that such recognition had to have a significant ritual component. The jades and other objects placed in Neolithic burials, no matter how significantly they may have identified their owners in their lives, rarely present, at least to the modern eye, surfaces that carry individual iconographic messages. They were by their very nature impersonal objects whose magico-religious powers may have resided in their very impersonality. The Shang bronzes, however, once inscriptions started to be cast into them by about 1200 B.C., provide us with far more specific information.

4.1 Shang Bronzes, Temple Names, and the Day of the Dead

It is well known that some late Shang and early Zhou ancestors were given temple names, such as "Father Jia" and "Grandmother Keng," and that these temple names employed the same "heavenly stems" (*tian gan*) given to the ten days of the Shang week, jia, yi, bing, ding, and so forth. Further, we know that Father (Mother, Grandfather, or Grandmother) Jia received cult on a jia day, the first day of the week, Father Yi on an yi day, the second day of the week, and so on. There were ten *gan* stems available for naming ancestors, just as there were ten days to the Shang week.

These temple names are of interest to scholars of Chinese mortuary practice because they were frequently cast into the sacrificial vessels used in the ancestral cult. The inscription on a late Shang *jue*, for example, ends with the phrase "Made this vessel for his accomplished Father Yi."[25] I assume that even in the case of the shortest inscriptions, which may consist of only two words, like "Father Ji,"[26] the full but unrecorded message was "This is a vessel that I, the maker, made for my late Father [or Mother, Grandfather, etc.], whose temple name is Ji and who is to receive cult, on ji days, in this vessel."

This is all clear enough. A problem arises, however, when we try to understand why vessels inscribed in this way were buried in graves and what the connection was between the grave occupant and the inscriptions on the vessels. Tomb M5, for example, which was excavated at Anyang in 1976, contained 210 ritual vessels, 190 of which were inscribed.[27] Some 90 of the bronze objects bore the inscription "Fu Hao"; this was the name, well documented in the oracle-bone inscriptions, of a consort of the Shang king Wu Ding (circa 1200-1181 B.C.). It is generally agreed that the burial, which contained at least 16 human victims, was that of Fu Hao herself, whose bones, be it noted, surrounded with bronzes and other grave goods, had rotted away.

What, however, are we to make of the 7 out of the 190 inscribed vessels in the Fu Hao tomb that bore temple names? The title Si Tu Mu Gui (Queen Tu Mother Gui) had been cast into two large, square *zun*; the title Si Mu Xin (Queen Mother Xin) had been cast into five other bronzes. The most popular theory is that "Mother Xin" was the temple name of Fu Hao herself. This seems plausible at first glance, for there were more Mother Xin than Mother Gui vessels in the grave. Nevertheless it is puzzling to find that two Mother Gui vessels were also present. If Fu Hao was Mother Xin, who was Mother Gui and why were her bronzes also buried with Fu Hao?

The anomaly disappears if we accept the view that no member of the Shang elite knew, when alive, what his or her temple name was going to be when dead. I believe, on the basis of the oracle-bone inscriptions, that the stem of the day of cult, and thus the temple name, was chosen by divination after death. If this is true, it follows that Fu Hao, when alive, could not have known that she would be named Mother Xin (or Gui or any other stem). I suspect that the Mother Xin (and Mother Gui) vessels were in Fu Hao's tomb not because her temple name was Xin—in fact, it probably was not—but because she had used the vessels in her lifetime to worship some other Mother Xin (or Gui). The vessels would have belonged, like the stem names themselves, to the dead not to the living.

I believe that all late Shang bronze vessels bearing temple names and buried in graves generally shared this similar role. They had been used during the deceased's lifetime for the worship of his or her ancestors or ancestresses, whose names were cast into the vessels. The bronzes then, like the human victims, accompanied the deceased in death, presumably to identify the status of the deceased and to exemplify the belief, discernible in grave goods since at least the Neolithic, that premortem roles and activities survived into the postmortem period.

What this means in terms of the quest for eternity is that the elites of late Shang China were buried with the bronzes they had used in their lifetimes. Some of those bronzes carried their secular names while alive, such as Fu Hao, which served to identify the deceased as the owner and user of the vessels. This form of status assertion was obviously important. Objects inscribed with Fu Hao in M5 constituted nearly 50 percent of all inscribed objects in the tomb. It is clear that the deceased was also identified by the ritual vessels that belonged to his or her ancestors and ancestresses. M5, in this view, was the tomb not just of any Fu Hao but of the Fu Hao who had worshiped Mothers Xin and Mother Gui. Fu Hao's ritual activities were thought to be an enduring part of her identity. And in burying the bronzes in this way, the Shang also continued to commemorate, in this underground world of the dead, the Mother Xin and Gui.

To return to the question I raised at the start of this paper. What kind of commemoration was this? What can these temple names tell us about Shang Chinese conceptions of eternity?

It is evident that the names commemorated an association with particular days of the week, which were in turn associated with the ten suns of Shang legend, so that there were ten different suns for the ten different days of the week, a sun for the jia day, a sun for the yi day, a sun for the bing day, and so on. Indeed there seems to have been a totemic association between the jia, yi, and bing suns, and so on, and the Jia, Yi, and Bing ancestors worshiped on the days of those particular suns.[28] Furthermore my research indicates that not all days were equal. A study of approximately one hundred divinations about lucky days as forecast in the reign of Wu Ding indicates that there was a striking preference for *geng* day events, which were regarded as auspicious 95 percent of the time (Table 1). Yi, ding, and jia days were also regarded as more favorable than unfavorable; bing, ji, and gui days were more unlucky than lucky. Lucky days and king names were, in fact, related, for the distribution of lucky days does not differ greatly from the distribution of the *gan* names of the Shang kings (Tables 2 and 3). The match is not perfect, but both distributions show a preference for jia and ding (and a dislike for bing, wu, ji, ren, and gui) both as lucky days and as king names. Jia, ding, yi, and geng, in fact, were among the most popular four *gan* for both king names and lucky days.

Conceptions of eternity, which we in the West tend to associate with timelessness or being out of time, in Shang China thus appear to have been associated with the presumably unending round of the ten-day weekly cycle. The extent to which the Shang experience was similar to or differed from that of other cultures, like that of the ancient Egyptians, that also organized their religious life around the days of the week, requires more research. The importance of Sunday—the first day of the week, the "day of the sun"—in the history of Christendom suggests that the Shang ritualists were far from unique. The ten-day week, rather than the sixty-day *ganzhi* cycle, or the lunar months, may be seen as the fundamental unit of Shang time. As has been written of our own culture:

> Imagine for a moment that the week suddenly disappeared. What a havoc would be created in our time organization, in our behavior, in the co-ordination and synchronization of collective activities and social life, and especially in our time apprehension....We think in week units; we co-ordinate our behavior according to the "week"; we live and feel and plan and wish in "week" terms. It is one of the most important points of our "orientation" in time and social reality.[29]

When we consider that the Shang named their ancestors by the days of the week and sacrificed to them on their name days in order to maintain the flow of ancestral blessings, we gain some sense of how fundamental the question of lucky days and their ritual ordering must be to any understanding of Shang kingship, Shang culture, and Shang conceptions of eternity.

Once again, furthermore, we notice that humans were remembered and commemorated in terms of general, ordered structures rather than particular, individual characteristics. The world of ancestor worship, the world of the temple names by which the ancestors were to be long remembered, was not the world of shining helmets. It was a world of suns, each shining in the sky for one day out of ten but individualized only by its position in the weekly cycle and eternally recurring. It was a world, once again, of general order and concept, not of specific detail and percept.

4.2 The Evolution of Mortuary Ritual in Zhou

When we turn from the Shang to the Zhou we find that there were significant changes in the ways the dead were commemorated and the ways that eternity itself was pursued.

4.2.1 The Evolution of the Temple Names

There were, for example, some significant changes in the temple names that were preferred. A count of ancestral *gan* names in 1,295 (some Shang, but presumably mainly Western Zhou) bronze inscriptions yields the rank order shown in Table 4. Three conclusions stand out. First, five *gan* names—yi, ding, xin, gui, and ji—were far more popular than the other five—wu, geng, jia, bing, and ren; as K. C. Chang has noted, they represent 86 percent of the total corpus.[30] Second, as Chang has also noted, these five were all even names; that is, in day terms they were, in order of popularity, days 2, 4, 8, 10, and 6. Third, whereas the popular Shang king names and lucky days ding and yi (both even) maintained their popularity, jia and geng (both odd), which had been so prominent in Shang lucky days and king names (Tables 1 and 2), had by Zhou times been replaced by ji and gui, two *gan* (both even) that had played only a minor role under Wu Ding. (The comparative rankings are provided, for convenience, in Table 5.) This striking preference for even days implies that ancestral sacrifices were generally being performed every other day. Even more than in Shang times, therefore, we see that ancestors existed, as it were, on schedule; they were defined so as to suit the needs of the ritualists rather than to express their own particularity.

4.3 The Function of the Bronzes

Turning to a second change, it is well known that the function of the bronzes dedicated to the ancestral dead appears to have changed with the advent of the Zhou. Unlike the Shang, the Zhou elites tended not to bury their ritual with the dead but to keep on using them above ground. Many bronze inscriptions, which were far longer in Zhou than they had ever been in Shang, end with the incantation "May sons of sons, grandsons of grandsons, forever treasure and use this vessel." The ritual vessels were no longer to be buried with the sacrificer; they were to be passed on to his posterity for use in this life. The inscription on the *Shi Qiang Pan*, for instance, records in more than 280 characters the names and attributes of the first six Zhou kings, together with the official posts of the members of the Wei lineage who served them.[31] The vessel,

which ends with the phrase "May [this vessel] be forever treasured and used for a myriad of generations" (*qi wan nian yong bao yong*) was not found in a grave, but in a horde of 103 bronzes, 74 of which were inscribed, with 55 of those belonging to the Wei lineage itself. The bronzes had apparently been buried in the ground to avoid their loss as the lineage was driven from its homeland in Fufeng county in the Wei River valley.[32] Eternity in such inscriptions was increasingly conceived in terms of the "myriad generations" of the living lineage rather than in terms of the dead underground. It was the lineage that was to be preserved; and the commemoration of the dead ancestors, as the vessel continued to be "forever treasured and used by sons of sons and grandsons of grandsons," was to be the symbolic indicator of eternal existence. This concern with biological perpetuation became so developed that, by the fourth century B.C., the philosopher Mencius (circa 372-289 B.C.) could declare that the greatest act of unfiliality was to have no posterity.[33] The greatest act of filiality, in short, was to become an ancestor one's self, thus maintaining the eternal existence of the family. Individual death—never, as we have seen, a subject for detailed artistic scrutiny—was to be conquered by an emphasis on the immortality of the social unit.

4.3.1 Longevity and Immortality

Turning to a third change between Shang and Zhou, there was, as Yü Ying-shih has shown, an increasing interest throughout the Zhou in personal longevity and, eventually, in personal immortality. The blessing most desired in Zhou bronze inscriptions was *shou*, long life. From the eighth century on, one finds references to "retarding old age" (*nan lao*) and to "no death" (*wu si*). And a longevity cult, that had originally been concerned with the prolongation of physical life, came to coexist with and in part be replaced by new conceptions of an otherworldly immortality that was to be achieved by philosophic discipline and by the ingestion of various drugs and elixirs. This ethereal conception of immortality was in turn to be challenged or even accompanied by, increasingly material conceptions of secular life prolonged indefinitely.[34] The first emperor of Qin, Qin Shi Huang Di, who died in 210 B.C., was by no means the only ruler of this time to indulge in extravagant expeditions to reach the Isles of the Blessed Immortals and obtain longevity elixirs. At the same time, he decreed that his dynastic successors should abolish the use of posthumous names. He was simply to be the first emperor (*Shi Huang Di*) and his successors were to be known as emperors of the second generation, the third generation, and so on, "for a thousand myriad generations (*qian wan shi*), passing the dynasty on without end (*chuan zhi wu qiong*)."[35] This piling of numbers on numbers—"one thousand myriad" generations—is perhaps the most explicit expression of eternity we are likely to encounter in early Chinese texts. It was a wish that had its roots at least as far back as the bronze inscriptions of Western Zhou. And it is a wish that has continued to exert its magic even in the communist society of the twentieth century, where millions of banners across China proclaimed in the 1970s the hope that Chairman Mao and his thought would last for "a myriad years" (*wan sui*, the Japanese *banzai*). It is mildly ironic that the great revolutionary was to be commemorated by the use of such a traditional formula.[36]

5. Death as Continuity

The secular quality of many of the grave goods found in the present exhibition surely reflects this hopefulness that postmortem existence would be a continuation of premortem existence. Such optimism had been present, indeed, since the Neolithic, as we can tell from the large numbers of the utensils of daily life, marked with traces of use, that were buried as grave goods with the dead. It had continued to exist in Shang times, as seen in the burial of ritual bronzes that the deceased had used in his or her life. What we witness in the changes I have described seems to have been concerned less with a belief in the continuity of the kinship unit and more with differing emphases in the way the quality of postmortem existence and the nature of the individual himself was conceived.

This is a complicated matter, with many interrelated strands. Speaking very generally, there seems to have been a shift, in the period of the Shang-Zhou transition, from burying ritual utensils with the dead to preserving them for the living, who continued to employ them in the commemoration and worship of their ancestors. This shift suggests that greater skepticism may have developed about the needs and efficacy of the dead. It may have been felt that the living could do more good by continuing the sacrifices to ancestors than the dead could do in their postmortem existence. Furthermore by the Eastern Zhou and Han there was increasing emphasis on the continuation of the nonreligious, nonritual aspects of life. Both of these trends presumably reflected the increasing humanism of Zhou culture in general, evidenced in the reduced role of human sacrifice, the moralized political doctrine of the Mandate of Heaven, and the general humanism of Eastern Zhou philosophical concerns. Unlike the Shang elites, who had been buried with their ritual vessels, the objects that had presumably given meaning and joy to their lives, Eastern Zhou elites might be buried with their orchestras and musicians. The ruler of the small state of Zeng, for example, who died in 433 B.C., was buried in a tomb that resembled a feasting hall, with a complete orchestra of sixty-five chiming bells hung on their frames and attended by twenty-one musicians who had presumably been buried alive. The eleven tons of bronze objects that, it has been estimated, he took with him into the ground also included more than forty-five hundred bronze weapons.[37] Clearly he conceived of his privileged status as continuing beyond death, and he conceived it less in terms of the performance of rituals to his ancestors—which did not, so far as I know, require the music of sixty-five bells—and more in terms of his own secular activities and enjoyments.

Since we cannot tell the proportion of available wealth given to the dead in either the Neolithic or the Bronze Age, there is, in fact, no way to quantify the precise nature of these shifts with certainty. But in general terms we can conclude that early Chinese culture was consistent, over the millennia, in devoting significant quantities of wealth to the care and commemoration of the dead. The pots in Neolithic graves in Gansu from the end of the third millennium B.C., the 468 bronze objects weighing more than one-and-a-half tons found in the unrifled tomb of Fu Hao from around 1180 B.C., the eleven tons of bronze objects found in the Lord of Zeng's tomb of 433 B.C., and the seven-thousand-man terra-cotta army that guarded the tomb of the first emperor, who died in 210 B.C.—a tomb, incidentally, whose treasures have not yet been excavated—all indicate the degree to which the provisioning of dead kin and of dead rulers—whose political power derived to a significant extent from their fatherlike, familial role in the polity—was one of the central values of early Chinese civilization. The quest for religious endurance was intimately bound up with the political culture as a whole.

6. The Quest for Endurance: Limited and Human

What then was the nature of eternity in early China? Eternity—as Henry Vaughn, who "saw it the other night," reminds us—is very much in the eye of the beholder. The Chinese who made, who paid for, and who buried so many of the objects about which I have spoken, and which appear, several millennia later, in the current exhibition, hardly expected that they were making their objects for this kind of preservation, this kind of museumification. This was not the eternity they had in mind, and we should not attribute it to them.

The term *yong*, which Western scholars have generally translated as "long, constant, eternal," did appear in some early texts, including, as we have seen, the bronze inscriptions of Western Zhou. Apart from these prayers for genealogical endurance, the early texts reveal little if any interest in such questions as origins and ends and the nature of time. The nature of my present inquiry, in fact, led me to return to the passages in the *Shi jing, Shang shu,* and other early texts, and I now believe, for three reasons, that to translate *yong* as "perpetual" or "eternal" is unjustified. First, the root meaning of the word is certainly related to "length," particularly the length of a river or a drawing out, as in singing, but nothing in the etymology of the word or its early dictionary and commentary definitions implies "length *without end*."[38] Second, the early contexts in which the term appears justify only the meaning of "long enduring." Even though the inscriptions speak vaguely of "a myriad generations" and of "a myriad years without end" I believe that my previous translation of the bronze-inscription prayer *zizi sunsun yong bao yong* as "May sons of sons, grandsons of grandsons, forever treasure and use this vessel" might better be rendered by the more prosaic but more accurate "treasure and use this vessel for a long time." Similarly the closing prayer in the *Shi Qiang Pan* inscription should read, "May (this vessel) be long treasured and used for a myriad generations." Third, I am struck by the fact that the one passage in the *Shang shu* that does require an "eternal" translation—*yong shi wu qiong*, literally "long generations without exhaustion," but which Legge in fine Christian style translates, not inaccurately but influenced I suspect by the King James Version of the Lord's prayer as "for ever and ever without end"— comes from a late and spurious section of the work.[39] I believe, in short, that in every pre-Han use of *yong* in which duration of time is involved, "long, very long, extended" is more accurate than words like "eternal" and "forever."[40]

I would suggest, in fact, that early Chinese conceptions of eternity were quite different from our own, which, at least in the Christian view have involved conceptions of eternal salvation and damnation and, not unsurprisingly, conceptions of the particularity of the individual soul that were quite at variance with those current in ancient China. The Chinese concern was generally with the lineage and with preserving the memory of the ancestors. We cannot tell how long this concern for remembering the dead was maintained in the Neolithic. It is of some significance, perhaps, that burials found in Neolithic cemeteries generally do not intrude on earlier burials, which suggests that the living preserved some memory of precisely where they had buried the dead. Nevertheless the lack of mounds or other ritual structures above the early graves suggests that the commemoration of the dead was not, in general, to last more than one or two generations. The oracle-bone inscriptions reveal clearly that the late Shang kings commemorated (or claimed to commemorate), in their systematic cycle of ancestral rituals, at least 17 generations of previous rulers, stretching back some 340 years. One assumes that the Zhou kings and the great rulers of the independent states were able to do the same for their own royal lineages.

These long-lived ritual remembrances of the ancient dead, however, may well have been the exception. The general rule by the late Zhou and the Han dynasties, as we see it expressed in the ideal mourning regulations, seems to have been that, with the exception of founding ances-

tors of dynasties or lineages, the dead were only remembered for five generations and were then dropped from the ancestral cult.[41] This suggests that the cult of the dead, for all the human effort, both emotional and material, that it consumed was not prolonged inhumanly. Already in the oracle-bone inscriptions one can see a differentiation between the more recently dead, who were hostile, and the older, more senior dead, who were more benevolent.[42] The retrospective cult of the ancestors, in short, with the possible exception of certain royal and ducal lineages whose endurance presumably had great political significance, was not conceived in terms of eternity. It was not even conceived in terms of hundreds of generations. It was structured to take care of natural forgetfulness, to accord with the very human inability to remember those ancestors whom one, or one's parents, had never known. Conceptions of eternity were focused on an open-ended, generalized, biological future, not on the past.[43]

By the time of the Han Dynasty, if not earlier, we find stipulated in the *Li ji* (The record of rituals), in the "Da zhuan" (Great treatise) chapter that laid down the rules for ancestor worship and kin relations, that only the founder of a new branch of a great family was honored with an ancestral tablet that was not removed from the main hall of the ancestral temple "for a hundred generations" (*bai shi bu qian zhi zong*); the tablets of less notable ancestors were shifted, over a period of five generations, from one ancestral hall to another and were then removed from the temple entirely.[44] Conceptions of endurance— and I am now going to give up my quest for eternity— were familial and biological. It is true that we are poorly informed about the degree to which such ritual regulations were observed, even by the Zhou and Han elites for whom they were intended.[45] The very fact that the rules were referred to in a variety of Han texts, however, suggests the degree to which mortuary rituals were a matter of central concern to the theologians and philosophers—the early Chinese equivalent of social scientists, in short—at this time. Good social order was thought to depend on good ritual order, and good ritual order was expressed in terms of one's relations to living and to dead kin over a finite period of time.

I would like to conclude with two final observations. First, I have stressed the great value that the early Chinese laid on ritual procedure, in the placing of the vessels in Neolithic burials, in the scheduling of ancestral sacrifices on certain days of the Shang week, in the highly detailed prescriptions for ritual order found in the *Yi li*. To fully understand the role of many of the objects in this exhibition and indeed in most museums around the world, we would need to know more than we frequently do about the context in which they were found. Where were they placed in the grave? In what sequence? Next to what other objects? What did they contain? The context can tell us as much about their function as their material nature can. If we lack that context, we lack important information in our own quest for the ancient Chinese.

Second, the quest for endurance, as we see it in this exhibition, was increasingly a humanistic quest with its roots in the living, a quest that paid great ritual respect to the dead but did so less with ritual vessels buried with the dead and more with a wonderful variety of lifelike statues of persons and animals that may have incarnated the optimistic hope that you can in some sense "take it with you." The quest for endurance kept its main focus on the immediate family unit with a retrospective embrace no more than five generations deep, as it moved through history, watched over by the close ancestors and producing the sons who would in turn commemorate for a time, but not for eternity, the fathers who gave them birth. There was in this view no "great ring of endless light." There was, rather, something more like a spotlight, highlighting the five-generation unit, but continually moving on with the passage of time.

It is the virtue of exhibitions such as this one that they can expand the scope of that spotlight to cover millennia. The quest for eternity, it would seem, is indeed best conducted in modern museums. The early Chinese were too busy staying alive, being alive, and celebrating the life of the kinship unit to give the matter their fuller philosophic and religious attention. Who can say, given the wonderful objects presented in the exhibition before us and given the extraordinary endurance of Chinese culture itself, that their optimism was not justified?

Table 1: Lucky and Unlucky Days in the Reign of Wu Ding: All Topics				
Gan (day)	regarded as auspicious or lucky	regarded as inauspicious or unlucky	total no. of days regarded as lucky or unlucky and percent of total	favorable/ unfavorable ratio
jia	14	6	20	18%	2.3:1
yi	6	2	8	7	3:1
bing	5	10	15	14	0.5:1
ding	11	3	14	13	3.7:1
wu	5	3	8	7	1.67:1
ji	0	3	3	3	0:3
geng	20	1	21	19	20:1
xin	7	5	12	11	1.4:1
ren	4	3	7	6	1.3:1
gui	1	2	3	3	0.5:1
Totals	73	38	111		

For days regarded as auspicious or lucky: N = 73. Expected frequency for each *gan* day = 7.3. Threshold measure = 15.51. Chi-square index = 45.88. We can conclude with 95% confidence that the distribution of days regarded as lucky for all topics does not reflect a random process.

For days regarded as inauspicious or unlucky: N = 38. Expected frequency for each *gan* day = 3.8. Threshold measure = 15.51. Chi-square index = 16.23. We can conclude with 95% confidence that the distribution of days regarded as unlucky for all topics does not reflect a random process.

For the total number of days regarded as lucky or unlucky: N = 111. Expected frequency for each *gan* day = 11.1. Threshold measure = 15.51. Chi-square index = 33.17. We can conclude with 95% confidence that the total distribution of days regarded as lucky and unlucky for all topics does not reflect a random process. Constructing a 95% confidence interval for the probabilities involved for particular days indicates that the probability of the number of *geng* and *bing* days being prognosticated lucky or unlucky as given in Table 7 is greater by circa 89% and 35% respectively than the probability of such prognostications occurring on these days had they been prognosticated randomly. Had they been prognosticated randomly, the result would have been an equal-rate pattern of 11.1 lucky and unlucky prognostications per *gan* day.

For sources, see Keightley, "Lucky Days," Appendix B. For the lucky days placed in rank order, see Table 3.

Table 2: Number of *Gan* Names of Shang Kings

gan name	number of kings	percentage of total
jia	6	20%
yi	5	17
bing	1	3
ding	6	20
wu	1	3
ji	1	3
geng	5	17
xin	4	13
ren	1	3
gui	0	0

N = 30. Expected frequency for each *gan* day = 3. Threshold measure = 15.51. Chi-square index = 17.33. We can conclude with 95% confidence that the distribution of the kings' *gan* names does not reflect a random process.

Source: Keightley, *Sources of Shang History*, pp. 185-87. I include Lin Xin and also Wu Geng, the Shang descendent, in this list but exclude the predynastic ancestors from Shang Jia to Shi Gui, as well as Wu Ding's "son," Zu Ji.

Table 3: Rank Order of *Gan* King Names and Lucky Days as Recorded in the Oracle-bone Inscriptions

rank order of king names by number of occurrences	lucky days by number of occurrence	luckydays order by favorable/ unfavorable ratio
1. jia, ding (6 cases)	geng	geng
2. ——	jia, ding	yi
3. yi, geng (5 cases)	——	ding
4. ——	wu, xin	jia
5. xin (4 cases)	——	wu
6. bing, wu, ji, ren (1 case each)	yi, bing, ren	xin
7. ——	——	ren
8. ——	——	bing
9. ——	gui	gui
10. gui (0 cases)	ji	ji

Table 4: Rank Order of Names in 1295 (?) Shang and Zhou Bronze Inscriptions

gan name	number of occurrences	percent of total
1. yi	270	21%
2. ding	268	21
3. xin	205	16
4. gui	202	16
5. ji	172	13
6. wu	55	4
7. geng	42	3
8. jia	33	3
9. bing	22	2
10. ren	19	1

N = 1288 (see below). Expected frequency for each *gan* name = 129. Threshold measure = 15.51. Chi-square index = 760.6. We can conclude with 95% confidence that the distribution of *gan* names on Shang and Zhou bronzes does not reflect a random process.

Source: I derive these figures from the chart given by K. C. Chang, *Shang Civilization*, p. 170, fig. 44, "Frequency of occurrence of the ten celestial signs in 1,295 bronze inscriptions." Chang does not identify the "catalogue of inscribed bronzes" or the 1,295 inscriptions he has selected. In retranslating his bar chart back to numbers I have had to estimate what the original figures would have been; some error has clearly crept in since the number of occurrences listed above totals only 1288.

Table 5: Ranking of the Most Common Shang King Names, Shang Lucky Days, and *Gan* Names on Zhou Bronzes

Shang king names (by number of occurrences)	Lucky days (Wu Ding) (by favorable/ unfavorable ratio)	On 1295 Bronze Inscriptions
1. jia, ding	geng	yi
2. ——	yi	ding
3. yi, geng	ding	xin
4. ——	jia	gui
5. xin	wu	ji
6. bing, wu, ji, ren	xin	wu
7. ——	ren	geng
8. ——	bing	jia
9. ——	gui	bing
10. gui	ji	ren

Notes

1. John H. Finely, Jr., *Four Stages of Greek Thought* (Stanford: Stanford University Press, 1966), pp. 3, 4, 28. Similar observations about Homer's compulsion to externalize in the *Odyssey* may be found in "Odysseus' Scar," the opening chapter of Erich Auerbach's *Mimesis: The Representation of Reality in Western Literature* (Princeton: Princeton University Press, 1953).

2. For a more detailed discussion, see Keightley, "The Hero, Art, and Culture: Early China and Early Greece," prepared for the regional seminar, Center for Chinese Studies, University of California, Berkeley, 21 March 1987, esp. pp. 30-33.

3. The numbers in parentheses in this paragraph and figure numbers in this footnote refer to catalog items in the exhibition *The Quest for Eternity*, Los Angeles, Los Angeles County Museum of Art, 1987. See, e.g., "Qin Shi Huang bingma yongkeng chutu di taoyong taoma zhizuo gongyi," *Kaogu yu wenwu* 1980.3: 113, fig. 6. Note, for instance, the similarity in that figure between mustaches 1 and 21, 2 and 21, 3 and 24, 5 and 22, and so on. Yuan Zhongyi, one of the archaeologists involved in the find has apparently reached different conclusions. He Fei's English translation of his text refers to portraits of "real warriors and horses," to "a genuine likeness of real persons," to "portraits of real persons," and suggests that the different facial types represented may be linked to different regions of China (*Qin Shi Huang Di ling bingma yong* [Beijing: Wenwu, 1983], pp. 13-15, 17.). Yuan's original Chinese text, however, does not refer to portraiture but only to imitations of reality and the lifelike quality of the results. Yuan, in fact, notes that the sculptors "used a method that is simple...and not overloaded with details. Attention is paid only to...the main features. In order to make the image vivid and lifelike, emphasis on certain parts of the body and artistic exaggerations have been given" (p. 15). The fact that "ten odd clay figures are disproportionately modeled, with either arms being too short or too long, or with one long arm and another arm short, or with feet too small or hands too big" (p. 16) is further evidence that the figures were not modeled from individuals, but were constructed componentially from a varied repertoire of body parts (see "Qin Shi Huang bingma," pp. 111-112). The goal was to produce the appearance of individuality without its substance, realism without portraiture. As Yuan himself concludes, "On the whole the sculpture of the Qin clay figures is general rather than detailed" (p. 17).

4. Keightley, "The Hero," p. 27.

5. Herrlee Creel, *The Origins of Statecraft in China. Volume One: The Western Chou Empire* (Chicago: University of Chicago, 1970), pp. 485-86.

6. John Steele, trans., *The I-Li or Book of Etiquette and Ceremonial*, vol. 2 (London: Probsthain, 1917), pp. 49-50.

7. See, e.g., Laurence G. Thompson, *Chinese Religion: An Introduction* (Belmont, California: Wadsworth, 1979, 3d ed.), pp. 36-37.

8. "Death and Time," in S. C. Humphreys and Helen King, *Mortality and Immortality: The Anthropology of Death* (London: Academic Press, 1981), p. 267.

9. On this point, see David Cannadine, "War and Death, Grief and Mourning in Modern Britain," in Joachim Whaley, ed., *Mirrors of Mortality: Studies in the Social History of Death* (London: Europa, 1981), p. 191.

10. *Xi'an Banpo* (Beijing, 1963), pp. 205-6, for M3, 8, 32, 42, 69; see also fig. 150, pls. 177.1,2, 181.1, 182.2.

11. *Yuanjunmiao* (Beijing, 1983), pp. 19-20.

12. E.g., M11 at Xixiahou (*Kaogu xuebao* 1964.2:64 [fig. 8]; other cases at pp. 62-64); M17 at Dafanzhuang (*Kaogu* 1975.1:14 [fig. 3]).

13. *Dawenkou* (Beijing, 1974), p. 24 (fig. 17), pl. 12; p. 26 (fig. 18), pl. 13.3.

14. On the role of intoxication at funerals, see Richard Huntington and Peter Metcalf, *Celebrations of Death: The Anthropology of Mortuary Ritual* (Cambridge: Cambridge University Press, 1979), pp. 114-16.

15. Such as Daxi, Qujialing, and Liangzhu (all of the Middle Yangzi Late Neolithic), and Dawenkou.

16. Chen Lihua, "Jiangsu Wujin Sidun yizhi di xinshiqi shidai yiwu," *Wenwu* 1984.2:22. It must be noted, of course, that as with all discussion of prehistoric objects we cannot tell if the historical names assigned to jades and pots were those actually employed at the time of their manufacture and use.

17. A perforated ax made of shale (M3:45) and a perforated jade ax (M3:86), both showing no traces of use, were broken into over ten pieces by the fire; a similar ax (M3:94) was broken into seven or eight pieces, again as the result of burning ("1982 nian Jiangsu Changzhou Wujin Sidun yizhi di fajue," *Kaogu* 1984.2:115-16).

18. "1982 nian Jiangsu Changzhou Wujin Sidun," pp. 113-14 (fig. 5); Wang Zunguo, "Liangzhu wenhua 'yu lian zang' shulue," *Wenwu* 1984.2:29.

19. E.g., Max Loehr, assisted by Louisa G. Fitzgerald Huber, *Ancient Chinese Jades from the Grenville L. Winthrop Collection in the Fogg Art Museum, Harvard University* (Cambridge, Mass.: Fogg Art Museum, 1975), p. 11 n. 24, citing *Bencao gangmu*, chap. 8.

20. E.g., *Kaogu* 1977.4:263, 264, 265, 267; *Shanghai gudai lishi wenwu* (Shanghai: Jiaoyu, 1981), p. 15.

21. For a strong assertion of the view that the squareness of the Neolithic *cong* symbolized earth, its roundness heaven, and the central tube the communication between them, see the views of Zhang Guangzhi, in his conversation with Gao Yude (Jeffrey Kao), Deng Shupin, and Chen Qinan, presented under the title "Yuqi li di wenhua," in *Dangdai* 17 (1 September 1987), pp. 65-75. Zhang believes that the animal designs on the *cong* symbolized the spirits that served as intermediaries between the two realms. The *bi* (disks), he believes, symbolized heaven.

22. "Chinese Jades: The Role of Jade in Ancient China: An Introduction to a Special Exhibition at the Museum," *Expedition* 20.3 (1978): 5.

23. Robert Hertz refers to "a well-known belief: to make an object or a living being pass from this world into the next, to free or to create the soul, it must be destroyed....As the visible object vanishes it is reconstructed in the beyond, transformed to a greater or lesser degree" (*Death and the Right Hand*, trans. R. and C. Needham with an introduction by E. E. Evans-Pritchard [New York: Free Press, 1960], p. 46; quoted by Huntington and Metcalf, *Celebrations of Death*, p. 63.

24. For glass paste and stone *bi* in Chu burials in Changsha, see Robert L. Thorp, "The Mortuary Art and Architecture of Early Imperial China" Ph.D. diss. (University of Kansas, 1979), p. 79. *Bi* (disks) made of wood in the Han burials at Mawangdui are referred to by Michele Pirazolli-T'Serstevens, "The Art of Dining in the Han Period: Food Vessels from Tomb No. 1 at Mawangdui" (paper presented at La Civilta Cinese Antica, Venice, 1-5 April 1985), p. 7.

25. Rene-Yvon Lefebvre d'Argencé, *Bronze Vessels of Ancient China in the Avery Brundage Collection* (San Francisco: Asian Art Museum, 1977), pl. 21, left; fig. 25; B60 B1049.

26. A *zun*, ibid., pl. 12, center; fig. 15; B60 B768.

27. I derive these figures and the others that follow from the excavation report, *Yinxu Fu Hao mu* (Beijing, 1980).

28. Sarah Allan, "Sons of Suns: Myth and Totemism in Early China," *Bulletin of the School of Oriental and African Studies* 44 (1981): 290-326.

29. Pitirim A. Sorokin, *Sociocultural Causality, Space, Time*, quoted by

Eviatar Zerubavel, *The Seven Day Circle: The History and Meaning of the Week* (New York: Free Press, 1985), p. vii. I am grateful to Thomas Laqueur for calling Zerubavel's book to my attention.

30. Chang Kwang-chih, *Shang Civilization* (New Haven: Yale University Press, 1980), p. 169.

31. I use the term "lineage" with James L. Watson's definition in mind: "A lineage is a *corporate group* which celebrates *ritual unity* and is based on *demonstrated descent* from a common ancestor" ("Chinese Kinship Reconsidered: Anthropological Perspectives on Historical Research," *The China Quarterly* 92 [December 1982]: 594). It is not easy in regard to the Shang and Zhou to demonstrate the kind of corporate, economic base that Watson's definition requires, and more work is required on the social, political, and economic institutions that enabled elite kin groups in ancient China to persist for generations. Although there is little doubt that the nature of the early corporate base would have been different from that of the post-Song period (Watson, pp. 616-17), there is also little doubt that, at least in the case of dynasties and long-lived elite families, some form of corporate structure was involved. The great emphasis placed on mortuary rituals and on the five mourning grades suggests that the religious dimension of this structure would have been particularly strong. On this point, see David Johnson, "Comments on James Watson's 'Chinese Kinship Reconsidered,'" *The China Quarterly* (June 1983).

32. The scholarship on this important inscription is voluminous. One might start, for example, with the articles by Tang Lan and Qiu Xigui in *Wenwu* 1978.3.

33. *Mengzi* 4.A.26.

34. Yü Ying-shih, "Life and Immortality in the Mind of Han China," *Harvard Journal of Asiatic Studies* 25 (1964-65): 80-122.

35. Takigawa Kametarô, *Shiki kaichû kôshô* (Tokyo, 1934), chap. 6, pp. 22-23; Edouard Chavannes, trans., *Les mémoires historiques de Se-ma Ts'ien*, vol. 2 (Paris: 1895), p. 128; Derk Bodde, *China's First Unifier: A Study of the Ch'in Dynasty as Seen in the Life of Li Ssu* (Leiden, 1938; Hong Kong: Hong Kong University Press, 1967), pp. 34 n. 1, 124; 114-16, 119-20. The first emperor did away with the posthumous names (*shi*) because he felt that they allowed descendants and subjects the impermissible opportunity to criticize fathers and rulers. The attempt to abolish such names, however, can also be seen as a further attempt to impersonalize the dead.

36. I will not go here into the traditional continuities and discontinuities presented by Mao's mausoleum, the Memorial Hall that now dominates the square of Heavenly Peace in Beijing and preserves for all to see the Chairman's embalmed remains. On these and other issues, see Frederic Wakeman, Jr., "Revolutionary Rites: The Remains of Chiang Kai-shek and Mao Tse-tung," *Representations* 10 (Spring 1985): 146-93.

37. I derive these figures from K. C. Chang, *Art, Myth, and Ritual: The Path to Political Authority in Ancient China* (Cambridge, Mass.: Harvard University Press, 1983), p. 105.

38. See, e.g., Bernhard Karlgren, *Grammata Serica Recensa* (Stockholm: Museum of Far Eastern Antiquities, 1957), no. 764; the entries at Zhang Qiyun, ed., *Zhongwen da zidian* (Taibei: Zhonghua shuju, 1973) 5:7834, no. 17461.

39. The passage is in the "Wei Zi zhi ming," a chapter not found in the *jinwen* version of the *Shu*; Legge's translation is on page 376 of *The Chinese Classics. III: The Shoo King* (Hong Kong and London, 1865). For similar spurious references, see Legge, op. cit., pp. 57, 183.

40. There are certainly several passages that would permit a translation of *yong* as "eternal," but they do not require it. At best one could use "forever" only in the weak sense of "habitually, always," as in, "I forever think of the hardships" (*Shang shu*, "Da gao," para. 8; cf. para. 14). By contrast, and more significantly, there are some passages where a translation of "eternal" is excluded by the context (e.g., *Shih jing*, Mao. 280, 299; *Shang shu*, "Gao zong yong ri," para. 3, "Jin teng," para. 10, "Wen hou zhi ming," para. 2).

41. On the *wu-fu* mourning system, based on a five-generation group, see, e.g., Marcel Granet, *The Religion of the Chinese People*, trans. Maurice Freedman (New York: Harper and Row, 1975), p. 87 n. 66; Henri Maspero, *China in Antiquity* (Folkestone, Kent: Dawson, 1978), pp. 109-10.

42. Keightley, "The Religious Commitment: Shang Theology and the Genesis of Chinese Political Culture," *History of Religions* 17.3-4 (February-May 1978): 218.

43. Chiang Yee recounts a story relevant to this point. Speaking of the first ancestor of the lineage, who lived at the end of the first century B.C., his father said, "The rule he made for his family is printed in large characters in the clan book. It consists of only four words: 'Benevolence,' 'Righteousness,' 'Sincerity,' and 'Endurance.' He commanded that each member of the family should be trained in these four qualities" (*A Chinese Childhood* [New York: Norton, 1963], pp. 9f.; cited by Thompson, *Chinese Religion*, p. 55.) The concern was with endurance, and I suspect that it was a concern that expressed itself in the cultural training of one generation at a time, just as Chiang Yee was being trained by his father, not in more rarefied conceptions of eternity.

44. Seraphin Couvreur, trans., *Li Ki, Mémoires sur les bienséances et les cérémonies*, vol. 1 (Ho-kien-fou: 1899; reprinted, Paris: Cathasia, 1950), p. 785.

45. For the conclusion that "the five degrees of mourning were already in practice in Han times" and an excellent introduction to their precise nature, see T'ung-tsu Ch'ü, *Han Social Structure*, ed. Jack L. Dull (Seattle: University of Washington), p. 313 n. 274. The newly discovered Qin and Han law codes may throw more light on this subject.

Mountain Tombs and Jade Burial Suits: Preparations for Eternity in the Western Han

Robert L. Thorp

Washington University, St. Louis

The early imperial era, especially its first two centuries, played a pivotal role in the long history of Chinese burial practices. Between the late Zhou period (fifth-third centuries B.C.) and the Eastern Han (25-220) fundamental changes in many aspects of burial rites, tomb structures, and furnishings transformed the nature of the passage from life to death. These developments reflect changes in Chinese society, as imperial unification became a reality and new philosophical ideas and social values emerged. Few archaeological discoveries mirror the processes of change as well as the pair of Han tombs excavated in 1968 near Mancheng County in Hebei Province. This essay analyzes features of the Mancheng tombs and their contents from the perspective of the broader Qin-Han transformation of burial practices underway at the time of their creation.

The Qin-Han Transformation

Qin and Han tombs can be analyzed as material expressions of a system by which the values and ideas of society were translated into burial rites and equipment. Many components within this system have their own history and may be properly studied by social, cultural, and intellectual historians. When, however, beliefs and practices came together to produce burial chambers and tomb furnishings, this topic also becomes an important aspect of the archaeology of ancient China. The study of tombs and their contents will remain academic, however, unless it is situated within Chinese social and intellectual history. Then sites and artifacts speak eloquently about the meaning of life

and death in early imperial China. It is the purpose of this essay to read the artifactual and site data for information about the society and ideas of Qin and Han times.

The impact of unification has been too little appreciated by modern archaeologists and art historians. The final victory of the Qin First Emperor (reigned 221-210 B.C.) was a prelude to the beginning of the imperial system under the Han, but the processes that made unification so powerful a force in Chinese society began even in the first decade of Qin rule. Political integration was accompanied by cultural fusion, a process that quickened throughout the two centuries of Western Han (206 B.C.- A.D. 9). As the political center (the imperial capital) gained more power over the realm and as national elites were created and circulated, values and customs that had been peculiar to one region in late Zhou times became more widely practiced. Economic integration also spurred cultural fusion. Disparate cultural traditions came together most dramatically in the crucible of the imperial capitals, first at Qin Xianyang and then nearby Han Chang'an. The unprecedented power and wealth of the imperial court was a force for patronage in all the arts; imperial patronage encouraged competition and rewarded bold ideas. State patronage and the economic prosperity of the Western Han period allowed a sizable elite society to indulge a life-style that had once been restricted to the feudal ruling class of late Zhou times.[1]

In burial practices one sees the creation of a new, imperial system of burial and the gradual spread of new structures and furnishings for the elite more generally.[2] The former was the creation of court specialists in ritual who, first, articulated a unique statement of imperial identity in the burial of the Qin First Emperor, and, second, perpetuated much of that accomplishment in tombs erected for the Western Han emperors and empresses.[3] When working for the Qin and Han sovereigns, court specialists could glean ideas from the accumulated customs of more than a thousand years. Yet they were also able to create unprecedented features. While the degree of continuity with preimperial, Bronze Age burials is striking, so too is the degree of innovation evident in the design and furnishings of imperial tombs of this era. Several innovations feature prominently in the analysis of the Mancheng tombs below.

The diffusion of burial customs can be charted decade by decade, as brick chamber tombs and ceramic surrogate furnishings appeared in areas outside Shaanxi and Henan (the location of the two Han capitals) during the middle and late Western Han. By the first century A.D. elite burials in most areas of the empire, from Lelang (modern North Korea) to Guangzhou, shared many common features of plan, construction, furnishings, and decoration.[4] The process appears at first to be one of homogenization. Unique local customs and styles might be expected to vanish in the face of such a new, unitary system emanating from the capital region. In fact strong local styles characterize the Eastern Han period as a whole. Tomb figurines of identical subject type or purpose were rendered in markedly different materials and styles throughout the realm. To the extent there was homogenization, it was a matter of goals and purposes rather than of artistic styles.[5]

A marked taste for "rich burials" (houzang) characterized Western Han times. The rationale for investing enormous economic resources in the burial of the dead was part ideological and part social. Filial submission (xiao) demanded sincere and appropriate obsequies at the passing of a parent, but if genuine sincerity was in short supply, public display was nonetheless available, at a price. This cynical analysis sounds like a modern complaint, but it was at the core of contemporary Han critiques of the custom. The learned scholars who represented traditional values in the so-called "Debate on Salt and Iron" were echoing the criticisms of the preimperial Mohist thinkers, but no amount of righteous indignation could derail the freight train of rich burials in Western Han times. The social rank of the deceased as well as expectations for social mobility by the living demanded conspicuous demonstrations of public grief and expenditures on the graves of the newly deceased ancestors. There were moral and pecuniary rewards for such behavior. Like imperial patronage, rich burials stimulated innovation, but unlike the imperial court, the elite were spread across the empire, and so affected developments of burials far and wide.

The Rock-cut Mountain Tombs at Mancheng

The first emperor of Western Han, Gao Zu (Liu Bang, reigned 206-195 B.C.), reintroduced a limited feudalism in state administration. A number of Liu Bang's most trusted associates from the campaigns against the Qin and other claimants for the throne were rewarded with kingdoms (wang guo) that functioned as quasi-independent entities among the commanderies (jun) that were the normal units of administration within the realm. These kingdoms were also bestowed on imperial relations, including sons who could not succeed to the throne. Whoever sat as king in these fiefs enjoyed the perquisites of the highest possible social rank, just below those of emperor and empress. Income in the form of tax revenue derived from the population of the kingdoms sustained the king's courts and permitted the luxurious life-style befitting royalty. Over the course of the second century B.C. the number of kingdoms shrank, especially after the revolt of 154 B.C., but some were always maintained for scions of the imperial line.[6]

Among these was the kingdom of Zhongshan, occupying the eastern slopes of the Taihang Mountains in west central Hebei Province. In the census of A.D. 2 the Zhongshan kingdom had a population of more than 160,000 households, perhaps as many as 668,000 people.[7] At that time it was the second largest kingdom in population and the third largest in area. The capital of the Zhongshan kingdom was located at modern Ding County (then known as Lunu). The Mancheng area, situated about twenty kilometers northwest of modern Baoding City, was known in Western Han times as Beiping. This populous fief was the economic foundation for the court of Zhongshan. When a tomb site was to be selected and the burial designed and furnished, it was the economic resources of this kingdom that determined what could be realized.

A single example of the costs created by such a burial will suggest the magnitude of the demands made by the Mancheng tombs. Tomb 2 contained two bronze basins (xuan), one of which bares an inscription that includes its cost: 840 cash.[8] This price was equivalent to the head tax on a family of five for two years. Moreover it is estimated this amount of money would have purchased enough grain to feed an adult for a year to a year and a half.[9] These basins are among utilitarian kitchen furnishings placed in the tombs. Nothing about their materials or workmanship catches the eye of a modern connoisseur. They are among dozens of bronze vessels found in the two tombs and merely a minute fraction of the total wealth invested in the burials. Without the economic base of the Zhongshan kingdom household furnishings like these, much less burials on this scale, could not have been realized.

The site of the two tombs is about a kilometer from the Mancheng County seat on a rocky mountain called

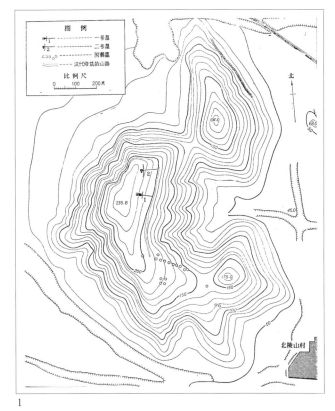

1

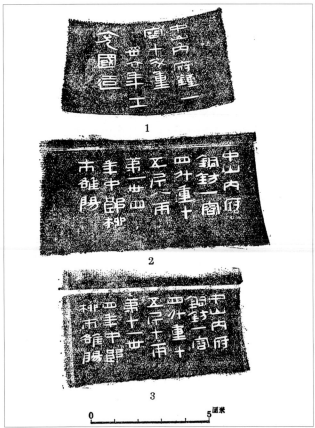

2

Figures

1. Map of Lingshan showing position of the two royal Zhongshan tombs. After *Mancheng Han mu*, vol. 1, 8 (fig. 3).
2. Rubbings of inscriptions on bronze vessels from Tomb 1. After *Mancheng Han mu*, vol. 1, 51 (fig. 33).

Lingshan (Tumulus mountain). Local tradition associates the mountain with an ancient tomb, and several nearby villages have names that suggest this area was used for important burials. Under Western Han practice a princely or imperial tomb had other burials nearby and was accompanied by a settlement (*ling yi*) whose revenue and population were dedicated toward their support. For example, according to the Han histories the tomb of the great statesman Huo Guang, buried at the Maoling, the necropolis of Han Wudi, was sustained by the tax revenues of three hundred families.[10] It would be reasonable to assume a like number of households was installed near the Mancheng tombs for the king and his consort.

The tombs were sited on the east slope of Lingshan about 30 meters below its summit (fig. 1). A winding road provided access from the lower slopes to the two entrances, which were separated by about 120 meters, Tomb 1 on the south and Tomb 2 on the north. The roadway was widened using rubble excavated from the rock of the mountain when the tombs were constructed. A total of 18 small burial mounds of piled stone have been located on the mountain, each with square bases 10-20 meters on a side and heights of 5 meters. These mounds may be tombs of clan members and, with Tombs 1 and 2, could provide a factual basis for the mountain's name. None of these smaller burials has as yet been reported. Traces of a mortuary shrine were also located on the summit above Tomb 1.

The discovery of the two Mancheng tombs came in May 1968, when a detachment of the People's Liberation Army (PLA) bivouacked on Lingshan. The soldiers came upon a fissure in the rock that opened up into what we now know to be the south-side chamber of Tomb 1. The PLA soldiers reported their find to the provincial government, which in turn notified authorities in Beijing. Work was authorized by Premier Zhou Enlai himself, it is said, and a team from the Institute of Archaeology dispatched. Excavation began in late May under the direction of the provincial cultural relics administration, but the rear burial chamber was not opened until the team from the Institute of Archaeology had arrived in late June. Work was completed in early August. By this time traces of a second, similar tomb had been identified about 100 meters north. After receiving permission from the central authorities, work on Tomb 2 began in mid August and was completed by mid September.

The Mancheng tombs had not been molested since the time of their sealing, a distinct rarity among major tomb sites of this period. Their structures survived intact because they were artificial caverns dug out of the rock of a mountain. Their furnishings were also complete, found in precisely the position in which they had been left when the king's court officers exited the tomb chambers. The only losses were the result of natural decay due primarily to moisture. All perishable materials, fabric, wood, and the like, vanished due to the water that entered the chambers over a period of 2,000 years.[11] Nonetheless, because of the nature of the tomb furnishings, these two burials provide an exceptionally complete and accurate record of the burial rites accorded a king and his consort in the late second century B.C. In the absence of any excavated imperial tomb or other equally well-preserved comparable tombs, the two Mancheng tombs provide the best picture yet available for an imperial burial from the Qin-Han era.[12]

As soon as the excavators began to examine the tomb furnishings, it was evident that these tombs were datable to the first half of the Western Han period. Bronze and ceramic vessels as well as coins attested a second century B.C. date for these finds. In Western Han times Mancheng County was a part of the Zhongshan kingdom, and indeed many objects retrieved from the two tombs bear inscriptions naming that kingdom. The presence of a jade burial suit in each tomb further certified that these were royal tombs. The question then remained whose remains were interred here?

Han shu records ten kings of the Zhongshan fief, the first taking the throne in 154 B.C. and the last losing the rank in A.D. 8.[13] The reigns of these kings extended from three to forty-two years, but only one, Jing Wang Liu Sheng, sat on the throne for more than twenty-one years. A number of inscriptions on bronze and lacquer objects found in Tomb 1 bear dates of the years thirty-two through thirty-nine of an unnamed Zhongshan king's reign. For example, a pair of *fang* vessels have inscriptions noting that they were bought in Luoyang in the king's thirty-fourth year by the Gentleman-of-the-Household Liu (fig. 2). A *zhong* vessel inscription records its production in the state workshop during the king's thirty-sixth year, while a *xian* steamer set is described as a gift from the kingdom of Zhao in the king's thirty-seventh year.[14] The logical inference is that these objects were made for Liu Sheng and moreover that Tomb 1 was therefore his burial. Sheng was the son of Jingdi and a brother of Wudi; his biographies in *Shi ji* and *Han shu* record his death about 113 B.C.[15]

The second tomb at Mancheng also contained furnishings from the Zhongshan court contemporary in date with Tomb 1. The excavators concluded that the jade burial suit found here was that for a woman and hence attributed this find to Liu Sheng's consort, whose name, however, is not recorded in the Han histories. A seal found in the burial chamber bears the legends "Dou Wan" and "Dou Junxu."[16] From these texts it appears that the consort was related to Empress Dou, the mother of Emperor Jing and the grandmother of Liu Sheng. The date of this burial can be narrowed further. The presence of *wushu* coins minted from 118 B.C. establishes a *terminus a quo*, while an inscription using an official term changed in 104 B.C. pro-

vides a *terminus ad quem*.

The Tomb Structures

The first feature of the two Mancheng burials that sets them apart from the great majority of Western Han tombs is their structure. Each was carved out of the solid rock substance of a small mountain, presumably using the iron chisels and crowbars then available. This Herculean task could only have been accomplished over a period of several years. The excavators suggest that a gang of a hundred laborers working with such tools today would require a year's time to accomplish the excavation of a single tomb of the scale of either burial at Mancheng. It is difficult to establish plausible estimates of work in ancient times, but it should be noted that the Western Han sovereign who commissioned a similar burial for himself, Wendi (179-157 B.C.), had a work force of thirty-one thousand laborers employed on the construction of his eternal resting place.[17] There was no shortage of huge labor forces in ancient China.

Construction began by carving a ledge into the side of the mountain that became a roadway to the tomb site. Two large clefts on the east side of the mountain were removed before the digging of entry passages could begin. The final depth of the excavations was 52 and 50 meters, respectively, measuring from the outer doorways to the rear walls of each innermost chamber. The volume of stone removed was on the order of 2700 cubic meters and 3000 cubic meters, respectively, and the interior spaces created were far larger than the ceremonies and furnishings for the two burials actually required. For example, the central chamber of Tomb 1 was almost 15 by 13 meters square with a height of 6.8 meters from floor to ceiling.

The motivation for such an unusual structure must have been the desire to create an impregnable resting place for the two deceased, one that would never suffer from the eventual decay and collapse that awaited any burial using a wooden chamber in a vertical shaft. A more immediate impetus for the Mancheng design may have come from the arrangements made for the Baling, the mausoleum of Wendi.[18] Wendi's posthumous edict prescribed that the tomb be constructed without erecting an aboveground burial mound.[19] From the geography of the site Chinese archaeologists infer that the burial was dug from the side of a mountain, which itself then served as the tumulus, a fashion later revived by the Tang emperors. Superficially the reason for Wendi's requirements was economy. His plan eliminated the labor intensive stage of constructing a large man-made pounded earth mound after the funeral. Long-term security doubtless also played a part.

The two Mancheng tombs were inviolate until 1968 because of extraordinary measures taken to seal the two rock-cut burials. Tomb 1 was first entered from the south-side

3

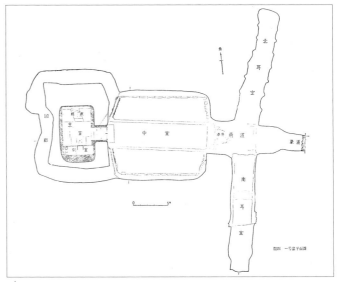

4a

chamber, but the excavators never actually cleared the approach to the interior along the corridor from the east. When they dug into that corridor from the mountain side, they found an adobe brick wall that sealed the passage from side to side and floor to ceiling. At the top of this wall was a crude clay trough; iron had seeped through cracks in the wall of adobe and were visible on the surface. The presumption therefore was that the tomb had been sealed by pouring iron on the spot. The more complete excavation of Tomb 2 revealed a similar arrangement, in this instance beginning with a brick wall (fig. 3) and followed by the cast-iron sealing wall, a layer of mud and straw, a second brick wall, a layer of loess soil, and a final brick wall. As at Tomb 1, the passage on both sides of the barrier was filled with rubble. The excavators did not report any evidence that grave robbers had attempted to enter the tombs. Their entrances were probably well hidden in post-Han times, and without aboveground indicators it is unlikely that anyone would have been drawn to such an elevated site as a potential treasure trove.

The plans of the two tombs differ slightly from each other but presage a disposition of spaces important in large Eastern Han tombs (fig. 4).[20] Each Mancheng tomb is entered through a long passage on an east-west axis. This approach arrives at a foyer flanked by two perpendicular side chambers. These chambers served two purposes: one contained a large investment of tomb furnishings and functionally was equivalent to a larder and storage facility; the other was filled with chariots, horses, and other animals, the equivalent of a stable. The north-side room of Tomb 1 and the south-side room of Tomb 2 were storage areas, while the south-side room of Tomb 1 and the north-side room of Tomb 2 were stables. These functional areas were within the underground chamber but outside the proper burial chambers. They correspond therefore to ancillary spaces within a courtyard plan subordinated to the princi-

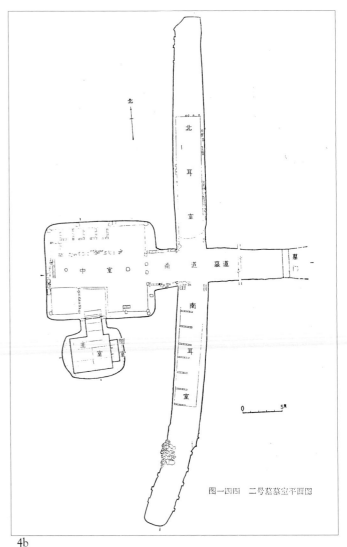

4b

Figures
3. Brick wall sealing entry passage of Tomb 2. After *Mancheng Han mu,* vol. 2, pl. 154.
4. Plans of the royal Zhongshan tombs. a. Tomb 1. b. Tomb 2. After *Mancheng Han mu,* vol. 1, opposite 11 (fig. 4) and 217 (fig. 144).

pal halls of a palace or estate, usually by being placed off axis.

Each tomb was dominated by its main chamber and an adjoining rear burial chamber. In Tomb 1 these two spaces were aligned on the principal axis, the doorway to the latter being determined by the line of approach. In Tomb 2, however, the burial chamber was placed on the south side of the central chamber in the middle of the wall and so was not visible from the entry corridor. Chambers differed from approach corridors in their general appearance. Whereas the latter seem to have been unadorned and undisguised, both central and the rear chambers were small-scale, stone rooms of rectangular plan with pitched, gabled roofs. The roofed area within Tomb 1 also included the north- and south-side chambers and the foyer; hence during the funeral most of its interior space was roughly equivalent in overall appearance to a palace compound. The main chamber may have been covered by a structure three to five bays across axis and three bays in depth. A tentative reconstruction published before the formal excavation report suggests such a hall, but the final report does not assess this possibility.[21] The final report does note the existence of a number of stone plinths in the chambers of Tomb 2, and it too was found to contain a large quantity of broken roof tiles at the time it was opened.

Rock-cut Tombs in Western Han

Tombs like the two Mancheng examples are not yet documented prior to the second century B.C. This lack of evidence, however, does not exclude the very real possibility that large tombs built for powerful patrons did closely mimic the plan and look of palatial architecture, as I have suggested elsewhere.[22] To date, however, the only likely candidates are large wooden chamber tombs placed within deep vertical shafts. The need to bear the enormous weight of the fill overhead precluded any very literal imitation of a pitched roof. There is, however, abundant evidence that floor plans and interior furnishings were modeled on palace halls. The equivalence of aboveground and below ground components is a marked trait of later imperial burials, such as the tombs of imperial princes and princesses near the Qianling of Tang Gaozong (died 683).[23]

This fashion was not unique in Western Han times to the sites at Mancheng. Other major examples are reported:

1. A group of five tombs with more complex plans at Jiulong Shan near modern Qufu City in Shandong Province.[24] This group is tentatively dated to the late second century B.C. and the following several generations. It is presumed to be the cemetery of the kings of the state of Lu, members of the Liu imperial clan.

2. An even more ambitious rock-cut tomb with many appended passages and chambers at Beidong Shan in the north suburbs of Xuzhou City, Jiangsu Province.[25] In this case the attribution is to a king of the Chu fief, with a date of mid second century B.C., prior to the Mancheng examples.

3. Another large tomb at Guishan, again near Xuzhou.[26] This burial has been attributed to a king and his consort; the probable date is late second century B.C.

4. A pair of tombs at Shiqiao, also near Xuzhou.[27] They may represent a king's burial (Tomb 1) and that of his consort (Tomb 2); their date is the middle of the first century B.C.

Most of these tombs share common features with the Mancheng examples. In every case a long passage leads from the cliff face to a series of caverns arrayed along a central axis and/or to one side of same. Outside the Zhongshan kingdom these approaches were sealed with large blocks of ashlar masonry, some weighing as much as seven or eight tons. No other examples have the cast-iron doors found at Mancheng. The caverns in all of the Lu and Chu tombs, however, are more ambitious than their Zhongshan counterparts, both in the complexity of their floor plans and in the care with which the chambers were cut. Like the two Mancheng tombs many of the Lu and Chu tombs had internal structures with tile roofs. The tomb of the King of Chu at Beidong Shan even had its wall surfaces covered with mortar colored with red lacquer.

This evidence at least demonstrates a fashion for large and complex rock-cut tombs in both the kingdoms of Lu and Chu during the same period that the Mancheng tombs were constructed. A hypothetical line of development might be sketched from the Baling of Wendi (circa 157 B.C.) to the kings of Chu buried near Xuzhou to the contemporary burials at Mancheng and Jiulong Shan. It is unlikely that this list exhausts examples of such construction among the kings of the imperial clan. The sophistication of cutting and design in the Lu and Chu kingdoms overshadows the Zhongshan examples, and the enormous scale of the two largest tombs near Xuzhou, the Beidong Shan and Guishan burials, suggests a significantly larger investment in preparations for eternity than made by Liu Sheng and Dou Wan. Many kings of Western Han times could command the creation of grand underground palaces as their eternal resting places.

These burials were also mountain tombs: natural topographic features appropriated and retrofitted as kingly tombs. The symbolism of the burial mound in Han times is obscure, but the philosophical writing and imaginative literature of the era are replete with images of the realm of the immortals, denizens of ethereal, elevated altitudes. Court preoccupation with the elixir of "no-death" is well documented both during the reign of the Qin First Emperor and during the time of Wudi.[28] Remaking a natural mountain into a king's or emperor's eternal resting place represented both a preeminent statement of the exalted status of the deceased as well as the creation of an abode attractive to the immortals. The combination of status and the cult of immortality is no less evident in another outstanding feature of the two Mancheng tombs, their jade burial suits.

Preparations for Eternity

The two caverns at Lingshan were furnished with objects that served many purposes. Some grave goods were favored personal possessions of the deceased; others necessary equipment and supplies for a wealthy household; still others tokens of royal rank. A final and vital component among the tomb furnishings, however, had a more specialized purpose: the maintenance of the mortal remains for all eternity. The gear created to meet this goal is not unique to the Mancheng burials, but its discovery in their chambers provided the first complete evidence of the elaborate steps taken in Western Han times to assure what Joseph Needham has termed the "terminal incorruptibility" of the corpse.[29]

Grave goods were installed in the tomb before and during the funeral proceedings, presumably by officials of the household of the king and his consort. As both an underground palace and eternal resting place, the tomb chamber required at least the simulation of all necessities. For this reason both the Mancheng tombs were designed with the formal hall, private apartments, stables, and storehouses of a noble. None of these areas could serve its purpose without a proper investment of furnishings, but unlike most tombs of the Han period, the great majority of the items placed in the Lingshan burials were utilitarian objects taken out of the palace rather than surrogates or "spirit articles" (mingqi).

The general layout of the furnishings in the two tombs was similar, although some objects had been disturbed by water and sediment that accumulated inside the caverns. In Tomb 1 the corridor and south-side chamber were occupied by six chariots and sixteen horses as well as a deer and eleven dogs. Together these offerings must constitute much of the king's entourage, specifically the chariots that accompanied him on any and all excursions from the palace. The dogs could have been a part of hunts; the deer perhaps a token of a royal menagerie. The comparable area of Dou Wan's tomb, the north-side chamber, had merely four chariots and thirteen horses, elements of a lesser entourage in keeping with her lesser status. The north-side chamber of Tomb 1 contained mostly ceramic vessels and storage crocks, the latter with inscriptions noting their alcoholic contents. A millstone with a horse beside it (a power source?) completed this investment of furnishings. In Tomb 2, by comparison, the comparable area was located on the south side of the passage and was subdivided into six bays, each filled with neatly arranged ceramic food container vessels.

The greatest number of valuables were displayed in the central chambers of the two tombs. A canopy occupied the center of Liu Sheng's chamber (fig. 5), midway between the passage and the door in the rear wall. Small ceramic figurines were found here. Before this canopy, just inside the chamber, was an array of large bronze vessels with a row of lamps. More ceramic lamps were disposed to the right (north) of center, with ceramic figurines and several rows of ceramic vessels. Nearest the burial chamber door, behind the central canopy, was an array of bronze drinking cups and a pile of coins. Flanking them to the left (south) of center was another canopy and another array of bronze vessels. The neat displays of vessels and drinking equipment suggest preparations for a ritual comparable to a banquet set out in the king's palace hall. Servants were represented by figurines, but neither the number of vessels nor the quantity of figurines was extravagant. Compared to the riches installed in the tomb of a feudal lord of the Warring States era, the chamber's contents are modest.[30]

The contents of Dou Wan's central chamber were even less extensive than those found in Tomb 1. The rear burial chamber was repositioned to the south wall, so the symmetry of Liu Sheng's chamber was lacking. Low brick walls were built along the north wall to create partially enclosed areas like the side chamber of the same tomb, but these

Figure

5. Central chamber of Tomb 1, view from entry corridor at time of excavation. After *Mancheng Han mu*, vol. 2, pl. 3.

bays were empty. Most of the furnishings were actually found in the southeast and southwest corners, flanking the door to the burial chamber. Rather than an impressive array of large bronze and ceramic vessels and figurines, however, the objects found here were clustered in several spots. Some of them must originally have been placed inside lacquered boxes and on trays. The assortment found directly in front of the door to the burial chamber included a number of miniature bronze vessel types regarded as "spirit articles" by the authors of the excavation report. Such miniatures are not a feature of Liu Sheng's tomb. Unlike her spouse, Dou Wan was not sent off to the afterlife with a conspicuous array of ritual equipment.

In each tomb the rear burial chamber corresponds to the private apartments of the deceased, and furnishings bear a logical relationship to this function. In Tomb 1 Liu Sheng was accompanied by large stone figurines (representing household servants) at the front door and at the door to the bathing room on the side. His multiple coffins were installed on a low couchlike platform at the right (north) side of the chamber. A lacquer tray had been placed in the center with wine and service vessels and the remains of a slaughtered pig. These vessels included four magnificent *hu* that must have been the pride of the king's possessions. Because the roof had fallen in, the weapons originally placed on the left side (south) wall were found in disarray in the center of the chamber. Iron lamellar armor was also found, as were the personal weapons of Liu Sheng originally placed within the coffins. The simulated bathing room on the left side (south) was equipped with large container vessels, lamps, and a magnificent gold-inlay incense burner crafted as a magic mountain floating amid the waves of the ocean.

Dou Wan's burial chamber shared the same general plan as that of her consort, but her coffin was placed opposite the door against the south wall rather than to one side. Much of the floor space here was originally taken up by lacquered wooden trays with metal fittings; their offerings, like the wood itself, had long since decayed by the time this chamber was opened. The "Changxin Palace" lamp was found right of center near the entrance, and two fine bronze *hu* were closer to the coffin on axis with the door. A small flanking chamber on the east, possibly analogous to the bathing room of Tomb 1, was in this instance entirely filled with bronze and ceramic vessels.

One component of elite burials not much in evidence in the two Mancheng tombs is figurines. Only five stone figurines in the rear chamber and eighteen ceramic ones in the central chamber were found in Liu Sheng's tomb, and none are reported from the burial of Dou Wan. Additional figurines may, however, have been created for the Mancheng burials. Based on the tomb at Beidong Shan near Xuzhou, it is possible that figurines could have been placed in

niches outside the tomb chambers. At Beidong Shan seven niches containing about thirty figurines each were found on the sides of the approach leading to the tomb's front door. If a similar placement were used at Mancheng, we would not know it; the entrance passage leading into Tomb 1 has still not been opened. Moreover there is the possibility that trenches placed somewhere else on the mountain might have been used for a large quantity of tomb figurines. Both the tombs at Yangjiawan near the Changling of Han Gaozu and the recent discovery of trenches on Shizi Shan near Xuzhou suggest this possibility.[31] In each case well over two thousand small warrior figurines were installed in proximity to a large tomb. The eighteen small "tombs" that lie on a lower portion of the mountain before the roadway leading to Tombs 1 and 2 could contain figurines in like quantities.

Although both Liu Sheng and Dou Wan took a great deal of personal and state wealth with them to the grave, the greatest expenses associated with their tombs were the cost of the excavation of the rock-cut chambers, on the one hand, and the cost of the two jade burial suits in which they were interred, on the other. In neither case was the palace of the deceased stripped of all of its furnishings to provide for the dead, even if one assumes that many perishable items (lacquer ware, silk textiles, etc.) once placed in the tomb did not survive the passage of time. This does not make the two tombs at Mancheng either modest or frugal; they certainly still qualify as "extravagant burials." Yet the effort and expense dedicated to assuring the eternal security of the corpse set these burials apart.

Jade and Immortality

Jades fashioned expressly for burial, usually for the corpse itself, are an enduring feature of Chinese mortuary culture. The love of jade (nephrite) is well attested long before Han times, and the use of this and related minerals in graves dates at least from the Neolithic. Some of the most hallowed jade types are documented in burial contexts as early as the third millennium B.C., and while we do not understand their significance in this early period, by the late Bronze Age and early imperial eras an elaborate ritual symbolism embraced these objects and provided a rationale for their use. By the Western Han, jades for burial can be assigned to several categories. Jade mouth amulets (*han*), frequently shaped as cicadas, are common throughout the realm, as are pieces meant to be clasped in the hands of the deceased, usually shaped as pigs. Jade plugs (*sai*) to stop up the bodily orifices were also in fashion but apparently less extensively used. Ritual forms, particularly the *bi* disk, are also common in burials, both as decoration within or on the coffin and as tokens placed on or near the corpse. Finally one must mention the remarkable jade burial suits (*yu yi; yu xia*) known now from several dozen

Han tombs. These full-length jade shrouds made from small plaques and metal "thread" were a prerogative of the imperial house sometimes shared with favored associates of the throne.

Plugs to stop the bodily orifices were known in late Zhou and Han times as *shen*, a term defined by the *Shuo wen* dictionary (circa 100) as "a jade to fill up the ears."[32] The same character was also in use in ritual texts for cloth bindings wrapped around the ears. Plugs for the ears are generally short tubes with a flaring end, while plugs for the nostrils are generally small bullet-shaped stones. One of the earliest complete sets of these plugs comes from the tomb of Liu Sheng (fig. 6).[33] That set included two flat plaques for the eyes, plugs for each ear and nostril, a large amulet for the mouth, a plug for the anus, and a sheath for the penis. Thus all nine bodily orifices were closed. Dou Wan was similarly provided for.[34] The belief that jade and related stones had magical properties, especially efficacious against physical decay, was deep-rooted in ancient China. Practitioners of the alchemical tradition continued to uphold this view in post-Han times. Hence Ge Hong's statement in *Baopuzi* (circa 320), "When gold and jade are inserted into the nine orifices, corpses do not decay."[35] Ge Hong's comment may be the earliest explicit literary statement of this belief, but the evidence of Han archaeology substantiates such concepts several centuries earlier.

The most frequent jade form found in Han burials is the *bi* disk, the type symbolic of Heaven in the canonical ritual literature.[36] In the two Mancheng tombs *bi* disks are especially prominent. Tomb 1 contained twenty-five disks, while Tomb 2 had eighteen. These jades were employed in several fashions. For Liu Sheng two sets of nine (the imperial number) were placed on the chest and under the back of the corpse; all had imprints of cloth cords, which suggests that they were in some fashion tied together. A similar usage is attested in Dou Wan's case, but the number of disks varies (seemingly one set of nine and another partial set). The most magnificent of all the disks found at Mancheng, the grand *bi* with a pair of addorsed dragons forming a crest on its upper edge (fig. 7), was one of two found between the decayed shards of the inner and outer coffins. Whether it was placed there or actually mounted to the wall of one or the other is uncertain.[37] It is known, however, that Dou Wan's coffin had twenty-six *bi* disks inset on the exterior of her coffin.

The ritual and symbolic significance of this form in a burial context is poorly documented. Painted disks feature as decorative elements on the coffin of the Western Han tomb at Shazitang, Changsha, and on the better-known coffins and banner paintings from Mawangdui, also Changsha.[38] On each coffin magical animals (cranes and dragons) entwine their bodies with a disk on one end panel, while other *bi* are shown tied by sashes to other

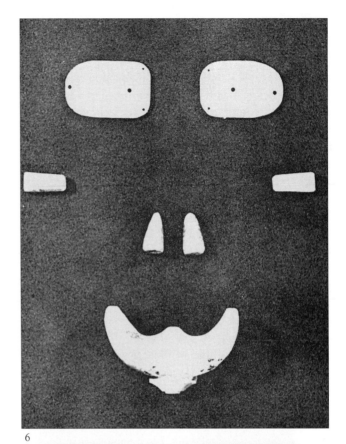

6

7

Figures

6. Jade plugs from Tomb 1. After *Mancheng Han mu*, vol. 2, pl. 105.

7. Jade *bi* disk with dragons from Tomb 1. After *Mancheng Han mu*, vol. 2, color pl. 15

faces. In the Mawangdui banners the *bi* serve as nodes through which the ascending dragons pass. The Mancheng coffins evidently took this decoration a step further by using real *bi*. The addition of dragon motifs on some disks may connote imperial status; two other examples of disks with dragon emblems are also reported from royal burials.[39] In every case the placement of such disks on or near the corpse must have had an auspicious effect, but the relationship between their mortuary usage and their normal ritual functions is not clear.

Jade Burial Suits

Archaeological evidence often supplements the historical record and not infrequently can solve a longstanding riddle. Research on the two "gold thread jade suits" (*jin lou yu yi*) found in the Mancheng tombs served exactly this function. While literary and archaeological data are not completely in agreement, the fit between them inspires heightened confidence in the work of the learned commentators whose notes to the early histories have become essential to reading those texts. In the interpretation of such finds, archaeology truly functions as a historical science.

Most jade suits were made in about a dozen parts, and the two examples from Mancheng are no exception.[40] The suit crafted for Liu Sheng required 2498 plaques of mottled green nephrite knit together with gold wire weighing about 1100 grams. Dou Wan's suit was a somewhat less demanding project: only 2160 plaques and 700 grams of gold thread were used. The plaques were thin sheets of stone in a variety of shapes and sizes, most rectangular or quadrilateral. Many plaques were specially designed and fitted together to fit the shape of the corpse. The face mask in each case incorporates eye slits and a rudimentary nose, while Dou Wan's stocking cap also has ear covers on the sides. The anatomy of the deceased is not revealed by these body suits, with the notable exception of Liu Sheng's paunch. The tunics for the torsos were made as two parts, and while each was originally backed with cloth, Dou Wan's chest piece also had silk ribbon bindings bordering and crossing each of the large plaques. Each suit had two arms, two hands, two leggings, and two boots. Unlike the chest pieces, these elements were not customized.

The excavators believe that Liu Sheng's corpse was improperly dressed at the time of his funeral. The chest piece was actually found under the back piece, but the remainder of the suit indicates the body was laid out in an extended supine posture. This anomaly seems to fly in the face of the solemnity and gravity of the occasion. Why would those in charge of the funeral of a king have so carelessly dressed his remains in the priceless shroud of jade?

About two dozen burial suits have been reported to date, half of them from the Western Han period and a like number from the Eastern Han.[41] The two examples from Mancheng may not be the earliest, but they were the first to be discovered intact and the first to be fully restored. Two finds could predate the suits from the Zhongshan kingdom: fragments found in the burials at Yangjiawan near the Changling of Han Gaozu associated with a pair of Western Han generals and a partial suit found at Linyi, Shandong Province.[42] The Linyi find has a special significance (fig. 8). This suit from the tomb of one Liu Ci, perhaps a relation of the imperial line, consisted only of face mask and stocking cap, two gloves and two boots, all made from jade plaques tied with gold wire. Several writers speculate that this may be an earlier form of burial suit created before the full-body shroud had appeared. Liu Ci's suit thus would be a handy intermediate stage for the evolution of this distinctive mortuary garment, since the only antecedents presently known are no more than remnants of cloth facial masks adorned with small plaques of jade. These distant precedents are dated to the late Zhou period and were found among burials at the Zhongzhou Road site in Luoyang.[43] Decorative jade plaques on cloth shrouds would constitute a logical first step in the history of the jade suits that flourished from the late second century B.C. onwards. The text *Lu shi chun qiu* (Master Lu's Springs and Autumns, circa 240 B.C.) seems to make reference to such predecessors in a passage noting that the well-to-do use "pearl mouth amulets and scale coverings." The commentator Gao You (flourished 205-12) glosses the latter phrase as, "to place jades like fish scales on the body of the dead."[44]

Lu Zhaoyin of the Institute of Archaeology believes that full-body suits appeared during the reign of Wudi (141-87 B.C.). He notes that there are no references to such mortuary accessories in *Shi ji* and no actual examples in such well-appointed early Western Han tombs as the burials at Mawangdui.[45] All of the Western Han examples are dated to the first century B.C., with the exception of the

Figure

8. Jade burial suit of Liu Ci, Linyi, Shandong. After *Dai koga bunmei no nagare* (Tokyo: Seibu Bijutsukan and Asahi Shinbunsha, 1986), no. 76.

Yangjiawan, Linyi, and Mancheng tombs, and most of those, like Mancheng, can be associated with the imperial family, especially the enfeoffed kings. The earliest references to a system of graded types of jade suits appears in the *Hou Han shu* (History of Later Han) "Treatise on Rites and Ceremonies" compiled by Sima Biao (240-306).[46] Here the suits of the Son of Heaven are described as made with gold thread, those of kings, marquises, honorable ladies, and princesses are to be made with silver thread, while those of elder honorable ladies and senior princesses are made with bronze thread. In *Han shu* accounts no such distinctions are observed, and indeed many of the Western Han examples are knit together with gold thread. The "Treatise" also suggests that jade suits were created by the imperial court workshop charged with the manufacture of mortuary accessories, the Artisan of the Eastern Garden (*Dong yuan jiang*).[47] It is self-evident that crafting a full-length body suit of jade would require the resources and expertise of a large jade workshop. Since most of the kingdoms are unlikely to have had such artisans in their employ, centralized production is a preferable explanation. One example, of Eastern Han date, evidently was too large when it arrived from the capital. The excavators found sections of both leggings neatly placed under the torso and concluded that these sections were taken off at the time the corpse was dressed.[48] The inference is that the suit was already made in the capital workshop and then sent when needed to the kingdom.

Both literary and archaeological sources suggest that jade suits more elaborately decorated than those found at Lingshan were also produced. *Han shu* records a "pearl robe jade suit" in its description of the funeral accorded the notorious eunuch Dong Xian.[49] The Tang commentator Yan Shigu (581-645) explains the phrase: "A pearl robe has pearls for the tunic like a suit of armor sewn together using gold thread. From the waist down the suit is jade [plaques], and down to the feet it too is sewn together with gold thread." If no archaeological corollary to this kind of shroud has yet been reported, there are at least two known examples of suits made from plaques that were engraved and then decorated with gold thread or foil on their surfaces.[50] The dragon, floral, and cloud patterns rendered in gold found on these plaques may indicate that over time jade suits became even more elaborate.

The Mancheng Tombs in Perspective

An assessment of the two burials on Lingshan must be conducted in the absence of several vital pieces of evidence for the mortuary culture of the Western Han period. Most obvious among these missing elements is the utter lack of any excavations of the Western Han imperial tombs themselves. As a consequence, the relative magnitude and "richness" of the two Zhongshan burials can only

be guessed; how rich a truly extravagant burial could be in this age remains to be seen. When, however, these tombs and their furnishings are compared to other kingly burials of the period and to pre-Han burials of roughly equivalent local lords, the Mancheng finds do not appear to set any records for either ambition or indulgence.

A second serious limitation in coming to grips with these finds is the incomplete condition of the tomb furnishings. What has survived to our day is a selection of the most durable goods. What has been lost is surely the most delicate and precious of the perishable materials, notably silk textiles and lacquer wares. The quantity of metal fittings found in the two chambers is sufficient evidence that fine lacquer wares were an important part of the life-style of Liu Sheng and Dou Wan. Nonetheless the evidence is far inferior to that derived from the two well-preserved tombs at Mawangdui or others like them. In this case the rock-cut caverns created for Liu Sheng and Dou Wan did a poorer job of preserving the tomb contents than the older tradition of vertical shafts and well-sealed wooden chambers. As a consequence, a further note of qualification may be in order. Perhaps the true extravagance of Liu Sheng and Dou Wan was in many hampers of silk robes that were taken to the grave, materials for which today we have only the most fragmentary evidence.

The Mancheng tombs and many other burials of the Western Han kings have an additional importance for the history of late Zhou and Han jade carving. The *bi* disk with dragons (fig. 7) is but one example of carving strikingly similar to jades associated with the rich, prewar finds at Jincun, a village near Luoyang.[51] The proper dating and attribution of the several Jincun tombs is still debated, but Li Xueqin has made a strong case for its affiliations with the royal Zhou domain of the middle and late Warring States era (fourth and third centuries B.C.). The jades from Mancheng and Qufu as well as those from the Nan Yue royal tomb at Guangzhou have much in common with the so-called Jincun style of working jade.[52] This raises several intriguing possibilities. It may be necessary to redate some of the Jincun material to the Western Han unless it can be shown that the opposite logical possibility—redating some jades in Han tombs to a pre-Han date—is more persuasive. If neither case can prevail, it is at least necessary to consider the possibility that a large jade workshop was active from the late Zhou into the Western Han serving first the Zhou kings and then the Han emperors.

In addition these two tombs must be evaluated in the context of the vogue for immortality in the reign of Wudi. Both the use of jade amulets, plugs, and ritual disks and the jade burial shrouds are strong evidence for the seriousness with which this king and his consort took the claims of practitioners of the various arts that promised "no death." Their infatuation with these claims was hardly unusual in their day, and the ritual specialists at court quickly accommodated these new accessories into the repertoire of perquisites defined for an imperial burial. The layering of beliefs evident in these tombs and their furnishings is typical. Rather than abandon old habits of thought in favor of new ones, ideas were grafted onto the existing structure of beliefs and practices. Ideas and customs first created in the early Bronze Age had an extraordinarily long life in the rituals and accessories of the dead. Even if Liu Sheng were totally committed to the pursuit of "no death," his burial nonetheless was in most respects a logical outgrowth of longstanding traditions that had grown from earlier (even conflicting) values and belief systems.

Finally the tombs at Mancheng remain prime evidence for understanding the development of the rites of burial for the Son of Heaven. Until the tombs of the Qin First Emperor or the sovereigns of early Western Han are excavated, these two burials are our best window into the rituals observed at the time of an imperial funeral. None of the other tombs of Han kings can match the furnishings found at Mancheng. The royal Zhongshan tombs provide a wealth of specific detail on the customs of the imperial court in this formative stage in the evolution of the institution of the emperor.

Notes

1. Martin J. Powers, "Artistic Taste, the Economy and the Social Order in Former Han China," *Art History* 9.3 (September 1986): 285-305.

2. Robert L. Thorp, "The Qin and Han Imperial Tombs and the Development of Mortuary Architecture," in Los Angeles County Museum of Art, *The Quest for Eternity: Chinese Ceramic Sculptures from the People's Republic of China*, exh. cat. (San Francisco: Chronicle Books, 1987), 17-37.

3. On the first emperor's tomb, see Robert L. Thorp, "An Archaeological Reconstruction of the Lishan Necropolis," in *The Great Bronze Age of China: A Symposium*, ed. George Kuwayama (Los Angeles: Los Angeles County Museum of Art, 1983), 72-83.

4. For a preliminary review of these processes, see Robert L. Thorp, "The Mortuary Art and Architecture of Early Imperial China," Ph.D. diss. (University of Kansas, 1979), esp. chaps. 4 and 5. While data have continued to accumulate, no more recent general treatments of this topic have appeared yet in either Chinese or Western languages.

5. Compare the Shaanxi, Henan, and Sichuan figurines in *Quest for Eternity* (nos. 11-38).

6. On the Western Han kingdoms, see Ch'u T'ung-tsu [Qu Tongzu], *Han Social Structure* (Seattle: University of Washington, 1972), 76, 165-67. Han administration is discussed in Hans Bielenstein, *The Bureaucracy of Han Times* (Cambridge: Cambridge University Press, 1980), 105-7.

7. Institute of Archaeology and Hebei Cultural Relics Administration, *Mancheng Han mu fajue baogao* [Excavation report of the Han tombs at Mancheng] (Beijing: Wenwu Press, 1980), 3-4. Unless otherwise cited, data pertaining to the Mancheng site are derived from this report.

8. *Mancheng Han mu*, vol. 1, 250, and vol. 2, pl. 171. Also illustrated in *Wenhua dageming qijian chutu wenwu xuan* [A selection of cultural relics unearthed during the Great Cultural Revolution] (Beijing: Wenwu Press, 1974), no. 14. Another vessel of comparable cost was exhibited in *The Genius of China* (London: Times Newspapers, 1973), no. 157.

9. "Mancheng Han mu fajue jiyao" [Summary of the excavation of the Han tombs at Mancheng], *Kaogu* [Archaeology] 1972.1: 15-16. This first report of the Mancheng discoveries is embellished with polemical passages including quotations from the Marxist canon printed in bold type but is nonetheless an accurate summary of the initial findings.

10. Ban Gu, *Han shu* [History of Han] (Beijing: Zhonghua Press, 1962), 68, 2948. Translation in Burton Watson, *Courtier and Commoner in Ancient China* (New York: Columbia University Press, 1974), 140.

11. Two fissures in the rock of the mountain developed after the time of the burial and allowed rainwater to enter the chambers. In addition to the south-side chamber of Tomb 1 an opening developed in the south-side room of Tomb 2 (*Mancheng Han mu*, 15, 219).

12. The tomb of the king of Nan Yue, excavated in Guangzhou in recent years, has yet to receive a thorough excavation report; once it does, it too will be a prime example of this highest social level. See "Xi Han Nan Yue wang mu fajue chubu baogao" [Preliminary report of the excavation of the tomb of the Western Han King of Nan Yue], *Kaogu* 1984.3: 222-30.
A popular introduction to the Mancheng finds is Edmund Capon and William MacQuitty, *Princes of Jade* (London: Nelson, 1973), but this volume is flawed by numerous errors. In addition to the excavation report the best illustrations are found in *Wenhua dageming*, 1-29, and *Out of China's Earth* (New York: Abrams, 1980), 126-37. A selection of objects from the tombs was included in *The Genius of China*, nos. 139-67.

13. *Mancheng Han mu*, vol. 1, 336.

14. *Mancheng Han mu*, vol. 1, 43-74 passim.

15. Sima Qian, *Shi ji* [Historical Records] (Beijing: Zhonghua Press, 1959), 59, 2099; *Han shu* 53, 2422-26. The former source records his demise after forty-two years on the throne; *Han shu* records the figure of forty-three years, which is believed to be in error. See also, Burton Watson, trans., *Records of the Grand Historian of China*, vol. 1 (New York: Columbia University Press, 1971), 456-57.

16. *Mancheng Han mu*, vol. 1, 274.

17. *Shi Ji*, 10, 434.

18. On the Baling, see Liu Qingzhu and Li Shufang, *Xi Han shiyi ling* [The eleven Western Han imperial tombs] (Xi'an: Shaanxi Renmin chubanshe, 1987), 34-39. The tomb site has not been systematically surveyed or excavated.

19. *Shi ji*, 10, 433-34, and *Han shu*, 4, 131-32. For a translation of the latter, see Homer H. Dubs, trans., *The History of the Former Han Dynasty*, 3 vols. (Baltimore: Waverly Press, 1938-55), 1: 266-72.

20. Yu Weichao, "Handai zhuhou wang yu liehou muzang de xingzhi fenxi" [An analysis of the plans of tombs of Han kings and marquises], in *Xian Qin liang Han kaoguxue lunji* [Collected essays on the archaeology of the pre-Qin and two Han] (Beijing: Wenwu Press, 1985), 117-24.

21. *Mancheng Han mu* [The Han tombs at Mancheng] (Beijing: Wenwu Press, 1978), 15. Reprinted in *The Great Bronze Age of China* (New York: Metropolitan Museum of Art, 1980), 326, fig. 112.

22. Thorp, "Archaeological Reconstruction of the Lishan Necropolis," 78-80.

23. Thorp, "Qin and Han Imperial Tombs," 30-35.

24. "Qufu Jiulong Shan Han mu fajue jianbao" [Brief excavation report of the Han tombs at Jiulong Shan, Qufu], *Wenwu* [Cultural relics] 1972.5: 39-44, 54.

25. "Xuzhou Beidong Shan Xi Han mu fajue jianbao" [Brief excavation report of the Western Han tomb at Beidong Shan, Xuzhou], *Wenwu* 1988.2: 2-18, 68.

26. "Tongshan Guishan erhao Xi Han yaidong mu" [Rock-cut tomb no. 2 of the Western Han at Guishan, Tongshan], *Kaogu Xuebao* [Acta Archaeologia Sinica] 1985.1: 119-33. A related burial is reported in "Tongshan Xiao Guishan Xi Han yaimu" [The rock-cut Han tomb at Xiao Guishan, Tongshan], *Wenwu* 1973:4: 21-35.

27. "Xuzhou Shiqiao Han mu qingli baogao" [Report of clearing the Han tombs at Shiqiao, Xuzhou], *Wenwu* 1984.11: 22-40.

28. Yu Ying-shih, "Life and Immortality in the Mind of Han China," *Harvard Journal of Asiatic Studies* 25 (1964-65), esp. 93-108.

29. Joseph Needham, *Science and Civilization in China*, vol. 5, *Chemistry and Chemical Technology*, pt. 2, *Spagyrical Discovery and Invention: Magisteries of Gold and Immortality* (Cambridge: Cambridge University Press, 1974), 297-304.

30. See, for example, the late fifth-century B.C. tomb of Marquis Yi of the small state of Zeng at modern Suizhou, Hubei; Robert L. Thorp, "The Sui Xian Tomb: Re-Thinking the Fifth Century," *Artibus Asiae* 43 (1981-82): 67-110.

31. For Yangjiawan, see "Xianyang Yangjiawan Han mu fajue jianbao" [Brief excavation report of the Han tombs at Yangjiawan, Xianyang], *Wenwu* 1977.10: 10-21. For Shizi Shan, see "Xuzhou Shizi Shan bing ma yong keng diyici fajue jianbao" [Brief report of the first excavation of the pit with warriors and horses at Shizi Shan, Xuzhou], *Wenwu* 1986.12: 1-16.

32. Na Zhiliang, *Yuqi tongshi* [A general account of jades], (Hong Kong: Kai-fa Press, 1964), 134.

33. *Mancheng Han mu*, vol. 1, 139-40. Illustrated in *Wenhua dageming*, 29.

34. Ibid., 295.

35. Needham, *Science and Civilization*, 284.

36. Xia Nai, "Handai de yuqi" [Jades of the Han period], *Kaogu Xuebao* 1983.2, esp. 129-32, and the same author's *Jade and Silk of Han China*, trans. Chu-tsing Li, The Franklin D. Murphy Lectures III (Lawrence: Spencer Museum of Art, 1983), 16-49.

37. On this disk and related examples, see my *Son of Heaven: Imperial Arts of China* (Seattle: Son of Heaven Press, 1988), 63-65.

38. For the Shazitang coffin, see Li Zhengguang, *Handai qiqi yishu* [The art of Han period lacquer wares] (Beijing: Wenwu Press, 1987), pls. 138-41; for Mawangdui, see *Changsha Mawangdui Yihao Han mu* (Beijing: Wenwu Press, 1973), fig. 24 (red lacquered coffin) and fig. 38 (banner painting).

39. See Yang Boda, ed., *Yuqi* [Jades], *Zhongguo meishu quanji, Gongyi meishu bian* 9 [Compendia of Chinese Arts, Arts and Crafts] (Beijing: Wenwu Press, 1986), pls. 190 and 193.

40. *Mancheng Han mu*, 36-37, 244, 344-57.

41. In what follows I am indebted to the research of Lu Zhaoyin, "Shilun liang Han de yu yi" [A preliminary discussion of the jade suits of the two Han dynasties], *Kaogu* 1981.1: 51-58, the most comprehensive analysis of the subject in print. See also Jeffrey Kao and Yang Zuosheng, "On Jade Suits and Han Archaeology," *Archaeology* 36.6 (November/December, 1983): 30-37.

42. "Xianyang Yangjiawan Han mu" and "Shandong Linyi Xi Han Liu Ci mu" [The Western Han tomb of Liu Ci at Linyi, Shandong], *Kaogu* 1980.6: 493-95.

43. *Luoyang Zhongzhou lu (Xi gong duan)* [Report of excavations at the west section of Zhongzhou Road, Luoyang], (Beijing: Science Press, 1959), 118-20.

44. *Lu shi chun qiu* (Sibu congkan edition), 10.5a.

45. Lu, "Shilun liang Han de yu yi," 52.

46. Fan Ye, *Hou Han shu* (Beijing: Zhonghua Press, 1963), zhi 6, 3141 and 3152.

47. On this office, see Bielenstein, *Bureaucracy of Han Times*, 62.

48. "Ding Xian 40-hao Han mu chutu de jin lou yu yi" [The gold thread jade suit unearthed from Western Han tomb no. 40 at Ding Xian], *Wenwu* 1976.7: 57-59.

49. *Han shu* 93, 3734.

50. A tomb at Ganchuan Shan near Yangzhou; see *Wenwu kaogu gongzuo sanshinian, 1949-1979* [Thirty years of cultural relics and archaeological work, 1949-1979] (Beijing: Wenwu Press, 1979), 205. See also "Hebei Xingtai nanjiao Xi Han mu" [The Western Han tomb in the south suburbs of Xingtai, Hebei], *Kaogu* 1980.5: 403-5.

51. For an introduction to these finds, see Li Xueqin, *Eastern Zhou and Qin Civilizations*, trans. K. C. Chang (New Haven: Yale University Press, 1985), 29-36. A contemporary account is William C. White, *Tombs of Old Loyang* (Shanghai: Kelly and Walsh, 1934).

52. See Yang, *Yuqi*, pls. 138-59, for Nan Yue jades.

A New Look at the Xianbei and their Impact on Chinese Culture

Albert Dien

Stanford University

As we learn from the catalogue for the exhibition *The Quest for Eternity*, after the fall of the Han, in A.D. 220, "four centuries thereafter China was divided and in turmoil. The government broke into competing states, armed conflict was frequent, and the economy stagnated."[1] It was during this period of political fragmentation that various non-Chinese peoples established a number of states in north China, many of which were short-lived and which make this period one of the most confusing and troubled in Chinese history.[2] Among these non-Chinese peoples were the Xianbei tribesmen, who came into China in the early years of this era, established several states that together lasted some two centuries or more, during which time there was a process of assimilation, and then they apparently were absorbed into the Chinese population. For years almost all that was known about them was from textual sources, and these have a strong bias since they were written from the point of view of the Chinese. In the last decade or so an unprecedented amount of archaeological evidence has appeared that enables us to be somewhat clearer about the Xianbei and the time in which they lived. In the light of this new information it would appear that the course of assimilation was not a simple one, and that in fact the Xianbei retained their own identity over most of this period. We wish here to view that archaeological record, informed by the historical sources, to see what it can tell us of the Xianbei. Further, we wish to make some tentative assessments as to the contribution these nomadic tribesmen may have made to the glorious Sui and Tang civilizations that followed.

On July 13, 311, Luoyang, the eastern capital of the Jin dynasty, a city with a population of some six hundred thousand, with walls over seven miles in circumference, with a history as cultural center and capital for more than a thousand years, fell to the Huns, or as the Chinese called them, the Xiongnu, and the city was burned shortly after.[3] This event was as important in the history of China, in a symbolic sense, as was the sacking of Rome in 410 by the Goths under Alaric. The event in China sent shock waves through the land and beyond. A letter written about that time and found in a corner of a watchtower of the Great Wall, a short distance west of Dunhuang, written in Sogdian (a Persian dialect), by a foreign merchant, Nanaivandak, back to his home office, as it were, in Samarkand, tells of the news and the difficult times into which China had fallen.[4] The burning of Luoyang, followed a few years later by the capture of the emperor in his western capital at Chang'an, can be seen as marking an important turning point in Chinese history, for when the imperial prince who was then governor of Jiankang, modern Nanjing, declared himself the legitimate successor to the throne, China fragmented, with the south remaining under the control of the Chinese and the north abandoned to the "barbarians." Unity would not be achieved again for almost three hundred years. This period of disunion has been called the "Dark Age" of Chinese history, when the "Five Barbarians" brought disorder to China.

The fall of Luoyang came as the end result of a long series of events that in some interesting ways may well have paralleled the situation in Rome at the time of its fall. The Huns, who originally lived in the steppes to the north of China, in modern Inner and Outer Mongolia, pressed on the northern frontiers of China for the same reasons as motivated the Goths on the Danube, which is to say that there were other peoples behind them who pushed them on.[5] During the first and second centuries larger and larger numbers of Xiongnu were settled within the territory of the Chinese state, to buffer the Chinese from the other, more savage peoples and to provide also a source for troops in the frontier armies. Later, as conditions became more unsettled within China, they also were enrolled in the private armies of the various warlords who came to power. Like the Goths in the Roman service, these barbarians served with loyalty and distinction until the rulers themselves fell out. The wars between the seven princes of the Jin royal house, during the infamous "Yungjia" period, brought about a loss of control of these professional armies, and northern China sank even further into turmoil and confusion. The various groups of nomads established one short-lived state after another, each attempting to assert undisputed claim to the rule of the heartland. There were sixteen of these states during this period, and their competition for supremacy meant that the armies ranged over the land, fighting was constant, and survival was difficult.[6]

One of the nomad groups was the Xianbei, whose origins are to be found in northern Manchuria. They practiced a hunting-gathering economy and probably spoke an Altaic language related to Turkish.[7] As they began moving south into steppeland during the first century A.D., they became nomadic pastoralists, and eventually they moved into northern China. The Tuoba, who had become the leading clan among the Xianbei, established the precursor to the Northern Wei state in 386 and by conquering their rivals one by one managed to unite northern China under their rule. Unlike some of the other nomad states, whose method of rule was to slaughter the peasants (thus turning the land into a pasture for their herds), or to supply their needs by raids on the native population, the Tuoba managed to establish a stable form of administration, using the Chinese themselves to administer and to tax the population.[8]

The Xianbei account of themselves has it that they had lived far to the north, herding and hunting. They believed that they had taken the name Xianbei from a mountain of that name in the area where they had originated and that they had bored out a stone cave there in order to worship their ancestral spirits. They left this area perhaps early in the first century A.D. as they began their trek south and their rise to power. But in 443, according to the Wei shu (their state history), a delegation from the Wuluohou people, as yet unidentified, reported that they had found this stone cave. The Tuoba ruler then sent a Chinese official to the cave to render thanks to the spirits, and an inscription was carved on the cave wall to commemorate the occasion; the text of the inscription is also given in the history.[9] The location of that place of origin has been argued for years because the evidence at hand was very unclear. Then, in 1980, an inscription dated that same year of 443 and differing only in a few words from the text in the Wei shu was found on the wall of a large natural cave ten kilometers northwest of Alihezhen, in the Oronchon Autonomous Banner, Hulunbeier League, northern Heilongjiang Province. Usually archaeological reports are written in scholarly, dry prose, but at that point in the text of the report, the archaeologist's excitement shows through, as he writes, "and I could not believe my eyes."[10] One can hardly blame him.

There appears to be general agreement that the origins of the Xianbei are to be sought in the area of that cave, in the forests of the eastern flank of the Daxing'an Mountains, on the Gan River, which flows into the upper reaches of the Nen River in northern Heilongjiang Province. The route by which the Xianbei subsequently came into the China of that time is not clear.

The traditional account of the Xianbei move south is contained in the opening chapter of the Wei shu, the history of the Tuoba Wei, which records the early legends of the Xianbei, albeit in an extremely concise fashion. A confederation of thirty-six tribes (the Chinese text says guo, or states) and ninety-nine clans (daxing) was formed under a leader named Mao. Several generations later, perhaps at the beginning of the common era, the Xianbei moved south to a large marsh, said to be over a thousand li square in size,[11] where the land was dark, low-lying, and damp. A second move is perhaps to be dated at the end of the second century A.D. The direction is again given as southward, through mountainous country and over so many natural obstacles that they wished to stop. But led by a strange beast with the shape of a horse and the voice of an ox, the tribesmen finally emerged into the former territory of the Xiongnu, presumably modern Inner Mongolia.[12]

On the basis of this account and archaeological evidence uncovered in recent years, Professor Su Bai has proposed that the terminus of the first leg of the journey is represented by sites at Wan'gong and Zhalainuoer, both in the Hulunbeier League; the Wan'gong site is about sixty kilometers east of Hulun Lake while Zhalainuoer is just north of the lake. The lake would be the feature that was measured as a thousand square li, while the swampy area on the margin of the lake, presumably, is the low-lying damp land (see map).[13]

At Wan'gong, the earlier of the two sites, there are multiple and single burials in vertical pit graves, the bodies laid out supine with straight limbs, the heads to the northwest. The graves yielded evidence of animal offerings, ranging from heads to complete bodies of horses, oxen, and dogs. Tools and weapons were primarily made of bone and stone but with some bronze and iron objects, including bracelets, buckles, arrow heads, and knives. Ornaments of silver, shell, turquoise, coral, and agate were also found. Such jewelry, a three-legged *li*-tripod, and fragments of silk cloth indicate connections with the Chinese far to the south, while small bronze ornaments, rings, and buckles give evidence of Xiongnu influence. Birch bark was used for containers of various sorts, and birch bark and birch boards were used to cover the bottom of one of the graves and in another were placed over and under the corpse, serving as a coffin. Distinctive pottery, all handmade, consisted primarily of *hu* (jugs) and *guan* (jars). Some were rather crude, sand-tempered, and low-fired, others were of a finer quality and high-fired. The surfaces were generally plain and polished or with a simple comb decor or grooves, and vertical striations on the neck of the vessels done with fingernails. One type that is rather distinctive is a *guan* (jar) with a symmetrical pair of handles at the midpoint (fig. 1).[14]

The graves at Zhalainuoer appear to be of a later stage. These burials are mostly single, with birch boards now used to make four-sided frames. Offerings are now represented by parts of the animal, sometimes only hooves. Pottery types are more varied and of a better quality, and wheel-made pottery appears. The bronze and bone implements increased, but more significant was the greater variety of iron implements. This site represents a stage of further development of the nomadic pastoral economy. Evidence of even greater contact with the Chinese is found in the variety of imported items, such as a TLV mirror, embroidery, and a lacquered toilet case. These objects date the site as not earlier than first century A.D. The Xiongnu influence also continues to be strong, especially in the area of horse gear and weapons (fig. 2).[15]

For the second stage of the legendary Xianbei journey, through the high mountains and deep valleys, and then into the old Xiongnu lands, Professor Su Bai has conjectured that the mention of a desire to stop indicates a break during which the tribe settled down for a short period before going on. He believes that the first part indicates a trek through the southern half of the Daxing'an Range, back to the eastern side where a site similar to that of Zhalianuoer was found in the valley of the Wuerjimulun River, a branch of the Liao River, east of Nanyangjiayingzi, Balin Left Banner, Liaoning. Dwelling sites and graves alike yielded handmade sand-tempered pots and jugs and wheel-made gray jugs. The bodies in the vertical pit graves were laid out in the supine position with straight limbs, heads to the northwest. The use of wooden coffins and

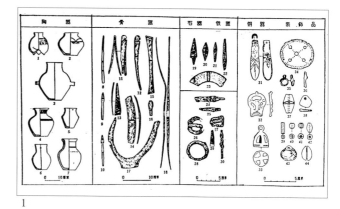

1

2

Figures
1. Material from Wan'gong. *Wenwu* 1977.5, 48, fig. 8.
2. Burials at Zhalainuoer. *Wenwu* 1977.5, 49, fig. 9.

sacrificial offerings of parts of animals was the same as at Zhalainuoer. Bronze and bone were not used as extensively as before, while iron objects had increased. A *wuzhu* coin of late Eastern Han, that is, second century A.D., helps in dating the site. The implements here, as compared with those at Zhalainuoer, seem more developed; there is greater social stratification in evidence in the graves, and the division of labor between men and women seems more defined. The paucity of remains at this site, Professor Su concludes, was due to the short-term stay here, and afterwards the Xianbei moved westward into Inner Mongolia.[16]

Professor Su's reconstruction of the Xianbei journey has not convinced everyone. On a number of grounds Qin Weibo has objected to the identification of Wan'gong and Zhalainuoer as the first stop. He says that Hulun Lake could not be described as a marsh, that the Wan'gong site was too early, and that the surrounding terrain, which he says is dry and gravelly, was not suitable for the herding and hunting in which the Xianbei said they were engaged at that time.[17] Rather, he proposes that the Xianbei simply followed the Nen River onto the eastern slopes of the Daxing'an mountains where there are still large stretches of marshland set amidst small reaches of woodland, an area ideally suited to a mixed economy of herding and hunting. A number of sites, such as those at Xinglongshan, Tongyuxian, Heilongjiang;[18] Laoheshencun, Yushuxian, Jilin,[19] and Xichagou, Xifengxian, Liaoning,[20] yielded material similar to those at Wan'gong and Zhalainuoer. Vertical pit graves, the typical pottery, and other such material point to these as being Xianbei. Qin Weibo thus concludes that the Xianbei arose in the upper and middle reaches of the Nen River, and after a period of conflict with the Xiongnu and the ancient state of Yan, during which they retreated to the northern part of the Daxing'an mountains, they came south into the foothills and adjacent plains of those mountains and the connecting ranges of mountains further south, where they were active during the first and second centuries A.D. At this point the theories of Su Bai and Qin converge. As Xiongnu power waned, a large number of the Xianbei turned westward, a move perhaps reflected in the second part of the legend, and they thus moved into the Xiongnu territory. Those who remained became a part of the Eastern Xianbei people, who were to establish themselves in modern Liaoning and Liaodong provinces.[21]

As the Xianbei appeared on the Chinese horizon, the Chinese officials no doubt became acquainted with their ways and were able to send descriptions of their customs to the capital where the reports would be properly noted and filed. The Wuhuan people were said to be the same in language and customs with the Xianbei, and the description of the Wuhuan in the history of the later Han, probably based on those field reports, may serve in part for the Xianbei as well.[22]

The description of the Wuhuan is rather typical in many ways for northern nomads. They are described as engaging both in hunting and herding, as living in domed structures (yurts?) with no permanent homes, as honoring the young and strong and despising the old and weak. The leader (or "big man") was selected on the basis of being the bravest and most judicious, but the position was not hereditable. The tribe was made up of smaller groups, numbering up to a thousand, each of which had its own leader. These smaller groups may have been the segmentary lineages found among modern nomads of the same area.[23] Many social customs correspond to nomadic societies in general, including bride's price and dowry, years of service in the bride's family, levirate, and an equality of the sexes, women in this case being said to be the decision makers in all but matters of war. The responsible role taken by women would seem to be confirmed centuries later by Yan Zhitui, who described the women of Ye, the capital of the Northern Qi, as handling family business, interceding on behalf of their husbands with the court and authorities, and seeking appointments for their sons. Yan concluded by surmising that such activity by women in public life was the heritage of the northern nomads.[24] Women shaved their heads, but upon marriage they let the hair grow and dressed it in buns with ornaments and the tall, horned cap later known in medieval Europe as the hennin.[25]

The *Hou Han shu* describes nomadic burial customs as follows: "By custom they honor death in battle. They lay out the corpse in a coffin, and grieve with weeping, but accompany the dead to the burial with songs and dance. They raise and fatten a dog and draw it along with colored rope and tassels, and together with the horse of the deceased and his belongings, all are burned to accompany him, saying it is all consigned to the dog to have it protect the spirit of the dead to return to Chishan. Chishan is several thousand *li* northwest of Liaodong; it is like the spirits of the Chinese dead returning to Taishan.

They pay respect to deities and make offerings to heaven, earth, sun, moon, stars, constellations, mountains, rivers, and those earlier chiefs of renown. In making offerings, they use ox and sheep, and when finished, they burn them."

Later in the same chapter of the *Hou Han shu*, the Xianbei are treated.[26]

"As for the Xianbei . . . their language and customs are the same as the Wuhuan, but they first shave the scalp upon marrying; only after feasting and drinking at the great meeting in the spring on the Raole River[27] do they pair off. Further, their animals are different from those of China: wild horses, primal sheep, and 'horn-tip' oxen. They use the horn to make their bows, which are commonly called horn-tip bows. They also have sable, the *nua* (monkey), and the *hun* (rodent). The furs of these animals are soft and plush, and so make the world's most famed fur garments."

As they moved closer to the borders of China, pushing some elements of the Huns before them, the Tuoba Xianbei became the center of a confederation of the tribes on the frontier. Such a confederation, like those of other nomadic groups, would have been composed of a variety of peoples, all taking their designation from the dominant group. This heterogeneous composition of tribal confederations helps explain what appear to be anomalies in language, race, and custom. They were drawn, whether willing or not, into the Chinese arena, exchanging hostages and entering into treaties with the Chinese state to the south. In 258 a walled settlement was built at Shengle, a short distance north of modern Holingol (fig. 3).[28] From the cultural deposits there it would seem it was primarily occupied by the Chinese who farmed for the Xianbei, while the tribesmen themselves remained largely nomadic herders, sticking with the old ways. There is a story in the *Wei shu* about the young prince who had spent years at the Chinese capital as a hostage. On one of his visits home he showed off with a bow that shot pellets for the purpose of hunting birds, and the fear that this aroused about new ways led to the prince's assassination.[29]

The Xianbei armies by now were an important factor in

the struggles going on in China. When the Huns captured the Jin capital of Luoyang in 311, the Xianbei were sending cavalry to prop up the Jin.[30] The grave of a warrior has been found at Xiaomincun, Anyang, and from it we can learn much about their gear. It is a vertical pit grave, the top slightly wider than the foot, with a ledge at the head on which had been placed two pots and the leg bone of an ox. At the foot were the skulls of a horse and a pig. The presence of nails indicated there had been a coffin. Most interestingly, a saddle had been placed under the head of the corpse and the horse equipage over the body. From the remains it has been possible to reconstruct the horse's trappings (fig. 4).[31]

As the Tuoba moved closer to the heartland of China, they increasingly took on elements of that culture. The effect of this adaptation to life in an agricultural society can be seen in a tomb found at Meidaicun, forty kilometers east of Huhehot. The tomb consists of a brick chamber with a high, vaulted roof, and the chamber and coffin within it are wider at one end than at the other (fig. 5). This differs much from the earlier vertical pit graves in that it has a ledge on which to place offerings. At Meidaicun there were no animal bones, bows and arrows, or objects of bone or horn, and yet the shape of the coffin and such grave goods as a bronze cauldron, typical of the steppes, and the same types of pottery seen earlier identify this as a Xianbei burial.[32]

Another contemporary tomb has an entryway, a square brick chamber with its walls slightly bulging, and a brick coffin platform. The chamber is rather small, measuring only 2 meters by 1.9 meters, but it contains some very interesting material. The pottery is about the same as before, but in addition there are figurines of warriors and horses as well as models of ox carts, oven, mill, and well, evidence that the Xianbei were moving from a herding economy to an agricultural one. The rough and crude modeling is an index perhaps of their cultural level at the time, but various seals and tallies give evidence of a high level of complexity in state formation, and jewelry of excellent quality would indicate increasing affluence.[33] One may say that the figures represent Xianbei, if for no other reason, because of the distinctive headdress and cloak that do not occur associated with other groups, especially not with the Chinese (figs. 6-7).

The Xianbei involvement in the internal affairs of China increased as the Jin state withdrew and the other nomadic groups staked out their claims. The decision was reached in 398 to enter fully into the fray. The leader of the Xianbei, Tuoba Gui, upgraded his status by having himself declared emperor of the state of Wei and, giving up the base in the steppelands, the court was moved to Pingcheng, at modern Datong in Shanxi, where the capital was to remain for the next 100 years.[34] State-building processes accompanied these developments, including attempts to transform the nomadic tribesmen into settled householders.[35]

The standard historical accounts of the Tuoba at this point suddenly burgeon with formal edicts written in elegant classical Chinese, setting up state schools teaching the Chinese classics and establishing the full panoply of officers and rituals; all of this might seem rather pretentious for a group so recently arrived from the steppes. The Chinese in the south, with a smugness rooted in centuries of cultural superiority, described the new capital in disparaging terms, telling of the consorts and concubines of the emperor living in earthen houses, the attendants dealing in cloth, selling wine, tending pigs and goats, and raising vegetables to sell for profit.[36] While the southern accounts emphasized the provincialism of this "barbarian" capital, giving the impression, as W. F. J. Jenner says, of a villa at the center of a *latifundium*, there are indications that there was much vitality in this burgeoning center. Near here, fifteen kilometers to the west, are the impressive caves of Yun'gang, begun in 460.[37] These were the accomplishments of a strong state, able to command the resources adequate to carry out such projects. Indeed, by the 430s all of northern China had been brought under Xianbei sway, and in 443 they were quite ready to send the mission to the place of their origins to give thanks to the ancestral spirits.[38]

The traces of Xianbei presence are rather fleeting; the evidence is there, but it is not a dominant theme. At Yun'gang, for example, there is almost no evidence in the elaborate ornamentation that this impressive complex of caves was constructed under the Xianbei regime. Only a row of worshippers, with the now-familiar hood, gives one a clue as to the identity of the donors (fig. 8). Similarly, at the Dunhuang caves in the far northwest the earliest surviving caves are from the Tuoba period, and yet the presence and patronage of the Xianbei does not come to the surface. It was indeed serendipitous that in the process of stabilizing the caves, the archaeologists found a piece of embroidery, some thirty inches by twenty inches, stuffed into a crack in the wall at Cave 126. This piece dates from 487 and was probably a part of a banner hung in a cave temple, a contribution by a Tuoba prince sent from Pingcheng, showing himself, his family, and a monk offering their devotion to the Buddha. Note the characteristic headgear, the long robe, trousers, and boots on the male, the long skirt on the female (fig. 9).[39]

It would seem that traces of Xianbei presence survive through adversity. In 1973 at Guyuan, Ningxia, which had been a strategic crossroad on the Silk Road, a railway survey team using a water-cooled drill accidently broke into a Northern Wei tomb. The tomb chamber again is described as being almost square, the side walls somewhat bulging out, the ceiling a cloister vault—a structure that became the standard form for tombs during this period (fig. 10).[40] The contents of the tomb were quite rich, including a surprisingly large number of bronze vessels as well as pottery vessels, iron sword and knife, stirrups, mirrors, cups, ornaments of gilt silver and other precious materials, and a

Sasanian silver coin of Firûz I (459-84). The water did much damage, but worse, the drill itself hit a lacquered coffin, and so only fragments were recovered in 1981 when the tomb was finally excavated. Still, it is a remarkable discovery.[41]

The coffin must have been a magnificent work of art. It

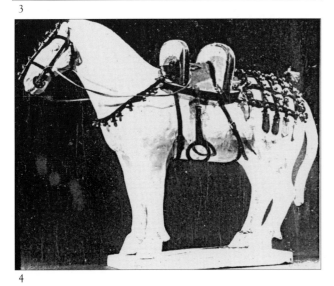

3

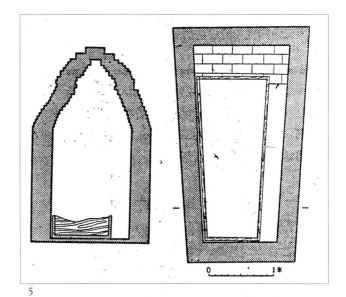

5

6

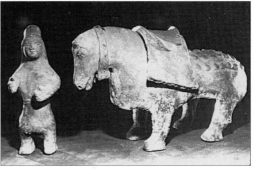

7

Figures

3. Plan of Shengle. *Wenwu* 1977.11,38 fig.1.
4. Reconstruction of saddle from Xiaomincun. *Kaogu* 1983.6, pl. 8.2.
5. Tomb at Meidaicun, Huhehot. *Kaogu* 1962.2, 86, fig. 1.
6. Figures from Northern Wei tomb Huhehot. *Chugoku Uchi Môko Hoppô kiba minzoku monbutsuten*, 58, fig. 57.2.
7. Figures from Northern Wei tomb, Huhehot. *Chugoku Uchi Môko Hoppô kiba minzoku monbutsuten*, 59, fig. 60.

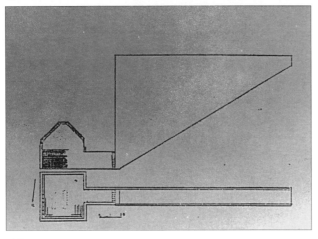

10

9

Figures

8. Worshippers at Yun'gang, Cave 11. *Yun'gang shiku* (Beijing: Wenwu chubanshe, 1977), pl. 63.

9. Figures from Northern Wei embroidery, Dunhuang. *Wenwu* 1972.2, 57, fig. 3.

10. Plan of Northern Wei tomb at Guyuan, Ningxia. *Wenwu* 1984.6, 47, fig. 4.

is wide at the head, narrower at the foot, harking back to the shape of the Xianbei coffins at Zhalainuoer and Meidaicun. The lid has a frame of a honeysuckle design. At the top are depicted two structures with hipped roofs, upturned ridge ends and a central bird, with bracketing and suspended, tied up curtains, all quite similar to what is found at the Yun'gang caves. Under each structure is seated a figure with the distinctive Xianbei headgear; some of the attendants also are similarly depicted. The figure to the left is labeled Dongwangfu, that is, King Father of the East, and therefore that to the right must be the Queen Mother of the West. A sun and moon are poised over the roofs, and down the middle of the coffin lid runs a wavy band of curlicues, representing the Milky Way. The remaining surface is covered with an intricate network pattern, and in each space two joined honeysuckle leaves form a base on which stands one of a variety of strange winged beasts. These include griffins, birds, long-eared dogs, and a creature with a bird's body and human head (fig. 11).[42] The sides of the coffin are decorated in a number of registers. The first is a series of panels, interrupted by triangular divisions, depicting traditional Chinese examples of filial piety, such as Guo Qu, who was digging a

pit in which he was going to bury his three-year-old son, in order to have enough food to keep his aged mother alive, when he found a pot full of gold. Another illustrates Shun, who was so badly treated by his father and stepmother, and yet he remained filial. Here he is shown escaping from the barn in which he was working after they had set it on fire in an attempt to kill him.[43] These stories of filial sons are of course Chinese, but note that the clothing depicted is Xianbei. What must be the occupant of the tomb is probably depicted on the headboard of the coffin. He is shown seated on a couch, within a gabled structure, holding a cup in one hand, a deer-tail whisk in the other (this is a common object in this period); his costume and that of his attendants are the same as already described. Below are figures of Buddhist deities. The roundels with pearl borders are West Asian (fig. 12).

Sun Ji, in a recent article, has commented that while the decor of the coffin reveals elements of sinicization, such as Queen Mother of the West and her consort, the Milky Way, and so forth, what is more striking is that the deceased is shown in a pose, holding a glass in a particular way, much like contemporary figural art of the Hephthalites, at the other end of Asia.[44] Other material in the tomb, particularly a gilded silver bowl obviously of West Asian provenance, may also point to contact with the Hephthalites, according to Sun. Sun concludes that the utilization of the stories of filial sons on the coffin is to be attributed to the almost religious significance the *Xiaojing* or Confucian *Classic of Filial Piety* achieved at this time, and these anecdotes, as with the depiction of the Queen Mother of the West, merely reveal that these were favored decorations of funereal objects of the time, and sinicization should not be considered the keynote of the coffin.[45]

Another Northern Wei tomb, that of Sima Jinlong, in the vicinity of the Northern Wei capital of Pingcheng, modern Datong, has been reported in great detail.[46] Sima Jinlong, who died in 484, was a descendant of the Jin royal house, and thus of Chinese descent, but he had a distinguished career under the Tuoba, serving as general, garrison commander, and governor. This serves to remind us that during these years not only were the Tuoba faced with adapting to Chinese culture but the Chinese, especially those in the service of the Tuoba, had to accommodate to the Tuoba culture as well.

The tomb is more complex than that at Guyuan, but each of the chambers (front, back, and side) has the same format as that one, square or almost so, slightly bulging walls, and cloister vault ceiling.[47] One does not find a lacquer coffin; instead, there was a lacquer screen with the themes not only of filial sons but of virtuous women, famed hermits, and others as well. Here, the figures are all in Chinese costume.[48] The Chinese archaeologists have made much of this and other objects that reflect Chinese culture, as such objects are taken as an index of the degree to which sinicization had proceeded, or in Sima Jinlong's case, maintained, among the elite in this Tuoba state. I would rather point to the large number (some 142) of male and female attendants in that distinctive Xianbei garb (fig. 13), and warriors, (122 on foot and 88 mounted) as well as figures of oxen, goats, pigs, dogs, chickens, and camels, but no models of stoves, buildings, or agricultural equipment, which would reflect an agricultural society.

There is one piece that is especially interesting. It is identified as a tomb guardian beast (*zhenmushou*), a kind of brooding beast with a human head and truncated cone representing some sort of hornlike growth (fig. 14). There are five rectangular holes along the back of its neck, perhaps for inserting a mane of hair. Its face is painted white, and the surface of the body is painted with white lines to represent scales. In earlier Chinese tombs of the Jin one occasionally finds a rhinoceros-looking beast, with two to four horns or spikes along the spine, poised to charge. In the south the guardian animal figurine in the tomb disappears; one has instead the chimera placed in front of the large, royal tombs. But here in the north one finds the start of a new tradition. Is this to be related to the old Xianbei belief

11

12

Figures

11. Coffin cover from Guyuan, Ningxia. *Meishu yanjiu* 1984.2, 8.

12. Detail of coffin from Guyuan, Ningxia. *Meishu yanjiu* 1984.2, 9.

of the dog that led the spirit to heaven, mentioned above, or perhaps to the winged animal that appears in the design of the lacquer coffin? One may observe, as the period progresses, how this creature developed during this period and culminated with baroque splendor in the Tang (fig. 15a).

The next stage in the cultural development of the Northern Wei state came in 493, when the emperor Xiaowen decided to make his state a thoroughly Chinese one. The city of Luoyang, which had lain virtually in ruins since its destruction in 311, was rebuilt and made into the new capital. Edicts were issued to erase a number of overt differences between the Tuoba and their Chinese subjects. The intention was to force the Tuoba to conform to Chinese standards by forbidding the use of the Xianbei language or dress at court, by forcing the adoption of Chinese names, and so forth.[49] This would seem to mark another instance of China's remarkable ability to acculturate and absorb the foreign invader. The immediate reasons for these new policies are still debated. Was it that the emperor sought to elicit support for his dynasty among his Chinese subjects? Or was it, as he claimed, to be able to press more firmly his plans for a conquest of the south? Or does it simply mark his own level of acculturation? My own sense is that Emperor Xiaowen sought to distance himself from the Xianbei military elite with whom he necessarily had to share his power. As emperor of a Chinese-style state, with a system of recruiting officials to serve him modeled on that of the Chinese court to the south, he could create a more highly centralized structure, one that gave him more autonomy. While Xiaowen had the force of character to push through his plan, his weaker successors could not sustain the effort.[50]

Not much remains of the Luoyang he built except some building foundations and traces of the wall,[51] but a short distance to the south there are the magnificent Longmen caves which were begun at this time. A huge relief, now divided between the Metropolitan Museum of Art, New York, and the Nelson-Atkins Museum of Art, Kansas City, shows the royal party, the emperor on one side, the empress on the other, as they might have appeared in a procession to the caves. There is nothing here that would have jarred the sensibilities of the most conservative Chinese subject.

The tombs of this period around Luoyang also reflect this assimilatory effort. The tomb of Yuan Zhao, who died in 520, is an example of this.[52] Yuan Zhao was a scion of the imperial house, the grandson of Emperor Xiaowen. Yuan, his surname, was the Chinese one chosen to replace Tuoba. The chamber is the same: square, walls bulged out, a peaked ceiling, but it was almost thirty feet below the surface. An airshaft, later backfilled, permitted some economy in the excavation of the passageway. It had been robbed, of course, and so it contained only what the robbers had left behind. In many ways it follows the new policies of his grandfather's court. Of the 115 pottery figures left, there is hardly one that is specifically Tuoba. The cavalrymen were standard for this time. The musicians perhaps are in the Xianbei mode, as are the guardian warriors who may well have derived from Xianbei prototypes (the cape with empty sleeves is significant as are the fierce, foreign-looking faces) but these are now standard protective figures in the tomb. What is most interesting is the guardian beast, which has now undergone some changes.

13

The beast we had seen in Sima Jinlong's tomb of 484 has now become a pair, one with an animal head, the other with a human one, still with the knob on its head, but both creatures now have a series of spikes, usually three, emerging from the spine, as well as a curled up tail. Perhaps influenced by the southern chimera or reflecting the image we had seen on the Guyuan coffin, there are scroll-like depictions of wings behind the front shoulders (fig. 15b).

While Yuan Zhao's tomb would appear to reflect the new age, it can be seen from tombs on the northern frontiers that the Xianbei who lived there were more conservative than those who had moved to Luoyang. A number of graves found at Guyangxian, Baotou, Inner Mongolia, and dated as Northern Wei yielded the same undistinguished pottery and bone carvings found in the Wan'gong and Zhalainuoer sites, which were centuries earlier, as well as new influences such as lacquer bowls. The two reported graves were in the form of pits with a crude, stepped approach, a ledge on each side, and a wooden coffin.[53] At Baotou a brick chamber tomb dated 499 yielded an animal skull and leg bones in the long passageway, recalling the frequent use of ox, horse, and sheep parts seen earlier at Zhalainuoer and elsewhere, indicating that some of these old customs were retained.[54]

However well Emperor Xiaowen's policies may have

14

15a

15b

been based on reasonable expectations of acceptance, they aroused much antagonism from the tribesmen who had been left on the frontier to guard against the other nomads still out on the steppes. These Xianbei soldiers felt they were not only being passed over in the distribution of the rewards for ruling the state but, in fact, were falling in status, coming to be considered no different from the exiled criminals being sent to fill in their ranks.[55] In the 520s and 530s the frontier armies turned south, and civil war erupted. When the dust settled, the north was divided into two parts, the western part, known as Western Wei, later Northern Zhou, with its capital at Chang'an, now Si'an, and the eastern, known as Eastern Wei, later Northern Qi, with the chief capital at Yeh, near modern Anyang. The policies of Emperor Xiaowen were reversed, the old names restored, and indeed the Xianbei culture seems to have had a renaissance.[56]

The last period of Xianbei rule of north China, that is, between the end of the Northern Wei and the takeover by the Sui in 581, is one that is remarkably rich in evidence of the Xianbei, especially in the northeast, but to some extent in the northwest as well, although archaeological evidence from the northwestern states, the Western Wei and Northern Zhou, is disappointingly sparse. A particularly significant discovery was the tomb of Li Xian, at Guyuan,

Figures

13. Figurine from tomb of Sima Jinlong. *The Quest for Eternity*, 122, fig 47.

14. Tomb guardian, tomb of Sima Jinlong. *The Quest for Eternity*, 124, fig. 52.

15a. Tomb guardians
   1. Cixian, Hebei, 547. Tomb of nee Zhao.
      Kaogu 1977.6, p.397, Fig.8.
   2. Anyang, Henan, 550. Tomb of the Avar Princess.
      Wenwu 1984.4, p.5, Fig.5.
   3. Anyang, Henan, 566. Tomb of Yao Jun.
      Wenwu 1984.4, p.18, Fig.9.
   4. Taiyuan, Shanxi, 570. Tomb of Lou Rui.
      Wenwu 1983. 10, p.8, Fig.18.
   5. Cixian, Hebei, 577. Tomb of Gao Run.
      Kaogu 1979.3, p.240, Figs.6.2-3.

15b. Tomb guardians, tomb of Yuan Zhao. *Kaogu* 1973.4, pl. 12.

Ningxia, in the same area where the lacquer coffin had been found in a Northern Wei tomb.[57] Li Xian, who died in 569, was from a prominent local family of this area, and he was one of the chief supporters of Yuwen Tai, who established the Western Wei-Northern Zhou state. Li's own ethnic identity has come under close scrutiny since his tomb was discovered. It had been thought that his family was of Xiongnu or Hunnish origin, since it claimed descent from Li Ling, the Han general who had surrendered to the Xiongnu, but recently it has been suggested that Li Xian was rather of Gaoju or Xianbei origin.[58] The tomb itself is an early and fine example of the type that became widely used in the Sui and Tang, a tomb chamber approached by a ramp with a number of shafts sunk at intervals, which enabled the long and deeply descending passageway to be carved out more efficiently (fig. 16). The tomb, as is generally the case, had been robbed, but the remaining contents are still most interesting. Some 239 figurines were found, of very crude workmanship; obviously these were a local product, perhaps especially made by an inexperienced artisan to emulate a funerary practice of the capital. A third or more represent military personnel.[59] Another third wear hoods; some of these have high brows, deep eyes, and prominent noses marking them as non-Mongoloid—they are simply labeled as *hu*. The remainder of these hooded figures are said only to be markedly chubby (figs. 17a, b). The guardian beast, *zhenmushou*, is a definite step backward in the evolution of this genre or perhaps it more closely represents the earliest stage of this beast despite its late date (fig. 15c). The tomb also contained a Sasanian gilded silver ewer and glass bowl that have attracted much attention and are cited as evidence of continuing trade between East and West.[60] This tomb also contained mural panels on all the walls, of which about half survive. These represent gate towers, guards, and attendants. The guards lined the passageway, while the attendants, including female musicians, were around the walls of the burial chamber. These are rather stiff in style, but incomparably of a higher quality than the pottery figurines.

The archaeological record for the eastern states, that is, the Eastern Wei and Northern Qi, is much more complete than that for the northwest. During the Eastern Wei and Northern Qi periods, the brick chamber tombs came to have rounded walls, high-domed ceilings, and long, ramped entryways that were filled in following the interment, after which a mound was raised over the whole site. Another feature of these tombs is the use of murals, covering the walls and ceilings of the chamber and in some cases the walls of the passageway as well. One of the most spectacular of these is the tomb of the Avar princess, dating to 550.

The Tuoba had left a vacuum in the northern

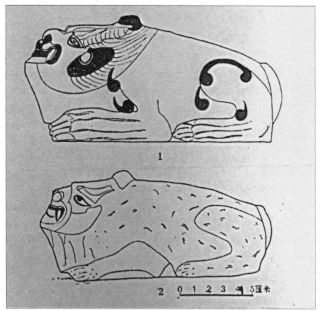

15c

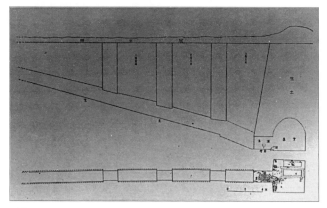

16

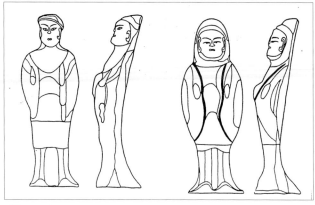

17

Figures

15c. Tomb guardians, tomb of Li Xian. *Wenwu* 1985.11, 9, fig. 16.

16. Plan of tomb of Li Xian, Guyuan, Ningxia. *Wenwu* 1985.11, 2, fig. 2.

17. Figurines, tomb of Li Xian (a,b). *Wenwu* 1985.11, 7, fig. 9. 3-4.

steppelands when they moved south, and the new power there was that of the Ruru, or Ruanruan, as the Chinese called them, perhaps the forerunners of the Avars, hence our designation.[61] The two northern states, east and west, competed with each other to win over these tribesmen, and the Eastern Wei proved to be more persuasive. The new alliance was celebrated by marriages, one of which was the eight-year-old granddaughter of the Avar khan to an eight-year-old prince of the Eastern Wei. She died only five years later, at the age of thirteen. The tomb of the princess is to be found two kilometers south of the modern Cixian, which would have placed it some eight kilometers north of the then capital at Ye.[62] The furnishings of the tomb are lavish, more than one thousand pottery figurines and fifty-two gold objects, even though the tomb had been robbed. Most important for us were the fragments of murals on the wall. What may be surprising is that the decor seems so completely Chinese.

The floor of the passageway, or *dromos*, was painted to resemble a carpet, and each side wall illustrated two of the directional animals, two drum beaters, and various bodyguards (fig. 18). The paintings within the entryway, or *stomion*, are badly damaged; perhaps these represented door guards, grooms, and attendants, apparently four on each side.

Inside the chamber only portions of the murals remain. The north or rear wall has seven women in all. The middle one, relatively more plumpish, wearing a tall hat, the right hand raised as if issuing an order, of course is a depiction of the Avar little princess; the other six women at her side are rather more slender, their hair combed into two buns, their hands holding such objects as a feather screen, decorated umbrella, large fan, cup, and basin—these must be the attendants of the princess (fig. 19). The other walls, also badly damaged, depict other attendants.[63] It is notable that what remains in the tomb is so Chinese; nothing would seem to reveal the steppeland origin of the deceased unless it is the figurine of what appears to be a shaman. A bronze figure with a very similar headgear was found in Xinjiang, at Xinyuan Xian, on the Gongnaisi River, but dated as Warring States, that is, fifth to third century B.C. It is perhaps to be related to the non-Chinese cultures of the steppes.[64] The connection between these two figures is not yet clear.

Another figure that deserves comment is a type of hooded figure, numbering 201 of the 1064 figurines found in the tomb (fig. 20). The description reads, "Wears a hood, dressed in a closed collar garment with two empty sleeves hanging down. The two hands are held before the chest. The clothing is painted red, the eyes are deep and nose high (or prominent). It is perhaps a Xianbei."[65]

This type of figure is distinctive because of its rounded, puffed out headdress, rounded face, and the overgarment

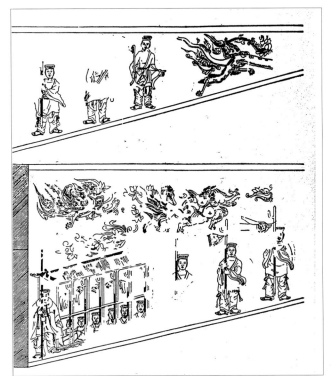

18

19

Figures

18. East wall, passageway of tomb of Avar princess. *Wenwu* 1984.4, 14, fig. 3.

19. Portion of mural, back wall, tomb of Avar princess. *Wenwu* 1984.4, 15, fig. 6.

with empty sleeves. It recalls some of the figurines found in the Li Xian tomb, mentioned earlier. One finds this type of tomb figurine as early as that of Gao Ya, 537, at Jingxian.[66] In the descriptions of these figurines in the reports of the tombs of Li Xizong (died 540), at Canhuang, Hebei, and Fan Cui (died 575), near Anyang, they are also said to represent Xianbei.[67] It is not clear why facial characteristics associated with non-Mongoloids are attributed to the Xianbei, but the round hood is characteristic, as we have seen. It may be that the authors of the reports have

Figure

20. Figurine from tomb of Avar princess. *Wenwu* 1984.4, pl. 3.5.

Mon-goloid.[69]

West of the Taihang Mountains, another group of Eastern Wei-Northern Qi tombs was clustered about Jinyang, near modern Taiyuan, Shanxi, which had been the secondary capital of these northeastern states. The tombs appear to have retained the more or less square chamber, albeit at times with rounded or bowed walls. These are the tombs of Zhang Susu (died 559),[70] Kudi Huiluo (died 562),[71] Han Yi (died 567),[72] and Lou Rui (died 570).[73] The figurines found in these tombs differ from those in the tombs further east. One does not find the type with hood and cloak, mentioned above as characteristic of that area. Rather there is another type, forming a large proportion of the tomb figures and described as having "minority people's," features, clothing, and headgear,[74] what I would take to be Xianbei characteristics. The hairline is high, perhaps indicating a shaved brow; there is a cloth covering the bun of hair at the top of the head with a band holding that cloth in place and a hood descending behind the ears. In some cases the gathered topknot is shaped into a three-peaked crown. The tunic may be worn with open or closed lapels; in figures found in Zhang's tomb, the tunic may have been slipped off the right shoulder (fig. 21), while that was not the case of those in Kudi Huiluo's tomb (fig. 22).

This same type of figure has been depicted in murals found in some of these tombs. Some fragments of the mural in the entryway of Kudi Huiluo's tomb show two such figures on each side. The belted tunics and trousers tucked into boots is the rather standard steppe costume, but the high brow and hood (which gathers the hair and draws it behind the ears to hang at the back of the neck) are distinctive (fig. 23). This can be seen much more clearly in the more complete murals preserved in Lou Rui's tomb.

Lou was a high-ranking Xianbei, cousin of a number of emperors, related by marriage to other eminent families, and while he was criticized by his contemporaries for his greediness and improper behavior, he did hold some of the highest offices in the state.[75] Therefore his tomb was especially grand. Further, a larger portion of the murals have survived—and while too little has been published,[76] one can see here how much stronger is the Xianbei influence.

In the passageway, at the topmost register there is a procession led by some racing dogs, then horsemen, and at the rear, loaded camels, resembling a caravan but perhaps here simply carrying the baggage of this procession (fig. 24). Much of the court's time was spent on the road between the two capitals, Ye and Jinyang, to the west. The second register, laid out like a scroll, has groups of cavalrymen interspersed by pairs of mounted men riding together (fig. 25). The third register shows a band blowing the long horns of that period that were characteristic of the nomad groups; next are a number of archers standing guard.

In the entryway, as at the Avar princess's tomb, there

in mind the incident reported in *Jin shu* in which Sima Shao, second emperor of the Eastern Jin, was referred to as a "yellow/brown bearded Xianbei," it being explained that his mother was a person of Yan-Dai, that is to say, the Xianbei states of Yan in Hebei and Dai in Shanxi. Nevertheless, there is no reason to suppose that the Xianbei, by and large, were anything but Mongoloids.[68] The same figure, with a top bun covered with a hood, swept back to the nape, and with facial hair, clad in a tunic, appears in the depiction of attendants in the tomb murals of Gao Run (died 576), at Cixian, Hebei, and they are clearly

21

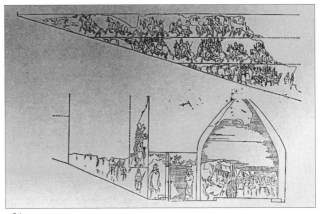

24

22

25

23

Figures

21. Figurines from tomb of Zhang Susu. *Taiyuan Kuangpo Bei Qi Zhang Su mu wenwu tulu*, 15.

22. Figurine from tomb of Kudi Huiluo. *Kaogu xuebao* 1979.3, pl. 8.1.

23. Mural in tomb of Kudi Huiluo. *Kaogu xuebao* 1979.3, pl. 12. 3-4.

24. Mural of west side, tomb of Lou Rui. *Wenwu* 1983.10, 3, fig. 4.

25. Detail of Lou Rui. tomb mural. *Wenwu* 1983.10, color plate.

are door guards and above, sacred beasts, clouds, flowers, and so forth. The door guard here resembles the door guard found in some southern tombs of this period. One of the scholars writing on this tomb comments that the similarity of these door guards to those found in the south reflects the historical tide that was moving toward unification, and so, in his opinion, the revulsion against Han culture and the restoration of Xianbei customs in the Northern Qi was not effective, but in view of the preponderance of Xianbei elements that occur in these murals, this is a surprising conclusion.[77]

Inside the chamber there are two or three registers, the upper ones devoted to celestial matters, while the lower one is devoted to human affairs. On the rear wall is the deceased sitting inside a curtain screen; to the left and right are the saddled horses and, as one may note, the ox and cart that are prepared for the deceased's journey. The depiction of such a vehicle in the tomb murals does not appear in later, Tang dynasty tombs but reappears in the tombs of the Khitans, another nomadic group, who came down into China some centuries later.[78]

On the upper registers are the usual feathered immortals, sacred beasts and, very interestingly, depictions of the twelve animals of the twelve animal cycle—this is the first recorded occurrence of the series in art. Unfortunately, the reproductions of the murals within the chamber are either illegible or have not yet been published, and we will have to wait for better photographs.

These murals are of high quality, and the tomb made a strong impact on the archaeological and art-historical community in China. The provisional report, for example, is followed by a special joint article by ten specialists.[79] It is indeed a most important find, and there is enough here to keep art historians busy for a decade. What has been known of Northern Qi painting heretofore has been the comments recorded in a history of painting written in the Tang, the *Lidai minghua ji*, by Zhang Yanyuan. The Northern Qi had only existed for twenty-eight years, and yet, as the modern scholar Tang Chi notes, of the twenty painters mentioned in that work who lived in the north during the three centuries of the dark ages, ten were active in the Northern Qi.[80] One of them, the court painter Yang Zihua, was especially noted for his paintings of horses. Given Lou Rui's high rank, there is some speculation that Yang Zihua had been called in to decorate the walls of his tomb.[81]

That three-peaked headdress, mentioned above, is also found in Lou Rui's tomb, both in figurines and in the murals (figs. 26-27). We see here Xianbei tribesmen in Xianbei traditional attire, which is apparently unaffected by the two hundred years the Xianbei had lived in China.[82]

If we came out of the tomb in that period, what would we have found? To what extent would Xianbei cultural traits have survived after so many years? How strong was the dichotomy between the Chinese and Xianbei? If the contemporary texts are any indication, the Xianbei still maintained a strong sense of identification. The Xianbei were the warriors and held most of the important military posts, which they jealously guarded.[83] All during this period there is much evidence that there was friction between the two groups. Gao Huan, the de facto ruler of the Eastern Wei, tried to make peace between the two. It is reported that he would say to the military in the Xianbei language, "The Chinese are your slaves, they farm for you, the women make your clothing, so they bring to you what you eat and what you wear, allowing you to be warm and full, why do you want to oppress them?" And to the Chinese he would say, "The Xianbei are your clients, you give them a measure of grain and a bolt of cloth, and they fight for you and enable you to have peace and order, why do you hate them?"[84] It was evidently not easy to rule over such a divided society.

We also have some insight into what it meant to be a high-placed Chinese in such a state. Yan Zhitui, who emphasized the importance of the study of the Confucian classics in order to prepare oneself to be a moral person and

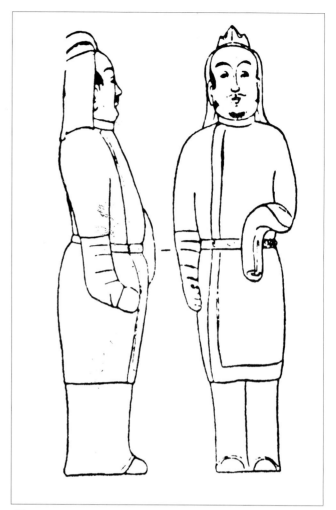

26

27

Figures

26. Figurine, Lou Rui tomb mural. *Wenwu* 1983.10, 5, fig. 7.2.
27. Detail of Lou Rui tomb mural. *Wenwu* 1983.10, pl. 3.1.

an effective administrator, served as a high official in the Northern Qi. As he reports, another high official told him, "I have a boy, already seventeen, who has a talent for literary studies. I am teaching him the Xianbei language and how to strum the bent-neck lute (piba), for I want him to know these in order to better serve the dukes and lords. It is also important for him to gain their favor." Yan's reaction at the time was to turn away from the man and later to say to his sons that he would not want them to follow such a course even if it were to enable them to reach the highest offices at the court.[85] An amusing anecdote concerns Lu Rui, prince of Pingyuan, who was to marry a girl of the Boling Cui family. The Chinese transcription of Lu's Xianbei name was Bulugu, and his prospective father-in-law mumbled that the young man's abilities and judgment were not bad, but he deplored the multisyllabic surname.[86]

Much is made of the intermarriage of the high-ranking Xianbei and prestigious Chinese families, but the cultural pull would seem to have been at least as much toward the Xianbei as toward sinicization. The Xianbei hold on the reins of state gave them the incentive to maintain their distinctiveness. They had, therefore, a vested interest in separateness. The attempt of Xiaowendi at the turn of the century had been ill-fated because his attempts to sinicize the Xianbei would have eroded the basis of Xianbei rule, and so, no doubt, there seemed little point in giving up the clothes, the military life, and even the language. Even Emperor Xiaowen realized that the Xianbei language could not be dispensed with immediately. After the move to Luoyang, as an aid in the learning of Chinese, he ordered that the Xiaojing be translated into the Xianbei language.[87] This would indicate that the process of assimilation had some distance yet to travel. As Xing Bingyan has pointed out, there was a resurgence of the Xianbei language under the Eastern Wei-Northern Qi as Xiaowen's assimilationist policies were abandoned and the less-acculturated northerners became dominant.[88]

The conquest of Northern Qi by the Northern Zhou in 577 united northern China. While we do not have adequate material to trace this process of assimilation in the conquering state, the organization of the army along Xianbei lines would seem to indicate a similar tendency toward retention of traditional Xianbei traits.[89] Only later when the main body of the Northern Zhou army came to be made up of Chinese did control of the state slip away, and then the transition was made through that group of Chinese military men who had served the Xianbei for generations, who seemed as much Xianbei as Chinese. The specifically Xianbei attributes were immediately dropped, and one does not hear again of the Xianbei language, but there remained that nomad emphasis on hunting and horsemanship such as one may see in the Tang tomb mu-

rals of the T'ang prince Li Xian, son of Tang Gaozong, the tomb dating from 706. There was a cultural continuity in the ruling classes, at least, that had its ultimate origins in the steppelands beyond the great wall but that came to the Tang through the mediation of the Xianbei, whom the founders of the Sui and Tang and their forefathers had served.

One may observe during these centuries the figure of the tribesman who is clearly distinguishable from his Chinese subjects. It is, however, difficult to say precisely what these tribesmen represented because, as has been noted, the Xianbei were a confederation of diverse elements. The hairstyles of the Tuoba (braided) differed from the Xianbei (clean-shaven); the language of the Yuwen (rulers of the Western Wei-Northern Zhou) differed from that of the Xianbei; and the faces of the figurines with this style of dress seem to be rather full, sometimes with features that are seen to be non-Han, which perhaps means non-Mongoloid. Nevertheless, very clearly this style of dress is to be identified with the Xianbei rule of north China and disappears once China came to be united under the Sui and Tang.

The format of the tombs of the Tang imperial family, such as that of Li Xian, reminds one of those that we have just seen: the tomb chamber, entry, passageway, skywells, all were worked out during the period we have been discussing. The guardian animal, to which we have alluded (fig. 15), continued to develop, until one had that magnificently baroque creature, whose antecedents are clear. One cannot claim that this particular type of tomb, the guardian beast, or other cultural artifacts that emerged at this time are necessarily Xianbei in origin. When we come to assess the impact of the Xianbei on Sui-Tang culture, it is of course difficult to say what aspects are peculiarly Xianbei. As Su Bai has pointed out, the archaeological evidence from Datong and Luoyang, while giving evidence of the impact of the higher level of Chinese civilization on the Xianbei, at the same time reveals that they retained elements of their original culture, some of which had some influence even into the Sui and Tang.[90] It certainly does harm to our understanding of Chinese cultural and artistic history to view the Xianbei only in terms of an inevitable progress toward assimilation, toward acculturation. Rather we need to remain sensitive to their role in the history of China. Sometimes they acted only as patrons and sometimes only facilitated an openness to other parts of the world, but as our knowledge of this fascinating people grows, we may be better able to discern in what ways they themselves contributed to that amalgam, that complex we know as Chinese culture. Perhaps only then can we give due credit to that people whose ancestors had come forth from that cave in the far north so many years before.

Notes

1. Los Angeles County Museum of Art, *The Quest for Eternity: Chinese Ceramic Sculptures from the People's Republic of China*, exh. cat. (San Francisco: Chronicle Books, 1987), 118.

2. For an excellent survey of the political developments of this period, see Han Guopan, *Wei Jin Nanbeichao shigang* (Beijing: Renmin chubanshe, 1983). Wolfram Eberhard's writings are especially insightful concerning the northern nomad states; see his *Das Toba-Reich Nordchinas* (Leiden: E.J. Brill, 1949), and his *A History of China* (Berkeley: University of California Press, 1977, 4th ed.), 109-68.

3. *Zizhi tongjian* (Beijing: Guji chubanshe, 1956), 87.2763. See also the essay by Arthur Waley, "Lo-yang and its Fall," in *History Today*, vol. 1, no. 4 (1951): 7-10, and reprinted in *The Secret History of the Mongols and Other Pieces* (London: Barnes and Noble, 1964), 47-55. The equation of Huns with the Xiongnu has long been debated; see Otto J. Maenchen-Helfen, "Huns and Hsiung-nu," *Byzantion* 17 (1944-45): 222-43, and "The Ethnic Name Hun," in Soren Egerod and Else Glahn, eds., *Studia Serica Bernhard Karlgren dedicata* (Copenhagen: Ejnart Munksgard, 1959), 223-38, and K. Enoki, "Sogdiana and the Hsiung-nu," *Central Asian Journal* 1 (1955): 43-62. For the contrary view, see Omeljan Pritsak, "Xun: Der Volksname der Hsiung-nu," *Central Asian Journal* 5 (1959-60): 27-34, and Maenchen's response, "Archaistic Names of the Hsiung-nu," *Central Asian Journal* 6 (1961): 249-61. William Samolin, "Hsiung-nu, Hun, Turk," *Central Asian Journal* 3 (1957-58): 143-50, also touches on the subject. For an overall discussion of the Huns and Hsiung-nu, see also Maenchen, *The World of the Huns: Studies in Their History and Culture* (Berkeley: University of California Press, 1973). It is, however, the reference to Hsiung-nu as *X'wn* in the fourth-century Sogdian letter that weighs heavily for the identification of the terms; see W. B. Henning, "The Date of the Sogdian Ancient Letters," *Bulletin of the School of Oriental and African Studies*, vol. 13, nos. 3-4 (1948): 601-15, especially 615. While there may be good reason to doubt that the Huns who showed up in Europe were the same people as those designated by the Chinese as Xiongnu, there is little doubt that the Chinese term was a transcription of the name Hunna or some form of it.

4. Henning, op. cit.

5. Arnold Toynbee, *A Study of History: The Growth of Civilization*, vol. 3 (New York: Oxford University Press, 1962), 395-452, argued for climate change as a significant factor in nomadic movements; however, Toynbee cites G. F. Hudson, 453-54, as one who casts doubt on this explanation. Frederick J. Teggart, *Rome and China: A Study of Correlations in Historical Events* (Berkeley: University of California Press, 1969), 225 ff., reviewed past explanations and argued for pressures applied by one group on another, creating chain reactions on the steppes. See also Kaare Grønbech, "The Steppe Region in World History, II," *Acta Orientalia* 24 (1959): 15-28.

6. See Chin Fa-ken, *Yung-chia luan-hou pei-fang ti hao-tsu* (Taipei: Chung-kuo Hsüeh-shu chu-tso chiang-chu wei-yüan-hui, 1964).

7. Peter A. Boodberg, "The Language of the T'o-pa Wei," *Harvard Journal of Asiatic Studies* 1 (1936): 167-85, and Louis Bazin, "Recherches sur les parlers T'o-pa (5e siècle apres J.C.)," *T'oung Pao* 39 (1949-50): 228-329. But E. G. Pulleyblank, "The Chinese and Their Neighbors in Prehistoric and Early Historic Times," in D. Keightley, ed., *The Origins of Chinese Civilization* (Berkeley: University of California Press, 1983), 452-53, on the contrary cites the work of L. Ligeti and states that the ruling group of the Xianbei, the T'o-pa and Yuwen, were proto-Mongols and that their language was basically Mongolian. See A. Dien, *The Biography of Yü-wen Hu*, Chinese Dynastic Histories Translations, no. 9 (Berkeley: University of California Press, 1962), 24, n. 2, for the literature cited there. In this paper Tuoba and Xianbei are used interchangeably, but one must keep in mind that one is dealing here with a confederation of diverse groups.

8. Eberhard, *Das Toba-Reich Nordchinas*, passim, and his *Conquerors and Rulers: Social Forces in Medieval China* (Leiden: E. J. Brill, 1965), 107-39.

9. For their origins, *Wei shu* 1.1 (Zhonghua shuju ed.); for the Wuluohou, *Wei shu* 100.2224; for the text of the inscription, *Wei shu* 108A.2738.

10. Mi Wenping, "Xianbei shishi de faxian yu chubu yanjiu," *Wenwu* 1981.2, 1-8. See also Tong Zhuchen, "Gaxiandong Tuoba Tao zhuwen shikekao," *Lishi Yanjiu*, 1981.6, 36-42.

11. On the interpretation of this term of measurement, see James Legge, *The Chinese Classics, Vol. 2: The Works of Mencius* (Hong Kong: Oxford University Press, 1960, reprint), 374, note.

12. *Wei shu* 1.2-3.

13. Su Bai, "Dongbei, Neimenggu diqu di Xianbei yiji—Xianbei yiji jilu zhi yi," *Wenwu* 1977.5, 42-54; Huang Lie, "Tuoba Xianbei zaoqi guojia di xingcheng," *Wei Jin Sui Tang shi lunji*, no. 2 (Beijing: Zhongguo shehui kexue chubanshe, 1983), 60-94. For the Su article, see also the translation by David Fridley, "Xianbei Remains in Manchuria and Inner Monglia—Record of Xianbei Remains, Part One," *Chinese Studies in Archaeology* (Fall 1979): 3-43.

14. "Neimenggu Chenbaerhuqi Wan'gong suomu faxian gu muzang," *Kaogu* 1962.11, 590, and Neimenggu zizhiqu wenwu gongzuodui, "Neimenggu Chenbaerhuqi Wan'gong gumu qingli jianbao," *Kaogu* 1965.6, 273-83; Cheng Daohong, "Yiminhe diqu di Xianbei mu," *Neimenggu wenwu kaogu* 2 (1982): 18-23.

15. Zheng Long, "Neimenggu Zhalainuoer gumuqun diaochaji," *Wenwu* 1961.9, 16-19; Neimenggu wenwu gongzuodui, "Neimenggu Zhalainuoer gumuqun fajue jianbao," *Kaogu* 1961.12, 673-80; and Neimenggu wenwu gongzuodui, *Neimenggu wenwu ziliao xuanji* (Beijing: Neimenggu renmin chubanshe, 1964), 101-14.

16. Su Bai, op. cit., 50-51; Zhongguo kexueyuan Kaogu yanjiusuo Neimenggu gongzuodui, "Neimenggu Balinzuoqi Nanyangjiayingzi di yizhi he muzang," *Kaogu* 1964.1, 36-43, 53.

17. But see *Neimenggu wenwu kaogu* 2 (1982): 18, which says the area is one of the best in Inner Mongolia.

18. "Tongyuxian Xinglongshan Xianbei mu qingli jianbao," *Xeilongjiang wenwu* 1981.3, not seen.

19. Jilinsheng wenwu gongzuodui et al., "Jilin Yushuxian Laoheshen Xianbei muqun bufen muzang fajue jianbao," *Wenwu* 1985.2, 68-82.

20. Sun Shoudao, "'Xiongnu Xichagou wenhua gumuqun di faxian," *Wenwu* 1960.8-9, 25-32, originally identified as a Xiongnu site.

21. Qin Weibo, "Guanyu Xianbei zaoqi wenhua di zairenshi," *Beifang wenwu* 1988.3, 12-17.

22. *Hou Han shu* 90.2979-80; the portion translated below is on page 2980. Fan Ye would seem to have based himself on the *Wei shu* of Wang Shen (fourth century) or a source common to the two. Wang's text, no longer extant, is quoted at length in *Sanguo zhi* 30.832-33 and 836-38.

23. William Irons, "Political stratification among pastoral nomads," *Pastoral Production and Society* (Cambridge: Cambridge University Press, 1979), 361-418, especially 370; Marshall Sahlins, *Tribesmen* (Englewood Cliffs: Prentice-Hall, 1968), 50-52.

24. Chou Fa-kao, *Yen-shih chia-hsün hui-chu*, Chung-yang yen-chiu-yüan li-shih yü-yen yen-chiu-so chuan-k'an, no. 41 (Taipei: Chung-yang yen-chiu-yüan li-shih yü-yen yen-chiu-so, 1960), 12a; Teng Ssu-yü, *Family Instructions for the Yen Clan* (Leiden: E. J. Brill, 1968), 19.

25. E. G. Pulleyblank, "The Chinese and their Neighbors in Prehistoric and Early Historic Times," in D. N. Keightley, ed., *The Origins of Chinese Civilization*, 453-54.

26. *Hou Han shu* 90.2985.

27. *Sanguozhi* 30.836 has Ruole River, while the *Wei shu*, cited in the commentary, has Zuole. Shiratori Kurakichi, "The Queue among the Peoples of North Asia," *Memoirs of the Research Department of the Toyo Bunko* 4 (1929), 8, identifies this river as the Shira-müren.

28. The walled enclosure was built on the Baobei River. It forms an irregular shape, some 2250 meters north to south and 1550 meters east to west. There is an inner city at the south end, 655 meters north to south and 670 meters east to west. In the thick layer of cultural deposits are many Han period tiles, iron farm implements, weapons, and bones of domesticated animals such as oxen, horses, sheep, and pigs. There are also many black-glazed thick tiles characteristic of the Northern Wei (386-534), which probably date to a later period when Shengle became an important military post. See Neimenggu zizhiqu wenwu gongzuodui, "Heilingeerxian Tuchengzi shijue jiyao," *Wenwu* 1961.9, 26-29; summarized in Zhang Yu, "Helingeerxian Tuchengzi shijue jiyao," *Neimenggu wenwu ziliao xuanji*, 69-74; Su Bai, "Shengle, Pingcheng yidai di Tuoba Xianbei—Bei Wei yiji: Xiangbei yiji jilu zhi er," *Wenwu* 1977.11, 38-46.

29. *Wei shu* 1.4-5.

30. *Song shu* 95.2321 and *Zizhi tongjian* 87.2752. In return, Tuoba Yilu was enfeoffed by the Jin as Duke of Dai in 310.

31. Zhongguo shehui kexueyuan Kaogu yanjiusuo Anyang gongzuodui, "Anyang Xiaomincun Jinmu fajue baogao," *Kaogu* 1983.6, 501-11. Another four graves are similar to this one, but they did not have any horse equipment. For reservations about the reconstruction, see Albert E. Dien, "The Stirrup and its Effect on Chinese Military History," *Ars Orientalis* 16 (1986): 33-34. It may be that these graves belong to the Eastern Xianbei rather than those of the Tuoba, since the capitals of the Murong Tuoba states of Former Yan (349-70) and Southern Yan (398-410) were at Ye, near Anyang. See *Kaogu* 1983.6, 510.

32. Neimenggu wenwu gongzuodui, "Neimenggu Huhehaote Meidaicun Bei Wei mu," *Kaogu* 1962.2, 86-7, 91. Su, "Shengle," 40-41.

33. Guo Suxin, "Neimenggu Huhehaote Bei Wei mu," *Wenwu* 1977.5, 38-41, 77. The best illustrations thus far have been those in *Chûgoku Uchi Môko Hoppô kiba minzoku monbutsuten* (Tokyo: Nihon Keizai Shimbunsha, 1983), pls. 53-59.

34. *Wei shu* 2.33; *Zizhi tongjian* 110.3470-1.

35. But those members of the confederation who lived in nonarable areas, and especially non-Tuoba members of the confederation, retained their traditional life-style and structure, being led by their *jiuzhang* or chiefs. See Mao Han-kuang, "Pei Wei Tung Wei Pei Ch'i chih ho-hsin chi-t'uan yü ho-hsin-ch'ü [added English title: The Ruling Group and the Key Area of the Northern and Eastern Wei and the Northern Ch'i Dynasties]," *Chung-yang yen-chiu-yüan li-shih yü-yen yen-chiu-so chi-k'an*, vol. 57 (1986): 250.

36. *Nan Qi shu* 57.984-6; W. F. J. Jenner, *Memories of Loyang: Yang Hsüan-chih and the Lost Capital (493-534)* (Oxford: Clarendon Press, 1981), 24-25.

37. On the Yun'gang caves, see now James D. Caswell, *Written and Unwritten: A New History of the Buddhist Caves at Yungang* (Vancouver: University of British Columbia Press, 1988). On the earlier literature, see Jenner, *Memories of Loyang*, 26, n. 35.

38. See *Wei shu* 4B.95 and n. 9 above.

39. Dunhuang wenwu yanjiusuo, "Xin faxian di Bei Wei cixiu," *Wenwu* 1972.2, 54-60 and pls. 11-12; a reproduction in color of part of the piece appears in Okazaki Takashi, *Chûgoku no rekishi 3: Gi Shin Nambokuchô no sekai* (Tokyo: Kodansha, 1977), pl. 5. The text on the banner allows one to identify the donor as Yuan Jia, Prince of Guangyang; see *Wenwu* 72.2, 57.

40. Guyuanxian wenwu gongzuodui, "Ningxia Guyuan Bei Wei mu qingli jianbao," *Wenwu* 1984.6, 46-56 and pls. 7-8.

41. Han Kongle and Luo Feng, "Guyuan Bei Wei mu qiguan di faxian," *Meishu yanjiu* 1984.2, 3-11; Wang Long, "Guyuan qiguan caihua," *Meishu yanjiu* 1984.2, 12-16. This issue of *Meishu yanjiu* includes seven pls. of color reproductions. Additional photographs are to be found in Zhang Anzhi, *Zhongguo meishu quanji: Huihuabian*, vol. 1 (Beijing: Renmin meishu chubanshe, 1986), 164-67. The most complete publication is Ningxia Guyuan Bowuguan, *Guyuan Bei Wei mu qiguanhua*, (Yinchuan: Ningxia renmin chubanshe, 1988).

42. For the human-headed bird, see Wang Kai, "'Ren mian niao' kao," *Kaogu yu wenwu* 1985.6, 97-101, who points to the apotropaic function of such creatures. During the Six Dynasties period these creatures most frequently appeared in pairs and held flowers, apparently symbolizing the happy life of the deceased couple in paradise (101).

43. The filial son incidents are identified in *Wenwu* 1984.6, 49-50.

44. For a contemporary description of the Hephthalites, see the translation of the account of Sung Yun, included in *Luoyang qielanji*, by Jenner, 259-60. An earlier translation by E. D. Chavannes, "Voyage de Song Yun dans l'Udyâma et le Gandhâra," *Bulletin del'École Francaise d'Extremé-Orient 3*, (1903):379-441.

45. Sun Ji, "Guyuan Bei Wei qiguanhua yanjiu," *Wenwu* 1989.9, 38-44, 12. Sun's reference to A. V. Pope, *A Survey of Persian Art*, vol. 7 (London and New York: Oxford University Press, 1938-9), pl. 137, appears to be in error. Nevertheless the scene of a seated figure holding a goblet and surrounded by attendants is certainly a common one in West Asian art. See also, in this regard, Gustina Scaglia, "Central Asians on a Northern Ch'i Gate Shrine," *Artibus Asiae* 21 (1958): 9-28.

46. Shanxisheng Datongshi bowuguan and Shanxisheng wenwu gongzuo weiyuanhui, "Shanxi Datong shijiazhai Bei Wei Sima Jinlong mu," *Wenwu* 1972.3, 20-33.

47. For the plan, see also *The Quest for Eternity*, 124, fig. 17.

48. The best reproductions thus far to appear are in *Zhongguo meishu quanji: Huihuabian*, vol. 1, 153-63.

49. For the attempt to impose a uniform ranking of family status, see Albert E. Dien, "Elite Lineages and the T'o-pa Accommodation: A Study of the Edict of 495," *Journal of the Economic and Social History of the Orient* 19 (1975): 61-88.

50. The reform movement is discussed in some detail in Jenner, *Memories of Loyang*, 38-52. See esp. 58, which lists the sequence of reform measures and the relevant sources in the *Wei shu*. See also John Lee, "Conquest, Division, Unification: A Social and Political History of Sixth Century Northern China," Ph.D. diss. (University of Toronto, 1985), chap. 2, "The Reform of the Late Fifth Century," 35-54; Lu Yao-tung, *Ts'ung P'ing-ch'eng tao Lo-yang* (Taipei: Lien-ching ch'u-pan shih-yeh kung-ssu, 1981) and Sun T'ung-hsün, *T'o-pa-shih ti Han-hua* (Taipei: Kuo-li T'ai-wan ta-hsüeh wen-hsüeh-yüan, 1962). There is an unfortunate tendency in some studies to view the reforms under Emperor Xiaowen as the culmination of the process of assimilation of the Xianbei into Han civilization, ignoring the continuing vitality of their native culture

51. Jenner, *Memories of Loyang*, and Yi-t'ung Wang, *A Record of Buddhist Monasteries in Lo-yang* (Princeton: Princeton University Press, 1984), are translations of *Luoyang qielanji* by Yang Xuanzhi, a description of that Northern Wei city written in 547, a decade or more after its destruction. See also Su Bai, "Bei Wei Luoyangcheng he Bei Mang lingmu—Xianbei yiji jilu zhi san," *Wenwu* 1978.7, 42-52; Ping-ti Ho, "Lo-yang, A.D. 495-534: A Study of the Physical and Socio-Economic Planning of a Metropolitan Area," *Harvard Journal of Asiatic Studies* 26 (1966): 52-101; Yan Wenru, "Luoyang Han Wei Sui Tang chengzi kanchaji," *Kaogu xuebao* 1955.9, 117-23; and Xu Jinxing and Du Yusheng, "Han Wei gucheng," *Wenwu* 1981.9, 85-87. For what has survived, see: Zhongguo kexueyuan Kaogu yanjiusuo Luoyang gongzuodui, "Han Wei Luoyang chubu kancha," *Kaogu* 1973.4, 198-208; Zhongguo kexueyuan Kaogu yanjiusuo Luoyang gongzuodui, "Han Wei Luoyangcheng yihao fangzhi he chutu di wawen," *Kaogu* 1973.4, 209-17; Zhongguo shehui

kexueyuan Kaogu yanjiusuo Luoyang gongzuodui, "Han Wei Luoyangcheng nanjiao di lingtai yizhi," *Kaogu* 1978.1, 54-57; Meng Fanren, "Bei Wei Luoyang waiguocheng xingzhi chutan," *Zhongguo lishi bowuguan guankan* 4 (1982): 41-48; Duan Pengqi, "Han Wei Luoyangcheng di jige wenti," *Zhongguo kaoguxue yanjiu: Xia Nai xiansheng kaogu wushinian jinian lunwenji* (Beijing: Wenwu chubanshe, 1986), 244-53; Zhongguo shehui kexueyuan Kaogu yanjiusuo Han Wei gucheng gongzuodui," Luoyang Han Wei gucheng beiyuan yihao mamian di fajue," *Kaogu* 1986.8, 726-30, 760; Luo Zixin, "Han Wei Luoyang chengzhi kaobian," *Zhongyuan wenwu* 1988.2, 63-68.

52. Luoyang bowuguan, "Luoyang Bei Wei Yuan Zhao mu," *Kaogu* 1973.4, 218-24, 243 and pls. 8-12. This tomb has been reconstructed in the Luoyang gumu bowuguan. The report gives his names as Shao, but it is now determined to be Zhao, according to Huang Minglang, director of the museum and author of the original report.

53. Baotoushi wenwu guanlichu, "Baotou Guyangxian faxian Bei Wei muqun," *Kaogu* 1987.1, 38-41 and 4.

54. Zheng Long, "Neimenggu Baotoushi Bei Wei Yao Qiji," *Kaogu* 1988.9, 856-57.

55. Yuan Shen, the prince of Guangyang, warned the court about the growing disaffection of the northern garrison troops, but his words went unheeded; see *Wei shu* 18.429-30 and *Bei shi* 16.617. He was the son of Yuan Jia, who had donated the embroidered banner at Dunhuang mentioned above. Wei Lan'gen issued a similar warning with the same lack of results; see *Bei shi* 23.329-30.

56. The events leading to the fall of the Northern Wei are told with admirable verve by Jenner, *Memories of Loyang*, 63-102.

57. Ningxia Huizu zizhiqu bowuguan and Ningxia Guyuan bowuguan, "Ningxia Guyuan Bei Zhou Li Xian fufu mu fajue jianbao," *Wenwu* 1985.11, 1-20, pls. 1-3 and color plate. See also Wu Zhuo, "Notes on the Silver Ewer from the Tomb of Li Xian," *Bulletin of the Asia Institute*, New Series, vol. 3 (1989), 61-70.

58. For a discussion of Li Xian's ethnicity, see Yao Weiyuan, *Beichao huxing kao* (Beijing: Zhonghua shuju, 1962), 300; Gu Tiefu, "Guanyu Li Xian shixing menwang, minzu di yixie kanfa," *Meishu yanjiu* 1985.11, 57-58; Luo Feng, "Li Xian fufu muzhi kaolue," *Meishu yanjiu* 1985.11, 59-60, and Wang Weiming, "Bei Zhou Li Xian fufu mu ruogan wenti chutan," *Meishi yanjiu* 1985.4, 62. The evidence for deciding the question is quite scanty, and any conclusion must be tentative.

59. For color photos of the figurines, see the inside back cover of *Meishu yanjiu*, 1985.4; *Tonkô Seika ôkokuten: Shiruko rôdo bi to shimpi* (Tokyo: Nihon Keizai Shimbunsha, 1988), 46-51; *Ningxia huabao* 1984.2, 32-33.

60. On the ewer, see Wu Zhuo, "Bei Zhou Li Xian mu chutu liujin yinhu kao," *Wenwu* 1987.5, 66-76.

61. H. W. Hausig, "Die Quellen über die Zentralasiatische Herkunft der Europäischen Awaren," *Central Asiatic Journal* 2 (1956): 21-43, especially 39, denies the equation of Ruanruan with Avars. However, Pulleyblank, "The Chinese and Their Neighbors," 453, offers an interesting solution to the problem, suggesting that the ruling element of the Ruanruan came from the Wuhuan, the Eastern Hu people mentioned earlier, and Wuhuan, Pulleyblank continues, is very probably a transcription of *Awar. For the history of the Avars, see H. Miyakawa and Arnulf Kollautz, *Geschichte und Kultur eines Nomadenvolkes in Europa: Die Jou-jan der Mongolei und die Awaren Karpatenbeckens*, 2 vols. (Klagenfurt, 1968). On the name Ruanruan (Juan-juan), see Boodberg, *Selected Works of Peter A. Boodberg* (Berkeley, 1979), 125-28, and A. Dien, *Biography of Yü-wen Hu*, 86, n. 104, for the literature cited there.

62. Cixian wenhuaguan, "Hebei Cixian Dong Wei Ruru gongzhu mu fajue jianbao," *Wenwu* 1984.4, 1-9, pls. 1-5 and color plate.

63. The murals of this tomb are described in detail by Tang Chi, "Dong Wei Ruru gongzhu mu bihua shitan," *Wenwu* 1984.4, 10-15. Tang's appraisal is that the murals are very well done and that such a high level of accomplishment in the Eastern Wei provided the basis for the famous artists who appeared during the Northern Qi. Very little had been known of the painting of the Eastern Wei before these murals were discovered, and their quality arouses much enthusiasm in China, although the reproductions that have thus far been made available do not do them justice.

64. *Wenwu* 1984.4, 4, color plate, and fig. 4.8, 3. A similar piece is said to be in the collection of the Museum of Fine Arts, Boston. Another was found in the tomb of Kudi Huiluo of 562; see Wang Kelin, "Bei Qi Kudi Huiluo mu," *Kaogu xuebao* 1979.3, 392 and pl. 9.3, where it is simply labeled as a dancing *hu* figure. For the Xinjiang figure, see Xinjiang Weiwuer zizhiqu shehuikexueyuan Kaogu yanjiusuo, *Xinjiang gudai minzu wenwu* (Beijing: Wenwu chubanshe, 1985), pl. 90.

65. *Wenwu* 1984.4, 4, pl. 3.5, and fig. 4.2.

66. *Wenwu* 1979.3, 20 and fig. 16.

67. *Kaogu* 1977.6, 385, and *Wenwu* 1972.1, 48, respectively.

68. *Jin shu* 6.161. The remark was made in 324 when Sima Shao made a daring reconnaissance of an enemy camp. The color *huang* may refer here to the dark reddish, off-black tint sometimes seen among Chinese in the north.

69. Cixian wenhuaguan, "Hebei Cixian Bei Qi Gao Run mu," *Kaogu* 1979.3, pls. 7-8. For a description of this type, see Tang Chi, "Bei Qi Gao Run bihua jianjie," *Kaogu* 1979.3, 244.

70. Shanxisheng bowuguan, *Taiyuan Kuangpo Bei Qi Zhang Su mu wenwu tulu* (Beijing: Zhongguo gudian yishu chubanshe, 1958), 2. This tomb, unlike the other three, was simply carved out of the soil and had no brick walls.

71. Wang Kelin, op. cit., 377-402 and pls. 1-12.

72. Tao Zhenggang, "Shanxi Qixian Baigui Bei Qi Han Yi mu," *Wenwu* 1975.4, 64-73. Both Zhang and Han appear to have been Han Chinese, but Zhang's family members and Han himself held high ranks in the Xianbei state hierarchy.

73. Shanxisheng Kaogu yanjiusuo and Taiyuanshi wenwu guanli weiyuanhui, "Taiyuanshi Bei Qi Lou Rui mu fajue jianbao," *Wenwu* 1983.10, 1-23, color plate, and pls. 1-7.

74. *Wenwu* 1975.4, 69.

75. Lou Rui's biography appears in *Bei Qi shu* 15.197.

76. In addition to the photo reproductions accompanying the original report, one may consult *Chinese Arts* 1 (1986?), published by the People's Fine Arts Publishing House, Hong Kong, which also has a number of articles on these murals. The best reproductions thus far are in Han Zhongmin and Hubert Delahaye, *A Journey through Ancient China* (New York and Florence: W. H. Smith Publishers, 1985), 198-203.

77. Yang Hong, *Wenwu* 1983.10, 36-37.

78. The occurrence of such vehicles probably does not require a specific rationale such as proposed by Linda Cooke Johnson in "The Wedding Ceremony for an Imperial Liao Princess: Wall Paintings from a Liao Dynasty Tomb in Jilin," *Artibus Asiae* 44 (1983): 107-36.

79. "Bitan Taiyuan Bei Qi Lou Rui mu," *Wenwu* 1983.10, 24-39. The contributors are Wu Zuoren, Su Bai, Shi Shuqing, Feng Xianming, Xu Pingfang, Tang Chi, Wang Qufei, Yang Hong, Li Zhiyan, and Tao Zhenggang. I wish to thank Tao Zhenggang for enabling me to view the murals at the Shanxi Institute for Archaeological Research, Taiyuan.

80. *Wenwu* 1983.10, 33.

81. *Wenwu* 1983.10, 27 and 29; Jin Weinuo, "Painting Heritage of the State of Northern Qi," *Chinese Arts* 1 (1986?): 21. For Yang Zihua, see William R. Acker, *Some T'ang and Pre-T'ang Texts on Chinese Painting* (Leiden: E. J. Brill, 1954), 167.

82. Unfortunately the hood that seems almost standard for the Xianbei conceals their hairstyle, about which there is some literary evidence and some scholarly discussion. The southern Chinese designation for the Tuoba Xianbei was *suo-tou*, which is usually taken to mean "braided," since they were said to be *pifa*, that is, "to wear the hair hanging down the back." See *Nan Qi shu* 57.983. In the *Song shu* account of them, they are called *suo-lu* "braided caitiff"; cf. *Song shu* 95.2321. For a discussion of the association of their name reconstructed as *Taqbac and the hairstyle, see Boodberg, "The Language of the T'o-pa Wei," 184-85. The association of braids and the Tuoba was cited in the case of the grave at Zhalainuoer where a complete hair braid was found; see Su, *Wenwu* 1977.5, 50. Since the grave was that of a female, the braid may not be significant. As we shall see, the distinctive hairdress of the Xianbei, as it occurs in depictions of them, is not braids that hang down, but it is rather of a rounded mass on top of the head, covered by a hood. See Boodberg, loc. cit., where the etymons he is discussing include Turkish *tüpe*- "braid of hair left on top of the skull," further related to the stem for "round" and with *dobo*- "protuberance." Shiratori Kurakichi, in his article "The Queue among the Peoples of North Asia," 1-69, explored the evidence found in the literary sources concerning hairstyles and concluded that while the Xiongnu wore their hair in queues, the Wuhuan and Xianbei had shaved heads. The tresses of hair found in Xiongnu tombs at Noin Ula would seem to confirm the texts regarding these people. See Camilla Trever, *Excavations in Northern Mongolia (1924-1925)*, vol. 3 (Leningrad: Memoirs of the Academy of History of Material Culture, 1932), 55-59, detailing the contents of Tumuli 1 and 6. However, S. I. Rudenko identifies these as those worn by women. For a photo of the braids and further description, see his *Die Kultur der Hsiung-nu und die Hügelgräber von Noin Ula* (Bonn: Habelt, 1969), 39 and pl. 19. Because there is reference to queues among the Murong, Tuoba, and Ruanruan, Shiratori conjectured that these peoples were more probably of the Xiongnu than the Xianbei race (18) and identified themselves as Xianbei only in order to avail themselves of the fame of that group (21). Shiratori's analysis places too much weight on hairstyle, especially since the literary sources are so sparse. Further, graphic representations may indicate that the situation is more complicated than one would suppose on the basis of texts alone. The Khitans, according to Shiratori's sources, were clean-shaven, but in the murals from Liao tombs one sees individuals with shaven crowns but with long tresses at the side of the head above the ear (see *Wenwu* 1973.8, 31). In *Bei shi* 98.3267 the Yuwen men are said to have cut their hair except for a tuft at the top of their head, several inches in length, which was retained for decorative purposes. It is this style that seems most closely to resemble what one sees in the figurines of this period. Whatever the case may be, the literary sources do not mention hoods and capes, which apparently covered some sort of topknot, which seem to characterize the Xianbei of this period.

83. This seems to have been a prevailing opinion among the Xianbei. See Jennifer Holmgren, "Politics of the Inner Court under the Hou-Chu (Last Lord) of Northern Ch'i circa 565-573," in A. Dien, ed., *State and Society in Early Medieval China* (Hong Kong and Stanford: Hong Kong University Press and Stanford University Press, 1990), 304 and 309. An exception was made of Gao Ang, who was apparently the sole high-ranking Chinese officer in his time; see *Bei Qi shu* 21.295 and *Zizhi tongjian* 157.4882. There was also a certain amount of vituperation recorded; see, for example, *Bei shi* 92.3053. Holmgren concludes that racial antagonisms came to the fore only in the last years of the Northern Qi (circa 573-77), when Chinese at the court began to aspire to military commands; see ibid., 322-23. I would, on the contrary, argue that the Chinese at the court attained positions of high office and important responsibilities at the sufferance of the Xianbei, and any perceived threat to the preeminence of the Xianbei was dealt with in a ruthless fashion; see my "Yen Chih-t'ui (531-591+): A Buddho-Confucian," in A. Wright and D. Twitchett, eds., *Confucian Personalities* (Stanford: Stanford University Press, 1962), 60-61.

84. *Zizhi tongjian* 157.4882.

85. Chou Fa-kao, *Yen-shih chia-hsün*, 5b-6a; Teng Ssu-yü, *Family Instructions for the Yen Clan*, 7-8.

86. *Bei shi* 28.1020.

87. *Sui shu* 32.935. There are a number of other works listed in the *Sui shu* bibliography as being in the "national" (*guoyu*) language as well as specifically in Xianbei; *Sui shu* 32.945. Manuals of military commands in the Xianbei language were compiled because the Xianbei soldiery had begun to lose their command of the language in the Northern Wei; *Sui shu* 32.947. In at least one case a work entitled as Xianbei rather than *guoyu* was credited to a Northern Zhou ruler, indicating that Xianbei was not considered the national language, and perhaps substantiating the surmise that the Yuwen rulers of the Northern Zhou spoke a different language.

88. Xing Bingyan, "Ye Tan 'Chilege' di yuanlai yuyan," *Guangming ribao* (July 26, 1983). He cites anecdotes about Gao Ang, *Bei Qi shi* 21.295; Sun Qian, *Bei Qi shu* 24.341, and Zu Ting, *Bei Qi shu* 39.515, as well as Yan Zhitui's dismay concerning the training of the seventeen-year-old cited above.

89. Albert E. Dien, "The Bestowal of Surnames under the Western Wei—Northern Chou: A Case of Counter-acculturation," *T'oung Pao* 63 (1977): 137-77.

90. Su Bai, "Dongbei, Neimenggu gudiqu di Xianbei yiji," 42. For a rare cautionary note in reference to the overwhelming emphasis on sinicization in modern Chinese scholarship, see: Lü Yifei, "Lizhen di Xianbei hua qingxiang", *Beichao yanjiu*, vol. 3, 1990, 105-8.

The Twelve Calendrical Animals in Tang Tombs

Judy Chungwa Ho

University of California, Irvine

The twelve animals—Rat, Ox, Tiger, Hare, Dragon, Serpent, Horse, Sheep, Monkey, Cock, Dog, and Pig—are the duodenary symbols in the traditional Chinese calendar. They form a distinctive group of burial objects, or *mingqi*, especially popular during the Sui (581-618) and Tang (618-907) dynasties. Made in a variety of forms they range from naturalistic animals to fantastic hybrids, such as the animal-headed figurines in the 1987 exhibition *The Quest for Eternity* at the Los Angeles County Museum of Art (fig. 1).[1]

Archaeological excavations have uncovered not only sets of the twelve calendrical animals but also images of the duodenary series in bronze mirrors, stone epitaphs, and murals.[2] The imagery seems to have progressed from animal to half-human then to fully human types. Within this broader development there are at least two regional variations: the anthropomorphic type first appeared south of the Yangzi River, especially in Hunan and Hubei provinces. The animal type appeared in the north and east coast areas, and the anthropomorphic type was later adapted from the south.[3] The animal type is the most common and enduring one, and it is in this form that the concept of the duodenary series survives in present Chinese communities such as Hong Kong and Taiwan.

The variety of imagery and extent of the mortuary use of the calendrical animals in the Sui - Tang period remain unsurpassed, a phenomenon that may have been related to special rituals and beliefs at the time.[4] Textual information concerning the mortuary function of the duodenary

Figure

1.　Calendrical Snake, from eighth-century tomb in Xian area, ceramic sculpture, 27.5 cm (height), Shaanxi Provincial Museum, photograph courtesy Los Angeles County Museum of Art.

series is scarce. Ritual manuals compiled before the ninth century, such as *Datang Liudian* (covering the period 673-740), compiled by Chang Jiuling and others, and *Datang kaiyuan li*, compiled in 732 by Xiao Song and others, made no reference to the series. The *Tang Huiyao*, compiled by Wang Pu (922-982), mentions the sumptuary edicts of 811, in which the duodenary series was stated as a component of *mingqi* for officials of all ranks, and the edict of 841 refers to its wider use, even by commoners.[5] Such official codification proves that the mortuary use of the series was a widespread phenomenon. Another point of interest is that the Tang code specifies the duodenary series as a whole. Although each calendrical animal has its own history of mythical and religious development, it is the entire series as such that has a special mortuary function. This is corroborated by the archaeological evidence, as tombs were designed to be furnished with complete twelve-piece sets of *mingqi*.[6]

The duodenary series had ancient origins and once pervaded all aspects of Chinese thought. However, there has been little study of its mortuary function. In particular, there has been little study concerning the following questions: What is the function of the series in the tomb context? Is there any correlation between the *mingqi* and bronze mirrors, stone epitaphs, murals, and the tomb plan and structure? What is the significance of the duodenary series in relation to the broader concerns of Chinese mortuary art?

This study will trace the development and mortuary function of the duodenary series. It will be shown that its divinatory role is the key to its mortuary function. The use of the duodenary series in this life was transferred to the afterlife, and mortuary art was perceived as a form of prognostication for the afterlife. Furthermore, it was religious faith that stimulated the creation of these images.

Duodenary Series and Prognostication

While the duodenary series had ancient calendrical origins, it played an increasingly important role in Chinese divinatory arts. Divination in its earliest form was restricted to affairs of the state and it was only during the Latter Han dynasty (25-220) that individual fate became a major concern. By the Tang period the most intricate forms of portent reading were established. This coincides with the time when the mortuary use of the duodenary series became fully developed.

The origin of the animal series—whether indigenous or imported from Turkic neighbors—has been a subject of scholarly dispute. With recent archaeological discoveries scholars now seem to favor the former view. Without further ado let us accept the antique origin of associating the pairing of animals with the "twelve earthly branches." While this concept was widespread in Asia, it was a commonly held Chinese notion by the first century.[7]

The sexagenary cycle is the most ancient Chinese day-count system, in which twelve characters called "earthly branches," or *diji*—*zi, qiu, yin, mou, chen, ji, wu, wei, shen, yu, xu, hai*—combine alternately with the ten "heavenly stems" or *tiangan*—*jia, yi, bing, ding, wu, ji, gang, xin, ren, gui*—to make sixty combinations designating a sixty-day cycle. This cycle can then be infinitely repeated. The sexagenary cycle is mathematical and abstract in nature with no apparent basis in astronomical observation. Characters for the stems and branches, often found in Shang oracle-bones strictly for day-count, were used in divination for affairs of state.[8] Without any animal association stems and branches were also used as an abstract numerical series for the calender, the compass, and for anything that could be divided into twelve, such as volumes, chapters, and sections in books.

Archaeological evidence for the pairing of branches with the animal series can be dated to the fourth century B.C., implying an even earlier date for its inception.[9] The pairing was as follows: Rat for *zi*, Ox for *qui*, Tiger for *yin*, Hare for *mou*, Dragon for *chen*, Serpent for *ji*, Horse for *wu*, Sheep for *wei*, Monkey for *shen*, Cock for *you*, Dog for *xu*, Boar or Pig for *hai*. The practice of using the system for the sixty-year cycle began around the first century, when a year was referred to by a particular stem-branch combination; this system is still used today. For example, the year of the 1911 Revolution is commonly referred to as the "*Xinhai* Revolution" according to the stem-branch characters of the year; it is also the Year of the Boar according to the branch *hai*.

Considered independently, the branches were also correlated to the calendrical system in which the sky was demarcated by twelve sectors along the equator called *chen*, a term with the original meaning of "chronogram" or "starry determinant," referring to the constellations for time-keeping along the path of the moon and planets. As the sidereal period of the planet Jupiter is almost exactly twelve years, a year would be the duration of the planet in each sector, which was also called "halt" or *ci* denoting Jupiter's station. As the sun takes two hours to move across each *chen*, the system was used to make the twelve double-hours (often broken down into twenty-four half-hours) of the day according to the Chinese calendar. The twenty-eight lunar lodgings, or *xiu*, were also incorporated. This system was then extended to mark the twelve months of the year, the seasons, and eventually, the term *chen* became a standard term for the hours. As the system was based on spatial demarcations along the horizon, the compass directions on earth were also included. The following diagram, an adaptation from the seventeenth-century encyclopedia *Wujing leipian*, illustrates the correlation of the duodenary series with the hours, months, years, *xiu*, and compass directions (fig. 2). The spatiotemporal correlations are represented in the form of a circular disc to represent the sky along the equator. Concentric rings starting from the center represent the following: the branches and twenty-four half-hours in the second ring; the twelve Jovian sectors, or *ci*, of the equator in the third ring; and the twenty-eight lunar lodgings in the outermost ring. The corresponding cardinal points are marked outside.[10]

While the sexagenary cycle was adopted officially for calendrical use by the first century, the Jovian cycle continued to influence Chinese thought, especially in astrology and popular religion. A divinatory system called *fenye* developed on the basis of celestial and terrestrial correspondences. By association the twelve branches also became inextricably bound with astrology. The very use of animal symbols could very well be related to other ancient animal asterisms, especially the twenty-eight *xiu*, popularly known as the "animal stars."[11]

Another type of prognostication based on the sexagenary cycle called *dunjia* applied correlative cosmology of the Five Elements and yin-yang principles to the stem-branch characters for the year, month, or day in predicting human affairs. Interpreted in terms of Five Elements and yin-yang theories, stem-branch combinations would signify ever more subtle and intricate cosmic interactions for creation and destruction as well as reflect the process of life and decay in nature.[12] The following chart summarizes the correlation mentioned above (fig. 3).

This type of prognostication probably developed in the Later Han (25-220), although Kuan Luo in the Three Kingdoms period (221-265) was known as the first to write on this subject. Apparently he also combined astrology into his calculation. For example, he predicted his life span of forty-seven to forty-eight years on the basis of his birth year of the Tiger in conjunction with the lunar eclipse.[13] By the fifth and sixth centuries, the belief that the calendrical animal of one's birth year influenced one's personality became widespread. Eventually, important events in an individual's life were governed by the "eight characters," or *bazi*, the eight stem and branch characters referring to the year, month, day, and hour of the day of an individual's birth, although the branch or animal of the birth year was always considered more important.[14] Among the most important human events for prognostication was burial. The date of burial was determined by one's birth year and its presiding calendrical animal.[15]

Portent reading also made use of the eight trigrams and sixty-four hexagrams based on the *Book of Changes*, or *Yijing*, to symbolize all permutations in nature and human events. The eight trigrams are also aligned with the compass directions according to two orders, one called the Anterior Order of Fu Xi and one the Posterior Order of the Zhou King Wenwang; and it is the Posterior Order that

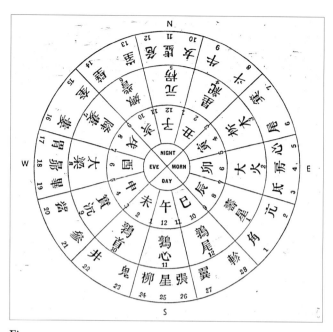

Figure

2.   Diagram of spatio-temporal correlations. After Percival Yetts, *The Cull Chinese Bronzes* (London: The University Press, 1939), p. 130, fig. 35.

was usually correlated to the branches. By the Former Han (202 B.C. - A.D 9) this system was applied in the form of a diviner's board, called *shi*, used to calculate fate according to the position of the pointer after rotating the circular disc of Heaven over the square board of Earth and the resulting alignment of markings on them. These markings included the branch and stem characters and trigrams symbolizing all cosmic forces and can be found in either the Earth or Heaven disc or both. One example discovered in a first century B.C. tomb in Mozuizi, Gansu province, used the duodenary series in combination with eight stems, omitting *wu* and *ji* from the series of ten (fig. 4). The branches functioned in both realms of Heaven and Earth and thus can be understood as a symbol of cosmic totality, representing the perpetual cycle of time as well as the infinite extension of the universe in all directions.[16] The *shi* is an antecedent of the standard Chinese magnetic compass (fig. 5), which had twenty-four compass points, composed of twelve branches and eight stems as in the Mozuizi *shi*, and the addition of four trigrams according to the Posterior Order: *gen* (northeast), *sun* (southeast), *kun* (southwest), *gian* (northwest). The duodenary series alone was also used as an abbreviation for all twenty-four points.[17] Almanacs and individual horoscopes based on a combination of various cosmological and astrological considerations further developed in Tang times and continued to influence popular thought in all subsequent ages.[18]

Prognostication for the Afterlife

Since life and death was understood in terms of cosmic

correlations, properly aligning the deceased with the cosmic forces for the afterlife journey was considered necessary for achieving immortality. According to the Chinese concept of multiple *hun/po* souls the *po* soul maintained some form of existence in the tomb itself.[19] The deceased could also influence surviving dependents, reinforcing the link between the dead and the living. Proper burial not only ensured happiness in the afterlife for the deceased but good fortune for the survivors in the living world.[20]

Recent archaeological finds help shed light on the evolution of ancient tomb design. By Han times the tomb was designed to create an ideal cosmic context for the deceased.[21] Tomb plans were patterned after imperial ritual halls, or *mingtang* and aligned with the cosmic forces according to the principles of yin-yang and the Five Elements. The entrance of the tomb chamber usually faced south, like the *mingtang*, the coffin occupied the center, and the rest of the tomb decoration was in concordance with the cosmic order. In this way the tomb functioned like a "mandala," which enabled the tomb occupant to be "in the sacred center," a locus of perfect balance and harmony with the cosmic forces in infinite space and time.[22] Analogous to the *shi* this ideal cosmic alignment would ensure a safe afterlife and even immortality for the deceased as well as provide happiness and prosperity for the survivors in this life. This cosmo-magical schema was exclusively used by the ruling class during the Han period. Later this schema provided the theoretical foundation for the development of *fengshui*, or geomancy.

Fengshui is a most elaborate and sophisticated form of portent reading for siting tombs that incorporated ancient astronomical, cosmological, as well as other principles of prognostication. Although *fengshui* had ancient origins (like other forms of divination), its application to calculations of personal fate was a post-Han development. Fully systematized by the Tang period, *fengshui* continued to influence a broad spectrum of Chinese society and is still practiced in Hong Kong and Taiwan today. As noted by other scholars, *fengshui* can be understood as a popular application of correlative cosmology.[23] For example, the geomantic compass called *luopan* used by the School of Cosmology was clearly based on the principles of correlative cosmology (fig. 6). A dial made up of as many as thirty-eight adjustable concentric rings with cosmic symbols, it was used to calculate the burial site and orientation of tomb furnishings in order to ensure maximal benefit from the cosmic forces not only for the fate of the deceased in afterlife but for the survivors in this life. The *luopan* is a more elaborate version of the earlier *shi*, using the twenty-four compass points as both celestial and terrestrial demarcations. Unlike the Han *shi*, with the square and circle as symbols of Earth and Heaven, the *luopan* has three discs symbolizing Earth, Heaven, and Man. By the Tang dy-

TRI-GRAMS OF FU HSI	DUO-DENARY SIGNS	ANIMAL SYMBOLS	LUNAR MONTH	HORIZON	YEAR	DAY	DUALISM
☷	子	RAT	11th	N	Winter Solstice	Midnight	Maximum *yin*
☷	丑	OX	12th			2 a.m.	
☳	寅	TIGER	1st	N–E	Beginning of Spring	4 a.m.	
☳	卯	HARE	2nd	E	Spring Equinox	6 a.m.	Equality
☳	辰	DRAGON	3rd			8 a.m.	
☰	巳	SERPENT	4th	S–E	Beginning of Summer	10 a.m.	
☰	午	HORSE	5th	S	Summer Solstice	Noon	Maximum *yang*
☰	未	SHEEP	6th			2 p.m.	
☶	申	MONKEY	7th	S–W	Beginning of Autumn	4 p.m.	
☶	酉	COCK	8th	W	Autumn Equinox	6 p.m.	Equality
☶	戌	DOG	9th			8 p.m.	
☵	亥	PIG	10th	N–W	Beginning of Winter	10 p.m.	

3

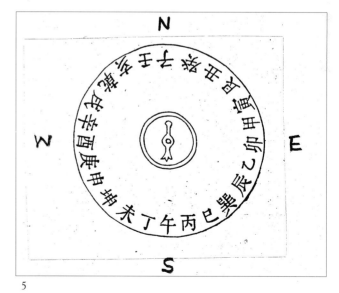

4

5

Figures

3. Table of correlations. After *The Cull Chinese Bronzes*, p. 133, fig. 36.

4. Diviner's board (*shi*), from tomb at Mozuizi, Gansu province, first century B.C., lacquered wood, 9 x 9 cm, inner square marked by 8 stems and 12 branches in seal script characters. After *Wenwu* 12 (1972): 15, fig. 8.

5. Chinese magnetic compass points.

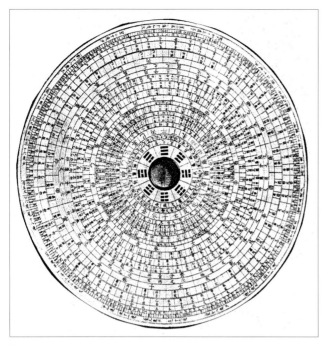

Figure

6. The John Couch Adams Compass (*luopan*), circa eighteenth century, 24 points on 5th, 12th, and 17th rings from center, the Whipple Museum of the History of Science, Cambridge, England. After Needham, *Science*, vol. 4, fig. 340.

nasty, the square-in-circle was not considered essential for cosmic symbolism. The square was often eliminated and circles were used to symbolize all cosmic realms, whether Heaven, Earth, or Man. There was also greater emphasis on the interactions of the different realms.[24]

The actual tomb plans, furnishings, and *fengshui* influences are not described in any detail in extant Tang codes. More detailed information, however, can be found in a later document, the *Dahan yuanling mizhang jing* (henceforth *Mizhangjing*), by an otherwise unknown author, Chang Jingwen. Although written in the twelfth century and probably with a northwest regional bias, the text still preserves many death rituals that were established earlier and were also used in other parts of China. Some furnishings found in Tang and even earlier tombs are still mentioned in the text.[25] Relying on *fengshui* theories, the *Mizhangjing* confirms that *fengshui* at the time was mainly concerned with proper alignment of the tomb and its furnishings with the cosmic forces. Several means could be used to achieve this end. One way was to arrange a southern orientation. Another way was to furnish the tomb with *mingqi* representing a pantheon of deities regulating the cosmic forces or with apotropaic and prophylactic talismans (*shensa*).

Especially illuminating is the section on "*mingqi shensa*" (on tomb sculptures and prophylactic spirits), with schematic plans for the proper placement of furnishings in tombs of the emperor, crown prince, dukes, barons, minis-

ters, officials, and commoners (figs. 7a-e). While the quantity of *mingqi* is obviously determined by the social status of the tomb occupant, the schema is the same for all. All tombs indicate a southern orientation. The tomb chamber is rectangular, with the coffin in the center. And except for commoners' tombs all others are furnished with *mingqi* labeled with the titles of court officials ranging from generals to cooks. They line the passageway from the tomb center to the south entrance, representing an elaborate assemblage modeled after the contemporary Chinese bureaucracy. They also emphasize the position of the tomb occupant as being "in the sacred center."

The four sides of the rectangular floor plan of the tomb chamber are marked according to the twenty-four points in the *luopan*, starting with *zi* in the middle of the top in clockwise direction. The use of the *luopan* demarcations not only indicates the influence of *fengshui* but the continuities with Tang and even pre-Tang mortuary traditions. Underlying the schematic layouts in the *Mizhang jing* is the concept of the tomb as a mandala, a cosmo-magical schema that was found already in the ancient concept of *mingtang* and the diviner's board *shi*.

Tombs for the upper and ruling classes have *mingqi* placed according to the stems and branches. Each branch is marked for a *Yuanchen* (Primal Asterism), each stem for a *Tianguan* (Celestial Official). *Yuanchen* and *Tianguan* refer to *mingqi* representing otherworldly officials charged with regulating the cosmic forces symbolized by the branches and stems respectively. This is undoubtedly the best clue to the mortuary function of the duodenary series. As we will discuss later, *mingqi* figurines representing the duodenary series in Sui and Tang tombs are positioned along the sides of the tomb, with the coffin in the center. Aligned with the compass points, the duodenary series symbolizes cosmic totality and infinity in space and time, and its presence would ensure the best possible fate for the deceased and his progeny.

The *Mizhangjing* mentions regulations promulgated in 811 and recorded in the *Tang Huiyao* specifying that the *mingqi* figurines of the duodenary series were not for lower-ranking officials and commoners. This is also confirmed by the archaeological evidence, as *mingqi* of the duodenary series from the Sui-Tang period were mostly from tombs belonging to the upper-ranking official classes.[26] This, however, does not mean that the duodenary series was excluded from use by lower-ranking officials and commoners. The *Mizhang jing* makes a distinction between *mingqi* and *shensa*, and while *mingqi* are not for commoners, *shensa* are for everyone. All tombs may have five *shensa* of the calendrical animals all placed according to their branch positions: Metal Ox at *qiu*, Tomb (earth) Dragon at *chen*, Jade Horse at *wu*, Metal Cock at *yu*, Jade Dog at *shu*, and Iron Pig at *hai*. These talismans correspond to the Five El-

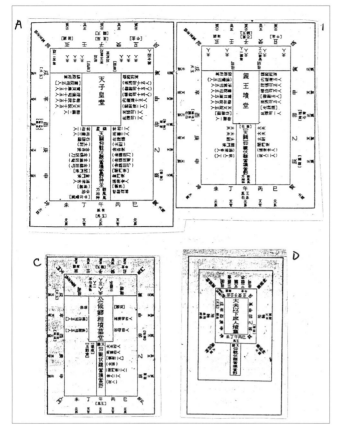

7a,b,c,d

7e

Figures

7. Tomb layouts from *Dahan yuanling mizhang jing*. After adaptation in *Kaogu* 2 (1963): 89-90, for (a) emperor, (b) Crown Prince, (c) dukes, barons, ministers (d) lower officials and commoners. Simplified diagram (e) showing 24 points used in all layouts.

ements, which control the interactions between the animals in the duodenary series. In other words the five talismans emphasize the dynamic relationship as such and can be understood to stand for the entire series also. The upper classes could use both *mingqi* and *shensa*, while commoners could only use *shensa*; but the purpose of tomb furnishings was the same—to evoke the presence of the duodenary series.

Archaeological evidence also proves that the southern entrance was a marked preference in Tang tombs of all social classes. Other *fengshui* considerations such as those followed by the School of Earthly Forms may have necessitated deviations from this southern exposure in some tombs, but the cyclical symbolism in the decorations and furnishings would compensate for this in symbolic terms, ensuring an ideal orientation at least in the tomb interior.[27]

The Duodenary Series as Potent Spirits

While the underlying purpose of tomb decoration was to ensure the best possible fate for the living and the dead, the iconographic development of the duodenary series was determined by religious beliefs. The duodenary series functioned as potent spirits and as objects of worship.

As pointed out by Benjamin Schwartz, correlative cos-

mology had an intrinsic religious dimension. In searching for correlates between the natural and human world, correlative cosmology led to the anthropomorphizing of nature, and in this way even abstract entities and mystical principles became incarnate.[28] Ancestor worship also contributed to the development of an otherworldly pantheon of cosmic deities and ancestor spirits capable of receiving ritual honors.[29] Beliefs in the calendrical animals as potent spirits can be understood as part of this religious development.

The duodenary series is represented as three basic types of beings: animal, human, and hybrid. The iconographic variation is the outcome of diverse mythicizing processes and religious beliefs.[30] Ancient shamanistic practices, correlative cosmology, and ancestor worship gave rise to popular faith in animal and nature spirits with apotropaic and prophylactic powers. The animal form of the duodenary series is the result of this development.[31] The hybrid and anthropomorphic forms evolved from two mythicizing processes: first, the identification of the animal and human world; second, the euhemerization of preexisting animal deities in anthropomorphic terms.[32]

Daoist references indicate how the calendrical animals were perceived of as animal as well as anthropomorphic spirits. *Tuiming* or fate- calculation, the practice of magical arts, and worship of spirits and deities were major components of religious Daoism. Absorbing ancient cosmological myths, shamanistic practices, and folklore concerning apotropaic and prophylactic animal and nature spirits, the Daoist pantheon naturally came to include the duodenary series. According to the Daoist Ge Hong (282-363) at least by the fourth century, the calendrical animals were already believed to behave like other nature deities, transforming themselves into humans and exercising magic on days under their branch signs.[33]

The paradigm of the "bureaucratic social order" is another pervasive influence in ancient China. Each of the Five Elements came to be known as having a presiding "official" in charge of all the phenomena governed by the Element.[34] Although there is no direct evidence of such images before the Tang, indirect evidence is provided by the fact that sixth-century cosmic chess games used chessmen named after the celestial and terrestrial forces and spirits. One game in particular used the twelve branches as chessmen. Each player started with six by throwing them on the board, and the contest would start with this chance placing. According to the sixth-century scholar Yu Xin some chess pieces were made in the form of celestial officials carrying ivory scepters.[35] The bureaucratic model should also be distinguished from the Daoist beliefs in the magical human and animal transformations mentioned by Ge Hong, although both mythicizing processes would lead to anthropomorphic representations of the duodenary series. According to Daoist beliefs, the duodenary series would be conceived of as magicians or shamans having a mystical identity with the animal forms. According to the bureaucratic model the duodenary series would be conceived of as cosmic officials similar to their mundane prototypes, presiding over the calendrical animals, who in turn control all the cosmic forces under their signs.

The animal, hybrid, and anthropomorphic types of the duodenary series had ancient roots in China. Image worship, however, must have received foreign impetus such as Buddhism. Reference to the animal cycle can be found in such Buddhist texts as the *Mahavaipulyamahasamnipata sutra* (Chinese: *Dafangdeng dajijing*, henceforth *Dajijing*) translated by Dharmaraksema at Wuwei near Dunhuang, Gansu Province, in 414-426.[36] This text contains a story of twelve animals. The Lion is used instead of the Tiger, but the series as a whole corresponds to the traditional animal correlates of the duodenary series. According to the story the twelve animals dwelled in caves that were originally occupied by bodhisattvas. Each animal took turns to circulate around the world performing miracles, saving those born under its sign. Later, Dao Shi in the *Fayuan Julin* (compiled 668) commented that this passage showed how bodhisattvas used animal and human transformations

as expedient means to save all sentient beings in the present world, and that it also proved that the Chinese concept of the twelve *chen* animals was in accordance with Buddhist teaching. Despite Dao Shi's comment the *Dajijing* is known to be a very mixed collection of texts from Central Asia, some of which are probably apocryphal. The concept of the calendrical animals that was already circulating in West and Central Asia was probably assimilated as a means of introducing the Buddhist doctrine to the native audience in a more palatable form.[37] At the same time, association with Buddhism inspired faith in the calendrical animals as benevolent spirits with the power to intervene in the fate and life span of believers.

The twelve *yaksha* generals serving the Buddha Bhaishajyaguru, or Medicine Buddha, were sometimes correlated to the twelve calendrical animals. By the seventh century they were depicted as armored ferocious guardians holding weapons and wearing headgear decorated with images of the calendrical animals.[38] Assimilation with the animal cycle must have enhanced the cosmic significance and prestige of these Buddhist deities; in turn, the *yaksha* generals must have also added a dimension to the calendrical spirits as fear-inspiring guardians. In the brick reliefs in the Northern Song (967-1126) tomb of Ge Zichang (died 1111), Jiangsi province, most of the calendrical spirits were depicted as animal-headed military officials wearing high boots and wielding weapons. The Tiger, Hare, and Dragon (fig. 8) also wear armor similar to those of Buddhist *yaksha* generals. Meanwhile South and Central Asia, where the concept of the animal cycle had been circulating for a long time, generated further iconographic variations, which were later transmitted to China and other East Asian countries such as Japan. They concern various correlations between major Buddhist deities, duodenary series, and the Eight Trigrams.[39]

The Duodenary Series As Tomb Art

Two related concerns, prognostication in this life and afterlife and religious faith in potent spirits, generated the rich repertory of images of the duodenary series. Every form of mortuary art in which the motif is used—such as bronze mirror, mural painting, stone epitaph, *mingqi* sculpture—is a talisman. The underlying cyclical design creates a mandala, a microcosmic version of the larger mandala of the tomb plan, hence reinforcing its efficacy. The imagery of the duodenary series as supernatural beings further invokes powerful deities and spirits to control such cosmic forces that would ensure the good fortune of the deceased and his progeny.

The duodenary series first appeared as tomb decoration in Han bronze mirrors, in the so-called T-L-V pattern, which became fully developed during the reign of the usurper Wang Mang (13-23) with the characteristic

8

9b

Figures

8. Brick relief of calendrical Dragon, from tomb of Ge Zhijang (died 1111), Jiangsi province, 17 x 30 x 4.5 cm. After *Wenwu ziliao congkan* 6 (1982), pl. 8: 5.

9a. Han T-L-V mirror, Wang Mang period (9-25), bronze, 17 cm (diameter), George Eumorfopoulos Collection. After Umehara Sueiji, *Omei ni okeru shina kokyo* (Tokyo, 1931), pl. 23.

9b. Diagram of typical T-L-V mirror. After Loewe, *Ways to Paradise*, p. 81, fig. 13.

9a

square-in-circle design (figs. 9a-b). A subject of intensive study by scholars, the T-L-V mirror is widely recognized as a schematic diagram of the Chinese universe. Earth is represented by the central square, while the outer circle symbolizes Heaven. The sides of the square correspond with the cardinal points, represented by four animal spirits (*sishen*): Xuanwu (Tortoise intertwined with Snake) in the North, Dragon in the East, Red Bird in the South, and Tiger in the West. The four demarcations extend to the celestial realm as well, representing the Four Palaces or constellations.[40] Together with the central boss, they also stand for the Five Elements. The branch characters are placed on the central square facing out, beginning with *zi* corresponding to Xuanwu in the north, and so forth, in a clockwise direction, clearly indicating their function as celestial and terrestrial demarcations.

The T-L-V mirror, with the "T" shapes attached to its sides and the "L" shapes attached to the outer circle, represents the ideal alignment of all the cosmic forces analogous to a diviner's board, or *shi*. In this way the T-L-V mirror has added divinatory significance in ensuring good fortune, all the better to escort the deceased in his afterlife journey.[41] T-L-V mirrors often bear inscriptions on the outer rim such as, "May your sons and grandsons be complete in number and dwell in the center" and "May you long preserve your two parents in happiness and good fortune."[42] Being in the center also means being in a position to receive maximal benefit from the cosmic forces. Usually placed near the coffin, the mirror serves as a mandala that enables the deceased to be "in the sacred center," i.e., in a state of perfect balance and harmony with the cosmic forces.[43] Those "in the center" would be the owner of the mirror, the deceased in the coffin, and anyone referred to in such inscriptions.

Other inscriptions invoke powerful spirits, such as, "Dragon on the left and Tiger on the right to ward off inauspicious forces, the Red Bird and Xuanwu to harmonize the Yin and Yang." The animals are the *sishen* with apotropaic and prophylactic powers and propitious qualities associated with ancient shamanistic practices and myths. After the Han period other phrases included references to "immortals" and the wish for "longevity to outlast metal and stone," reflecting the influence of the cult of transcendents (*xian*) and immortality in religious Daoism. The mirror is therefore a talisman that not only assures perfect harmony between the cosmic and human order but also invokes the protection of deities.[44]

Han mirrors, however, only used the characters, and the animal correlates of the duodenary series seemed to have appeared only in the sixth century according to the archaeological evidence. One of the earliest patterns used during the late sixth and seventh centuries is a square-in-circle pattern obviously derived from the Han T-L-V (fig. 10).[45] The inner square is marked with the *sishen*, while the animal cycle occupies the outer rim, in proper alignment with the directions. This new position on the outer rim not only provides extra space for the animal imagery, but the circular arrangement also emphasizes the symbolism of infinite space and time.[46] The animal heads are turned to the right, creating the illusion of counterclockwise movement. This way of depicting the animals also suggests that, for example, the Ox literally "follows" the Rat in the correct clockwise cycle of years, months, or hours of the day.[47] The resemblance to the Han T-L-V pattern is not coincidental. With the unification of the country and the desire for legitimization of the early Tang court, many attempts were made to restore the *mingtang* precisely during the late sixth and seventh centuries.[48] In a symbolic sense, the revival of the Han T-L-V pattern in Tang mirrors was also a restoration of the *mingtang* and the Chinese world order.

Another mirror with astronomical, astrological, and cosmological symbols was found in an eighth-century tomb, now in the Tianjin Municipal Museum (fig. 11a). Similar mirrors have been found, testifying to the popularity of this prototype.[49] The underlying pattern is the same in all examples. The innermost circle has the *sishen*; the next circle has the animals coordinated with the positions of the *sishen*, such as Rat corresponding to Xuanwu in the North. Then the next circle has the Eight Trigrams according to the Posterior Order, interspersed with floral designs; outside this is the circle with the constellations representing the twenty-eight lunar lodgings or *xiu*; then comes an inscription in fifty-four characters. The rim itself is decorated with a cloud pattern. Although the square is eliminated, the cosmic symbolism still holds, as the *sishen* and the duodenary series were widely understood as both celestial and terrestrial demarcations, Heaven and Earth, square and circle. This is similar to the case of the *luopan* for *fengshui* calculations wherein circular discs symbolized both Earth and Heaven.

The inscription also helps to clarify the religious significance of the mirror:[50]

> [This mirror] has the virtue of *Chang-keng*
>   [the Evening Star, Hesperus, Venus]
> And the essence of the White Tiger
>   [symbol of the Western Palace],
> The mutual endowments of Yin and Yang
>   [are present in it],
> The mysterious spirituality of Mountains and Rivers
>   [is fulfilled in it].
> With due observance of the regularities of the Heavens,
> And due regard to the tranquility of Earth,
> The Eight Trigrams are exhibited upon it,
> And the Five Elements disposed in order on it.
> Let none of the hundred spiritual beings hide their face
> from it.
> Let none of the myriad things withhold their reflection
> from it.
> Whoever possesses this mirror and treasures it,
> Will meet with good fortune and achieve exalted rank.

The above inscription clearly assumes that the mirror is a magic mirror, a talisman that can protect as well as determine the fate of the one who possesses it. The prototype of this mirror must have been in circulation at least by the sixth century, as testified by the story of Wang Du's mirror in the Tang compendium *Taiping guangji*. Wang Du, who lived during the Sui dynasty, was given a magic mirror complete with the animal cycle and other cosmic symbols that had the power to ward off baleful forces and bring fortune to the owner.[51] Since objects used in real life were sometimes used as tomb furnishings, concerns of this life could be easily transferred into the afterlife.

The tomb interior in ancient China was modeled after ritual interiors such as the *mingtang*, or ancestor temples. The ancient *zaojing* design was a cosmic symbol applied to the structure as well as decoration of ceilings. The dome or truncated pyramidal shape of the *zaojing* symbolized Heaven according to the Chinese "canopy (or *gaitian*) theory" and the lower rectangular chamber itself, a square,

11b

10

11a

Figures

10. Tang cosmic mirror, bronze, 20 cm (diameter), former collection of H. Ginsberg, Berlin. After *Omei ni okeru shina kokyo*, pl. 55.

11a. Tang cosmic mirror, bronze, 27 cm (diameter), Tianjin Municipal Museum. After Academy of Social Science, *Zhonggui gudai tianwen wenwu tuji* (Beijing: Wenwu, 1978), pl. 65.

11b. Diagram of same type of cosmic mirror from *Bogu tulu*. After Shen Congwen, ed. *Tang song tongjing* (Beijing: Wenwu, 1958), no. 43.

was an ancient symbol of Earth. With additional painted imagery, the ceiling easily created the illusion of cosmic totality.[52] By the sixth century the calendrical animals were included in such ceiling paintings in tombs. In the Northern Qi (550-577) tomb of Lou Rui (dated 570), in Taiyuan, Shanxi province, the truncated pyramid ceiling of the single tomb chamber is represented as the firmament with sun, moon, and stars as well as with mythical beings. The twelve calendrical animals are located along the springing of the vault on all four slopes (figs. 12a-c). Aligned with the *sishen*, they are in their proper compass positions, and the entire ceiling can be read as a dramatic and realistic version of the schematic cosmic design in bronze mirrors. Furthermore, in the company of the *sishen* and other mythical deities such as the wind and thunder gods, the calendrical animals had undoubtedly joined the ranks of cosmic deities.[53]

Stone epitaphs called *zhishi* also functioned as cosmic symbols. Such epitaphs were typically placed inside the entrance of the tomb chamber, as indicated in the tomb plan of Li Jingyu (buried 738) excavated in Henan province (fig. 13). The format of the epitaph was standardized by the fifth century. The use of epitaphs was restricted to the official class.[54] The center of the square bottom of the epitaph is usually engraved with the biography of the deceased, including a eulogy by a relative or friend, and wishes for everlasting glory and immortality for the deceased in afterlife, for his ancestors as well as his progeny. The dome-shaped cover is fastened to it with metal bindings and engraved with the reign period and official title or cognomen of the deceased in large characters. Other designs are engraved on the four slopes and sides of the cover

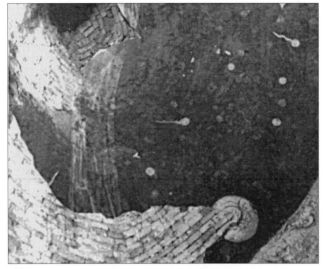

12a

12b

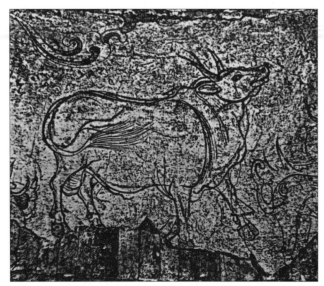

12c

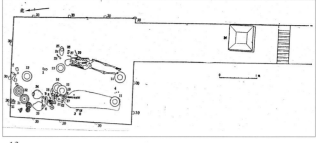

13

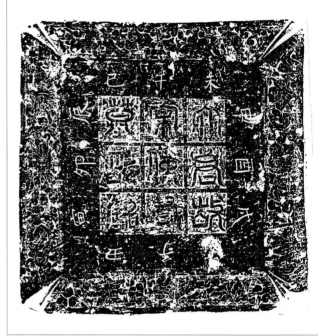

14

Figures

12a. Ceiling painting from tomb of Lou Rui (died 570), Taiyuan, Shanxi province, tomb chamber 5.7 x 5.65 x 6.58 (height) meters. Calendrical Hare in lower right. After *Wenwu* 10 (1983), pl. 4: 2.

12b. Detail of calendrical Tiger with Thunder deity below. After *Wenwu* 10 (1983), pl. 3: 2.

12c. Detail of calendrical Ox.

13. Floor plan of tomb of Li Jingyu (died 738), tomb chamber 3.3 x 2.6 x 1.1 (height) meters. After *Kaogu* 5 (1986): 443, fig. 23.

14. Rubbing of stone epitaph of Song Jing (died 706), Xian, Shaanxi province, 60 x 60 cm. After *Kaogu* 5(1986): 433, fig. 11.

as well as the sides of the bottom. The duodenary series usually forms a border design on the bottom or the cover. Another common motif is the *sishen*. The square epitaph can be understood as a miniature version of the tomb. The domed cover and square bottom are analogous to tomb structures from the Han through Tang and later periods, such as Lou Rui's tomb discussed above.[55] The same cosmic symbolism in the mirror or ceiling is therefore reflected in the epitaph.

In some epitaphs only the branch characters are used, such as the epitaph cover of Song Jing (dated 706), excavated in the Xian area (fig. 14). The central large characters in seal script refer to the deceased as "Datang gu song shijun muji ming" (Epitaph of Mr. Song, Former Imperial Censor of the Great Tang Dynasty) and around this inscription are branch characters arranged facing in, starting with *zi* in the middle of the bottom in a clockwise direction. The central cognomen symbolizes the presence of the deceased. The position implies that the deceased is "in the center." In surrounding this inscription, the branch characters create a form of mandala.

The duodenary series is more commonly represented as animals in epitaphs from the early Tang period. One of the most interesting designs made use of a couch motif. The earliest epitaph using this motif is from the Sui dynasty tomb of Duan Wei (dated 595), now in the Forest of Steles in Xian (figs. 15a-c). The illustration shows an ink rubbing of the epitaph bottom with the four sides folded out. The animals are arranged in threes on each of the four sides, starting with the Rat facing out in the mid-bottom and continuing around in a clockwise direction. Most animals seem to be scampering outdoors, as a few sweeping lines below them indicate valleys and hills. Puffs of clouds and vapors in the background exaggerate the speed of the animals as well as allude to the celestial atmosphere. Each animal is separated by a cusp-shaped frame that resembles the ornamental legs of chessboards and small couches. As pointed out before, cosmic chess games were already popular in the sixth century. *Mingqi* models of chessboards in tombs testify to the popularity and prestige of chess in general.[56] Applied to the stone epitaph, this couch motif creates the illusion of a precious object. The couch motif remained one of the most popular designs throughout the Tang period. The epitaph of Zhang Qushe (dated 747), though more stylistically refined, is almost exactly like Duan Wei's, testifying to the survival of this design over a long period.[57]

The couch is a familiar piece of Chinese domestic furniture, but the unusual arrangement of animals underneath suggests a more specific iconographic source. The juxtaposition of an outdoor panorama underneath the couch creates a sense of incongruity, enhancing the otherworldly nature of the calendrical animals. A narrative of miraculous

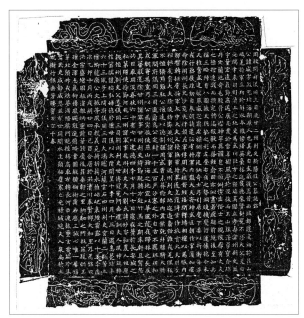

15a.

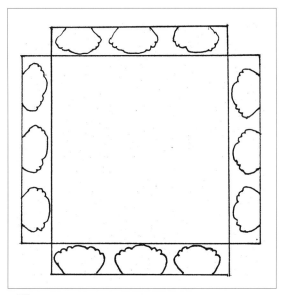

15b.

15c.

Figures

15a. Rubbing of stone epitaph of Duan Wei (died 595), 70.5 x 70 x 5 cm, Forest of Steles, Shaanxi Provincial Museum. After Nishikawa Yasushi, *Seian hirin* (Tokyo, 1966), pl. 168-69.

15b. Diagram showing frame of legs of couch.

15c. Detail showing running calendrical Dog with puffs of clouds and hilly landscape in background.

couches can be found in the *Vimalakirtinirdesa sutra*, one of the most popular Buddhist sutras in China since the fifth century. In one of the episodes Vimalakirti, the chief spokesman in the sutra, conjured up gigantic thrones in his tiny abode. These thrones were carried by fabulous flying lions from a distant universe. In the cave murals at Dunhuang one can find references to this episode, either as thrones carried by flying lions or as couch seats with small lions crouching underneath.[58] The similarity between the Dunhuang motif and the epitaph design may not be coincidental. The couch motif in stone epitaphs could be the result of Buddhist influence. Its meaning would have been enriched with a new sense of the magical by association with the Buddhist story. And the illusion of a magic couch must have greatly enhanced the potency of the stone epitaph as a talisman.

Other designs besides the couch motif are also used in epitaphs. A tenth-century epitaph shows the calendrical animals, constellations, divinatory symbols of the trigrams, and the *sishen* encircling the central inscription (fig. 16). Remarkably similar to the Tianjin Museum mirror, this epitaph illustrates the intimate connection with the bronze mirror.

By the mid eighth century animal-headed figures were a popular form representing the duodenary series. This can be seen in the epitaph of Gao Yuangui (dated 756) and another epitaph of Princess Wen An (dated 828), both from Xian (figs. 17a-b). Fantasy and realism are balanced in the characterization of these beings. The combination of animal heads and human torsos are fantastic, while the scepters and billowing garments are realistic details of contemporary official costumes. The swirling clouds in the back establish a celestial ambience, alluding to the figures as celestial officials.

The hybrid form of the duodenary series probably originated in the south. Tracing the source even further back in time, one can find in Han dynasty stone reliefs similar animal-headed figures, wearing long robes, paying homage to Xi Wang Mu or Queen Mother of the West, an ancient mythical figure that later became a prominent Daoist deity (figs. 18a-c). The garments worn by these hybrid figures indicate their official status. These figures may not be referring to the duodenary series, but they would be likely models for the depiction of the duodenary series as animal-headed officials. Although the myth of the Queen Mother was widely disseminated, these particular animal-headed figures can only be found in Han reliefs in the eastern and southern provinces, indicating a regional peculiarity.[59]

The animal-headed form of the duodenary series is also used with the couch motif. Unlike the running animals, these figures are seated dignified officials, and the stone epitaph itself can no longer be associated with the magical thrones carried by flying lions in the Buddhist story. The

couch motif becomes purely ornamental. The removal of Buddhist connotations can be understood in the light of the social and political context. The An Lu Shan rebellion of 756 and Buddhist proscriptions around 845 precipitated antiforeign sentiments with wide repercussions in Chinese life and culture.[60] The preference for the Han mythical creatures towards the end of the Tang dynasty reflects a conscious move away from Buddhist influences and a revival of native myths.

Toward the end of the Tang the fully human form of the duodenary series came into use. In the form of stone epitaphs an important dated example can be found in the tomb of Lady Cui (buried 850) in the Xian area (fig. 19).[61] The calendrical figures, fully human, are arranged in the standard form around the central inscription. The design therefore conforms to the schema of the mandala. Carrying scepters and wearing long robes, the figures are kneeling on mats. Their calendrical identities are referred to in the form of emblems of animals decorating their hats. Analogous to the official deities of the Five Elements, they represent officials in charge of monitoring the calendrical animals, which in turn control the cosmic forces. The background is left blank, without the couch motif or clouds. This form of the duodenary series as mundane officials became especially popular in the late Tang period. Again, this can be understood in the historical context mentioned above. The bureaucratic paradigm, like the animal-headed figures in the Queen Mother myth, signifies a more purely native tradition.

This late Tang development continued to influence epitaph designs in the next hundred years. The official type can also be found in the epitaph of Shi Yenqi (dated 910) of the Latter Liang (907-923) of the Five Dynasties, where the couch motif is used to frame each figure in the duodenary series (fig. 20). Another similar epitaph is from the tomb of An Shouzhong (dated 1000) from Xian.[62] A variation is the standing figure, and examples can be found in the epitaphs of the ruling class of the Liao dynasty (907-1125).[63] In all these examples the officials carry scepters and wear flowing Chinese robes and hats. The only reference to the animals is in the form of decorative emblems on their hats.

In the form of *mingqi* sculpture the duodenary series is used to enclose the deceased in the tomb. Although such *mingqi* were usually disturbed at the time of excavation, special niches built for them in the surrounding walls are clues that the *mingqi* were meant to circumscribe the coffin in the center. The earliest known *mingqi* figurines of the duodenary series are from the Northern Wei (386-534) tomb of the Cui family at Linzi, Shandong province, dated 525.[64] They are in the form of animals. Each calendrical animal is enclosed in a pottery niche framed by a pointed arch (figs. 21a-b). Marks where the niches were originally

16

17a

Figures

16. Rubbing of stone epitaph from tomb in Jiangsu province, dated 946, 40.5 x 58.5 cm, Yangzhou Museum. After *Zhongguo gudai tianwen wenwu tuji*, pl. 72.

17a. Detail of epitaph of Gao Yuangui (died 756), 76 x 75 cm. Side showing from left to right: Ox, Rat, Boar. After *Seian hirin*, pls. 257-58.

17b. Diagram of one side of epitaph of Princess Wen An (died 828), showing Ox, Rat, Boar, 74.5 x 17 cm. After *Kaogu yu wenwu* 4 (1988): 78, fig. 2.

17b

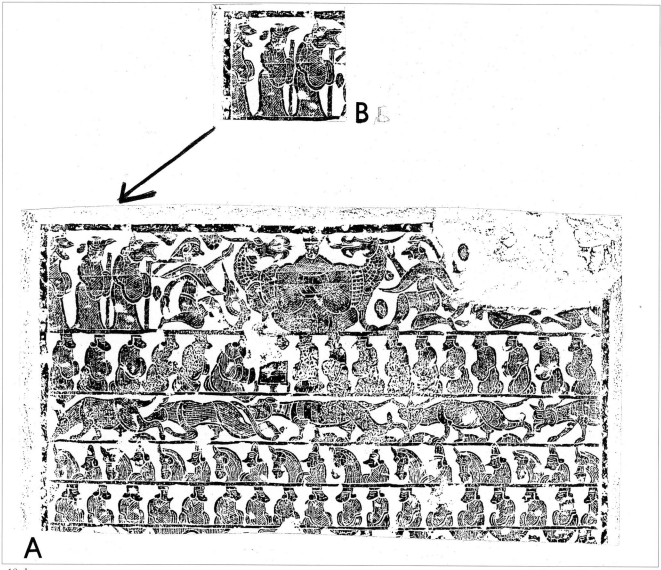

18a,b

Figure
18a. Rubbing of stone relief from Tengxian, Easter Han period, 82 x 82 cm. After *Han shandong hanhua xiangshi xuanji* (Shandong: Wenwu, 1985), pl. 217. (b) detail.

attached remain on the walls of the circular single-chamber tomb. In other words the calendrical animals originally surrounded the coffin.

Rectangular tomb chambers were more common. The calendrical figurines were first accommodated in special niches on the lateral walls of rectangular tomb chambers. In a mid seventh-century tomb from Sichuan province, besides the calendrical figurines in niches, a cosmic scene is represented on the lateral walls.[65] The Tiger and Dragon, referring to two of the four directional spirits *sishen*, are shown together with the corresponding constellations (fig. 22). This cosmic scene on the lateral walls can be understood as a variation of cosmic ceiling paintings. In Lou Rui's tomb mentioned earlier the calendrical animals are part of the painted ceiling; however, in the Tang tomb

from Sichuan the calendrical animals are sculptural images in niches. Painting and sculpture are therefore integrated in creating a three-dimensional cosmic environment in the tomb interior.

Gradually niches of the duodenary series were extended to all sides of the chamber. This development can be observed from many eighth-century tombs for the official classes.[66] The tomb of Li Jingyu from Henan province, dated 738, has three niches on each of the four walls, totaling twelve (fig. 13). In this way the calendrical figurines literally circumscribe the coffin.

A variation can be found in the tomb of Yang Siqu, dated 740, in the suburb of Xian, in which the figurines are placed on top of the house-shaped sarcophagus instead of in individual niches.[67] The position of the calendrical be-

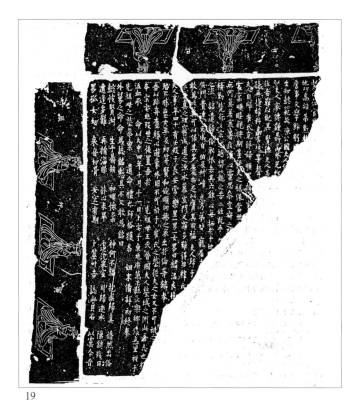

19

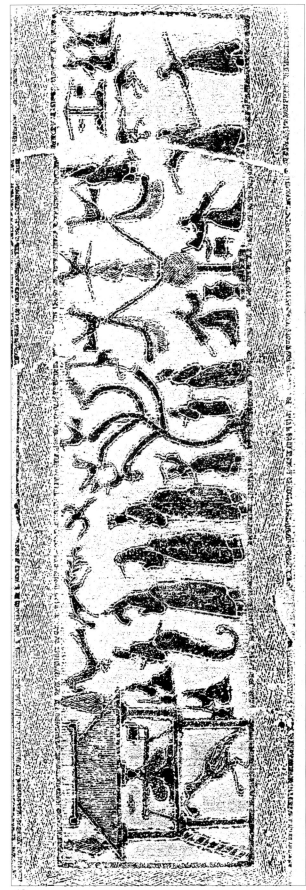

18c

20

Figures

18c. Detail of rubbing of stone relief from Xuzhou, Easter Han period, 265 x 80 cm. After *Xuzhou hanhua xiangji* (Jiangsu: Wenwu, 1985), pl. 11.

19. Rubbing of epitaph of Lady Cui (buried 850), Xian area, 57 x 57 x 9.5 cm. After *Wenbo* 5 (1987): 29, fig. 8.

20. Detail of rubbing of epitaph of Shi Yenqi (died 910), 94 x 94 cm., showing calendrical Hare. After *Seian hirin*, pl. 270.

21a

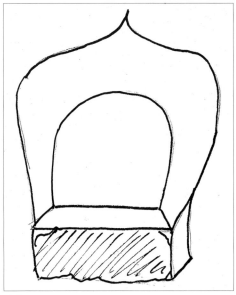

21b

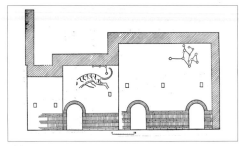

22

Figures

21a. Calendrical Tiger, from tomb in Linzi, Shandong province, dated 525, ceramic sculpture, 23 cm (height). Afer *Kaogu xuebao* 2 (1984), pl. 25: 4.

21b. Diagram of flame-shaped niche.

22. Diagram of east wall of tomb dated circa 650 from Wan Xian, Sichuan province, 4.2 x 3.2 x 4.5 (height) meters. After *Kaogu xuebao* 4 (1980): 504, fig. 2.

ings on the roof suggests a similar protective function as if they are surrounding the deceased from above instead of from the sides. In Han stone reliefs auspicious omens and mythical beings are often depicted on roofs of ancestral shrines.[68] This illustrates the ancient belief that creatures that settle on rooftops have special meanings, bringing good fortune and offering protection for those who dwell under the roof. The use of ceramic sculpture of calendrical and other mythical beings as roof top ornaments in traditional Chinese architecture is an extention of the same belief.

Whether in the form of animals, hybrids, or humans, the *mingqi* figurines clearly indicate the supernatural nature of the duodenary series. In the Linzi tomb each calendrical animal is placed in a niche with a pointed-arch frame reminiscent of the Buddhist flame halo, a symbol of enlightenment and supernatural status of the deity enclosed.[69] This niche therefore signals the supernatural status of the calendrical animals. It is also tantalizing to associate this particular set of *mingqi* with the Buddhist account of cave-dwelling calendrical animals in the *Dajijing* discussed above. The niches in the Linzi tomb can easily stand for caves and the animals inside as manifestation of the bodhisattvas according to Buddhist legend. Buddhism flourished under the Northern Wei dynasty as a state religion, permeating all aspects of society, and such Buddhist connotations would not be out of place in this Linzi tomb from the Northern Wei.[70] *Mingqi* figurines of the duodenary series are usually placed in their own special niches. Whether the niches are framed with a flame halo or not, they serve to exalt the status of the images placed in them.

The animal-headed form of the duodenary series underlines their otherworldly nature. The Sui dynasty tomb dated 610 from Hunan province is furnished with two calendrical sets, one in the form of hybrid creatures, the other in the form of human figures. The sets are combined and placed in twelve niches in the side walls.[71] The set of seated animal-headed figures are similar to those in epitaphs in the Xian area (fig. 23a). Similar figures carrying scepters are found in other tombs from the same area and period (fig. 24). By the mid seventh century, this type is commonly used in other regions.[72]

The standing pose is more commonly used in the north. Animal-headed figurines, such as those in the *Quest For Eternity* exhibition (fig. 1) can be found in many eighth-century tombs in the Xian area. A dated example is from Shi Suli's tomb of 744 (fig. 25).[73] While most figurines are ceramic, cast-iron ones are found in the tomb of Li Jingyu, dated 738, in Henan province.[74] A similar set of bronze figurines are now in the Avery Brundage Collection in the Asian Art Museum in San Francisco. Some of these figurines, like those from Shi Suli's tomb, are masterpieces of

23a

23c

24

23b

Figures

23a. Calendrical Hare, from tomb dated 610 at Xiangyin xian, Hunan province, ceramic sculpture, 22 cm (height). After *Wenwu* 4 (1981): 42, fig. 12.

23b. Calendrical figures, ceramic sculpture, from second set in same tomb. After *Wenwu* 4 (1981): 42, fig. 14.

23c. Side view of figures in 23b.

24. Calendrical Ox, from Sui dynasty tomb in Wuchang, Hubei province, ceramic sculpture, approx. 38 cm (height), Chinese Historical Museum, Beijing.

ancient Chinese sculpture. The animal heads, skillfully harmonized with their human torsos, seem to have human expressions of confidence and authority.

The second set of *mingqi* from the Hunan tomb of 610 is one of the earliest examples of the duodenary series in human form. These human figures all have miniaturized calendrical animals standing with their hind legs on their shoulders while their front legs are touching their hats (figs. 23b-c). These figures also have mysterious smiles on their faces. The simultaneous use of this set of human figures with the animal-headed set implies that human and animal-headed forms were both magical transformations of the same duodenary series.

Similar calendrical figurines have been found in other southern tombs in Hubei province. In one set the seated human figures are embracing the calendrical animals, which are not miniatures but life-size creatures. Figures with the Dragon and Snake coiled around their necks look almost like snake charmers (figs. 26a-b). In another set from a tomb in the same area the seated figure seems to be

25

26a

Figures

25. Calendrical Ox, from tomb of Shi Suli (died 744) from Xian area, Shaanxi province, ceramic sculpture, 42 cm (height). After *Shaanxi sheng qutu tang yong xuanji* (Beijing: Wenwu, 1958), pl. 82.

26a. Calendrical Dragon, (b) Snake, (c) Ox, (d) Monkey, from tomb in Wuchang, Hubei province, ceramic sculpture, approx. 38.5 cm (height), Chinese Historical Museum, Beijing.

restraining the slithery Snake with both hands (fig. 27). These figures from Hubei all wear tall hats and flowing robes; a few sport beards, such as the ones with the Ox and Monkey (figs. 26c-d). With half-closed eyes and enigmatic smiles, these figures seem to share a mystical bond with the calendrical animals. They are analogous to magicians or shamans. As these figurines are found only in the south and only in the Sui and early Tang period, they may be associated with localized beliefs and ritual practices that were discontinued in a later period. Their mysterious expressions suggest a connection with religious Daoism.

There is no archaeological evidence of the human form of the duodenary series in *mingqi* in north China from the Tang period. The animal-headed figurines are clearly more popular in north China. The only example of the human type from north China is the engraving on Lady Cui's epitaph. As mentioned before, in this epitaph the calendrical beings are represented as mundane officials, with little suggestion of their supernatural status. Although depicted as human figures, they are obviously different from the shamanistic figures from the south. While the human type was probably transmitted from south to north China, the

26b

26c

26d

religious overtones were left behind.

The mysterious Hunan and Hubei figurines reflect an interest that was not continued after the Tang even in the south. This is indicated by the findings in the tomb (dated 943) of Li Sheng, ruler of the Southern Tang dynasty (919-75), near Nanjing in Jiangsu province (fig. 28). In this tomb *mingqi* figurines of the duodenary series are depicted as dignified officials wearing prominent tall hats. The only reference to their identity as calendrical beings is that they are holding the calendrical animals in their hands. These animals are mere miniatures, unlike the dynamic lifelike animals in the Hunan and Hubei *mingqi*. The officials carry them like abstract symbols instead of embracing them as their mystical counterparts. In other words the *mingqi* from Li Sheng's tomb clearly follow the native bureaucratic model, and they represent officials presiding over the calendrical animals and their cosmic powers.

This official type continued to be used in the Northern Song, as exemplified by the figurines in a twin tomb in Jiangsi province (dated 1101). The duodenary series is in the form of civil officials similar to those from the tenth-century tomb of Li Sheng. They are no longer holding the

27

28

29

calendrical animals; rather, the calendrical animals associated with them are identifiable as small emblems on their hats, similar to those in Lady Cui's epitaphs and others. Closer to the date of the *Mizhangjing* and conforming to the model of a large underworld bureaucracy, the Jiangsi tomb furnishings are more elaborate than ever. Each of the calendrical figurines is accompanied by two attendants, placed in niches along the four walls (fig. 29). Other figurines in additional niches constitute a total of more than eighty-two.[75] In this progressive bureaucratization of the otherworld, the emphasis was no longer on the calendrical animals as mystical embodiments of cosmic power but rather on a pantheon of Chinese officials as purveyors of cosmic power.

Concluding Remarks

Concern for fate in this life and in the afterlife was a major force that shaped the development of mortuary art and ritual in traditinal China. This concern led to the use of an underlying cosmic schema, and the duodenary series or its corresponding animal cycle was naturally brought into the mortuary context as a symbol of ideal space and time. The cosmic schema was applied during the Han preriod to the planning of *mingtang* ritual structures and tombs of the ruling class. In the form of *fengshui* theories, the schema was extended to the broader social strata, and became the dominant influence in mortuary art and ritual throughout the imperial age in China.

The use of *minggi* figurines of the calendrical animals long predated the edicts of 811 and 841. Such edicts are indications of the Tang court's attempt to control a widespread and broadly based phenomenon. The *Mizang jing* further illustrates how tombs of the upper classes as well as those of commoners adhered to the same underlying schema. The duodenary series therefore represents one of the most enduring mortuary themes in Chinese tomb decoration, and illustrates the continuity between elite and popular cultures. Religous belief and devotional need gave rise to a rich and varied repertory of images of the calendrical animals. Different religous influences came into play, contributing to iconographic diversity during the Sui-Tang period. Buddhist influence later declined as the native bureaucratic paradigm gradually dominated the representation of the calendrical animals. This exemplifies a general trend in Chinese popular religion during the post-Tang period. The various representations of the calendrical animals provide a rich source for the study of popular culture and religous practices in traditional China.

Figures

27. Calendrical Snake, from Sui dynasty tomb in Wuhan, Hubei province, ceramic sculpture, 37.5 cm (height). After *Kaogu tongxun* 6 (1957), pl. 11: 6.

28. Calendrical figure, from tomb of Li Sheng (died 943), ceramic sculpture, 50 cm (height). After Nanjing Museum, *Nantang erling fajue baogao* (Nanjing: Wenwu, 1957), pl. 52.4.

29. Calendrical figure with attendants, from twin tomb in Jiangsi province dated 1101, ceramic sculpture, central figure 30 cm (height), attendant 25 cm. After *Kaogu* 4 (1988), pl. 1: 5.

Notes

1. For all twelve, see Los Angeles County Museum of Art, *The Quest for Eternity: Chinese Ceramic Sculptures from the People's Republic of China*, exh. cat. (San Francisco: Chronicle Books, 1987), 141-43, apparently assembled from two separate tombs.

2. Xie Mingliang, "Qutu wenwu sojian zhongggguo shier jishou de xingtai bianqian," *Gugung xueshu jikan*, no. 3 (1985-86): 59-105; Chen Anli, "Guwenwu zhong de shier sengxiao," *Wenbo*, no. 2 (1988): 41-50, concerns sculpture; and the earlier study of Éduoard Chavannes, "Le Cycle Turc des douze animaux," *T'oung Pao* ser. 2, vol. 7 (1907): 51-122, included discussion of mirrors.

3. Xie Mingliang, "Qutu wenwu...," 75; also Chen Anli, "Guwenwu...," 44-45.

4. As suggested by Xie Mingliang, "Qutu wenwu...," 73-79, and Chen Anli, "Guwenwu...," 49; no reference to the calendrical *mingqi* can be found in the monumental work by Jan J. M. de Groot, *The Religious System of China* [henceforth *Religious System*] 6 vols. (Leiden: Brill, 1892).

5. See *Tang Huiyao* compiled by Wang Pu (922-82) (Taipei: World Book, 1963), 695, 698.

6. Tomb robberies are the usual cause of missing pieces in the duodenary series. In one rare example a single Ram *mingqi* is placed in the tomb; e.g., see Jiangsusheng wuxian wenguanhui, "Jiangsu wuxian yaociaotou tang mu," *Wenwu* 8 (1987): 49-51. The epitaph includes a male's death date of 743, the year of the Ram, which suggests a relation between the death year of the tomb occupant and the *mingqi*; the use of *mingqi* in this tomb was also in direct violation of the *Tang Huiyao* code, as the deceased was a commoner.

7. See Wang Chung's (27-circa 89-104) comments on popular opinions concerning the animal correlation in *Lunheng*, vol. 1 (Beijing: Zhonghua, 1979), 210; Chavannes in "Le Cycle Turc des douze animaux," 51-98, for usage in other Asian countries and theory of Turkish origin; and for theory of Chinese origin, see Léopold de Saussure, "Le cycle des douze animaux et le symbolisme cosmologique des chinois," *Journal Asiatique*, ser. 11, vol. 15 (1920): 55-88, and Derk Bodde, *Festivals of Classical China: New Years and other Annual Observances during the Han Dynasty 206 B.C.-A.D. 220* (Princeton: Princeton University Press, 1975), 92f.

8. See Joseph Needham et al., *Science and Civilization in China* [henceforth *Science*], vol. 3 (Cambridge: Cambridge University Press, 1959-62), 396-401, for the sexagenary cycle; see also David Keightley, "Late Shang Divination: The Magico-religious Legacy," in *Explorations in Early Chinese Cosmology*, ed. Henry Rosemont, Jr. (Chico, California: Scholars Press, 1984), 11-34, for use in oracle bones.

9. The branches were identified with a set of animals closely related to the standard set in the bamboo documents from the Qin dynasty Tomb No. 11 in Hunan province; for complete archaeological report, see Rao Zhongyi and Zeng Xiantong, *Yunmeng qinjian yishu yanjiu* (Hong Kong: Chinese University Press, 1982).

10. For the meaning of *chen*, see Edward Schafer, *Pacing the Void: T'ang Approaches to the Stars* (Berkeley: University of California Press, 1977), 5; for calendrical development, see Needham, *Science*, vol. 3, 402-6, and vol. 4, 265-66; and Chen Mengjia, "Han jian nianlibiao xu," *Kaogu xuebao* 2 (1965): 113-30; for Chinese origin of the *xiu*, see Xia Nai, *Kaoguxue he kejishi* (Beijing: Science Press, 1979), 29-50; and de Saussure, "Le cycle des douze animaux et le symbolisme cosmologique des chinois," 55-88, for discussion of all correlations.

11. See Stephan Feuchtwang, *An Anthropological Analysis of Chinese Geomancy* [henceforth *Geomancy*] (Vientiane: Vithagna, 1974), 59; for astrological development, see Schafer, *Pacing the Void*, 54-84; Hou Ching-lang, "The Chinese Belief in Baleful Stars," in *Facets of Taoism*, ed. Holmes Welch and Anna Seidel (New Haven: Yale University Press, 1977), 200-209; see also Nakaura Shigeru, "Characteristics of Chinese Astrology," *Isis* 57 (1966): 442-54.

12. See Chao Wei-pang, "The Chinese Science of Fate-Calculation," *Folklore Studies* 5 (1946): 279-315.

13. See *Sanguo ji*, compiled by Chen Shou (died 297), completed by Pei Songji in 429, vol. 29 (Beijing: Zhonghua, 1959; reprinted 1975), 816-26; partial trans. in Kenneth Dewoskin, *Doctors, Diviners, and Magicians of Ancient China: Biographies of Fang-shih* (New York: Columbia University Press, 1983), 91-134; see also 25 on *dunjia*.

14. Peter Boodberg in "Chinese Zoographic Names as Chronograms," *Harvard Journal of Asiatic Studies* 5 (1940): 128-36, suggests popular use of cycle as chronogrammatic names among the northern nomads by the sixth century; see Chao Wei-pang, "The Chinese Science of Fate-Calculation," 281 and 299-308, for the Old Method, which takes the birth year as the chief factor.

15. See de Groot, *Religious System*, vol. 1, 44, 103-7.

16. For detailed coordination of trigrams, stems, and branches, see de Saussure, "Le cycle des douze animaux," 58-70; for *shi*, see Michael Loewe, *Ways To Paradise: The Chinese Quest For Eternity* (London: Allen & Unwin, 1979), 75-85 and appendix 3; Chen Mengjia, "Han jian nianli biao xu," 132-47; and Lian Xiaoming, "Shipan zhong de simen yu bagua," *Wenwu* 9 (1987): 33-36, 40.

17. According to the Anterior Order of Fu Hsi, *gen* is northwest, *sun* southwest, *kun* north, and *qian* south; for development of Chinese compass, see Needham, *Science*, vol. 4, 261-69.

18. See Needham, *Science*, vol. 2, 357-59, and 353, pl. XVII, for fourteenth-century horoscope.

19. For dualistic concept of the soul *hun* and *po*, see Yü Ying-shih, "O Soul, Come Back! A Study in the Changing Conception of the Soul and Afterlife in Pre-Buddhist China," *Harvard Journal of Asiatic Studies* 47 (1987): 363-95.

20. For the reciprocity between this life and afterlife in Chinese funerary rituals, see *Death Ritual In Late Imperial and Modern China*, ed. James Watson and Evelyn Rawski (Berkeley: University of California Press, 1988), esp. James Watson, "The Structure of Chinese Funerary Rites: Elementary Forms, Ritual Sequence, and the Primacy of Performance," 9.

21. For cosmic themes in tomb decoration, see Loewe, *Ways to Paradise*, 1-16; also Wilma Fairbank, "The Offering Shrines of 'Wu Liang tz'u,'" *Harvard Journal of Asiatic Studies* 6 (1941): 1-36; Wu Hung, "Myths and Legends in Han Funerary Art," in *Stories From China's Past* (The Chinese Culture Foundation of San Francisco, 1987), 72-81.

22. See John Major, "The Five Phases, Magic Square, and Schematic Cosmography," *Journal of the Association of Asian Religions* Thematic Studies L/2 (1986), 133-66.

23. See John B. Henderson, *The Development and Decline of Chinese Cosmology* [henceforth *Cosmology*] (New York: Columbia University Press, 1984), 49; for influence in mortuary ritual, see de Groot, *Religious System*, vol. 3, 935-1056.

24. See Feuchtwang, *Geomancy*, 11-12 and 18-88, for detailed analysis of the *luopan*; Needham, *Science*, vol. 4, pt. 1, 249-314, relates this to the invention of the magnetic compass.

25. See *Yongle dadian*, vol. 8199, 1-33; for textual and archaeological discussions also see Xu Pingfang, "Tang song muzhang zhong de mingqi shensa yu muyi jidu," *Kaogu* 2 (1963): 87-106.

26. According to Chen Anli, "Guwenwu ...," 48-49, a survey of stone epitaphs decorated with the duodenary theme indicates that they were used by high-ranking officials; for an exception, see note 7.

27. For a survey of Sui and Tang tombs in the Xian area see Sun Binggen, "Xian suitang muzhang de xingji," *Zhongguo kaoguxue yenjiu*, no. 2 (Beijing: Science Press, 1986), 151-90; also see

HO

Feuchtwang, *Geomancy*, 112-71 for discussion of the School of Earthly Forms.

28. Benjamin Schwarz in *The World of Thought in Ancient China* (Cambridge: Harvard University Press, 1985), 350-82, 390-400, asserts that correlative cosmology was fundamentally concerned with finding correlates between the natural and human world rather than being a pure "science" directed toward understanding natural phenomena as such, hence inextricably bound with religion.

29. See Evelyn S. Rawski, "A Historian's Approach to Chinese Death Ritual," in *Death Ritual*, in Late Imperial and Modern China, 20-34.

30. See Minakata Kumagusu, *Junishi ko*, 3 vols. (Tokyo: Heibonsha, 1972), for study of the narrative literature, myth, and folklore generated by each of the twelve animals.

31. Bodde, *Festivals*, 90-96, points out a possible connection with the Great Exorcism and refers to a Korean Yi court performance recorded by Song Hyon (1439-1504), in which a ritual dance involved the use of calendrical animal masks; also K. C. Chang, "The Animal in Shang and Chou Art," *Harvard Journal of Asiatic Studies* 41 (1981): 527-54, for the role of animal deities in shamanism and nature and ancestor worship.

32. See Michael Loewe, "Man and Beast: The Hybrid in Early Chinese Art and Literature," *Numen* 25 (1978): 97-117; also Derk Bodde, "Myths of Ancient China," in *The Making of China: Main Themes in Premodern Chinese History* (New Jersey: Prentice-Hall, 1975), 15-37.

33. See Ge Hong, *Baopuzi neipian jiaoxi* (Beijing: Zhonghua, 1982), 304; Eng. trans. James R. Ware, *Alchemy, Medicine and Religion in China of +320: The Nei Phien of Ko Hung* (Cambridge: M.I.T., 1966), 288-89, and Chen Anli, "Guwenwu ...," 49.

34. Swartz, *The World of Thought in Ancient China*, 373.

35. See Needham, *Science*, vol. 4, pt. 1, 320-21 and 327, for relation to the magnetic compass.

36. *Taisho shinshu daizokyo* (Tokyo. Daizo Shuppan Kabushiki Kaisha, 1924-1932) [henceforth *Taisho*] 13, no. 397, 167b-168a.

37. For *Fayuan Julin*, see *Taisho*, 53, no. 2122, 511a-c; Chavannes in "Le cycle turc des douze animaux," 85-98, considered this assimilation of the duodenary series in the Buddhist text to be evidence of Turkish influence in Central Asia and maintained the theory of Turkish origin of the animal cycle.

38. See Dunhuang Cave 220 (dated 642 by inscription), in Dunhuang Research Institute, *Chugoku sekkutsu: tonko bakokutsu*, vol. 3 (Tokyo: Heibonsha, 1980-82), pl. 27, for an example in painting; Luo Huaqing, "Dunhuang bihua zhong de dongfang yaoshi jingtu bian," *Dunhuang yenjiu* 2 (1979): 7, for iconographical discussion; for cult of Medicine Buddha, see Rauol Birnbaum, *The Healing Buddha* (Boulder: Shambala Press, 1979).

39. For references to Kuchean dance "Twelve Hours" and Manichean text concerning "Twelve Great Luminous Hours" or "Twelve Luminous Kings" see Schuyler Cammann, "The Lion and Grape Patterns On Chinese Bronze Mirrors," *Artibus Asiae* 16 (1953): 289; see also Chavannes, "Le cycle turc des douze animaux," 114-16; Mochizuki Shinkô, *Bukkyô daijiten* (Kyoto: Hôzôkan, 1954), vol. 3, 2331-333; and Alicia Matsunaga, *The Buddhist Philosophy of Assimilation: The Historical Development of the Honji-suijaku Theory* (Tokyo: Sophia University, 1969) [I owe this last reference to Professor Benjamin Ellman].

40. For discussion and Han illustrations of the Four Palaces either in the form of constellations or symbols of *sishen*, see Chen Jiangfeng, "Nanyang tianwen huaxiangshi kaoxi," *Handai huaxiangshi yenjiu* (Beijing: Wenwu, 1987), 141-54.

41. See Loewe, *Ways to Paradise*, 60-85, for the analogy between the diviner's board and T-L-V mirror.

42. See Umehara Sueji, *O-bei ni okeru shina kokyo* (Tokyo, 1936), 17-18, for inscription; Cheng Te-kun, in "Yin-Yang Wu-hsing and Han Art," *Harvard Journal of Asiatic Studies* 20 (1957): 176, suggests two alternative readings of the inscription—either wishing one's sons and grandsons well or wishing that a grandson will be born each hour of the day; also see Bernhard Kalgren, "Early Chinese Mirror Inscriptions," *Bulletin of the Museum of Far Eastern Antiquities* 6 (1934): 9-72.

43. See Major, "The Five Phases, Magic Squares, and Schematic Cosmography," 155-59.

44. Suzanne Cahill, "The Word Made Bronze: Inscriptions on Medieval Chinese Bronze Mirrors," *Archives of Asian Art* 39 (1986): 62-70.

45. See Kong Xiangxing, "Suitang tongjing de luixing yu fenqi," *Zhongguo kaogu xuehui diyiqi nianhui lunwenji* (Beijing: Wenwu, 1979), 380-99, and pl. 10:1-2, with mirror from tomb dated 583 in Henan province; see also Nancy Thompson, "The Evolution of the T'ang Lion and Grapevine Mirror," *Artibus Asiae* 29 (1967): 28-29 and fig. 1, for Six Dynasties mirror in the British Museum.

46. See Kong Xiangxing and Liu Yiman, *Zhongguo gudai tong jing* (Beijing: Wenwu, 1984), 139-43, for circular arrangement in other patterns; Schuyler Cammann, "The Lion and Grape Patterns in Chinese Bronze Mirrors," *Artibus Asiae* 16 (1952): 271-74, for Sui-Tang revival of Han cosmic pattern and circular symbolism.

47. A few show the heads turning to the left, creating a clockwise movement, as described in Thompson, "The Evolution of the T'ang Lion and Grapevine Mirror," 28-29.

48. See Howard J. Wechsler, *Offerings of Jade and Silk: Ritual and Symbol in the Legitimization of the Tang Dynasty* (New Haven: Yale University Press, 1985), 202-11, for history of restorations of the *mingtang* during the Sui and early Tang.

49. See Academy of Social Science, *Zhongguo gudai tianwen wenwu tuji* (Beijing: Wenwu, 1978), pl. 65 and 121, for another in the Hunan Provincial Museum; Needham, *Science*, vol. 3, 249, fig. 93, for one in the American Museum of History, another in the Field Museum of Natural History in Chicago; this prototype also discussed by Chavannes, "Le cycle turc des douze animaux," 104ff.

50. See Needham, *Science*, vol. 4, pt. 1, 249, based on interpretation by Chavannes, "Le cycle turc des douze animaux," 105.

51. See *Taiping guangji*, compiled by Li Fang et al., vol. 5 (Beijing: Zhonghua, 1981), 1761-67.

52 See Judy Chungwa Ho, "Tunhuang Cave 249: A Representation of the Vimalakirtinirdesa," Ph.D. diss. (Yale University, 1985), 193-98, for discussion of *zaojing*; Alexander Soper, "The 'Dome of Heaven' in Asia," *Art Bulletin* 29 (1947): 225-48, for fermentation with foreign influences; for Han through Tang tomb ceilings, see *Zhongguo gudai tianwen wenwu tuji*, pls. 44, 46-49, 55, 57-59, 66.

53. See Shi Shuqing, "Cong lourui mu bihua kan beicao huajia shoubi," *Wenwu* 10 (1983): 29-30, for discussion of ceiling imagery; also Susan Bush, "Thunder Monsters and Wind Spirits in Early Sixth-century China and the Epitaph Tablet of Lady Yuan," *Bulletin of the Museum of Fine Arts, Boston* 72 (1974): 24-55, for other examples of cosmic deities.

54. See *Datang kaiyuanli*, bk. 10, vol. 139, 5, and vol. 141, 8, for codification of its use; also de Groot, *Religious System*, vol. 3, 1133-40.

55. See Ho Xincheng, and Zhang Hongxiu, "Tang muji keshi," *Wenbo* 5 (1987): 55-60, for survey of more than three hundred examples from the Shaanxi Provincial Museum; see also Liu Fengjun, "Nanbeizhao shike muzhi xingji tanyuan," *Zhongyuan wenwu* 2 (1988): 80.

56. See Hunan sheng bowuguan, "Hunan changsha xianjiahu tang mu fajue jianbao," *Kaogu* 6 (1980): 509, fig. 3.7, for a ceramic model from a tomb dated circa 650; for example used in the living world, see *Treasures of the Shosoin*, ed. Shosoin Office (Tokyo: Asahi

82

Shimbun, 1965), pl. 31.

57. See Nishikawa Yasushi, *Seian hirin* (Tokyo: Kodansha, 1966), pls. 249-50.

58. For the Buddhist text, see *Weimo soshuojing*, a translation by Kumarajiva in 406, in *Taisho*, vol. 14, no. 474; a translation of the Tibetan version is by Étienne Lamotte, *L'Enseignement de Vimalakirti*, vol. 51 (Louvain: Bibliothéque du Museón Louvain, 1962); and a translation from the French by Sarah Boin *The Teaching of Vimalakirti* (London: The Pali Text Society, 1976), 138-41; for illustrations of thrones carried by flying lions, see Cave 335 (dated 686) in *Chugoku sekkutsu: Tonko bakokutsu*, vol. 3 (Tokyo: Heibonsha, 1981), pl. 61; for couch with lions underneath in Cave 138 (early tenth century), see ibid., vol. 4, pl. 193.

59. For complex origins of the Xi Wang Mu myth, see Riccardo Fricasso, "Holy Mothers of Ancient China," *T'oung Pao* 74 (1988): 1-47; although the cult was popular in Sichuan, animal-headed figures such as these are not found in Sichuan pictorial reliefs as illustrated in *Stories From China's Past*, 159-67.

60. See Camman, "The Lion and Grape Patterns On Chinese Bronze Mirrors," 282-83, for this phenomenon.

61. See Chen Anli and Ma Ji, "Xian xinqu tangji kaoxi," *Wenbo* 5 (1987): 26-30; see also Chen Anli, "Guwenwu...," 46-47, for other examples.

62. Nishikawa, *Seian hirin*, pls. 273-74.

63. For epitaph of Emperor Shengzong (circa 1000), see Jitsuzo Tamura, *Tombs and Mural Paintings of Ch'ing Ling*, vol. 2 (Kyoto: Zauho, 1953), pl. 133; epitaph of the Princess of the Chen Kingdom (died 1018), see *Wenwu* 11 (1987): 22, fig. 40.

64. See Shandong sheng wenwu kaogu yenjiuso, "Linzi beiqao cuishi mu," *Kaogu xuepao* 2 (1984): 221-44, for archaeological report.

65. Sichuan sheng bowuguan, "Sichuan wanxian tang mu," *Kaogu*

xuebao 4 (1980): 503-14; for similar structure from Hunan province, see Hunan sheng bowuguan, "Hunan zhangsha xianjiahu tang mu fajue jianbao," *Kaogu* 6 (1980): 506, fig. 1, and 506-11; see also Sun Binggen, "Xian suitang muzhang de xingji," 173, for general development of the twelve niches.

66. Sun Binggen, "Xian suitang muzhang de xingji," 168.

67. *Tang changnan chengjiao suitang mu* (Beijing: Wenwu, 1980), 66, pl. 92, for top view of sarcophagus, pls. 103-4, for figurines.

68. See Xin Lexiang, "Lun handai de muxiang xitang jichi huaxiang," *Handai huaxiangshi yenjiu*, 180-203.

69. See Alexander Soper, "Aspects of Light Symbolism in Gandharan Sculptures," in 3 pts., *Artibus Asiae* 12 (1949): 252-283, 314-330, and 13 (1950): 63-85; also Benjamin Rowland, "The Iconography of the Flame-halo," *Bulletin of the Fogg Art Museum* 11 (1949): 10-16.

70. For Buddhism under the Northern Dynasties, see Ocho Einichi, *Hokugi bukkyo no kenkyu* (Kyoto: Heirakuji, 1970).

71. See Xiong Juanxin, "Hunan xiangyin xian sui daye liunian mu," *Wenwu* 4 (1981): 39; how the twenty-four figurines were arranged in the twelve niches is not clear, due to past vandalism.

72. See examples from Sichuan in Sichuan sheng bowuguan, "Sichuan manx ian tang mu," *Kaogu xuebao* 4 (1980): pls. 4: 1-3.

73. For another example from a tomb dated 791, see Chen Anli and Ma Ji, "Xian zijiao tang xichang xianling furen shisi mu," *Kaogu yu wenwu* 3 (1988): 38, fig. 2.

74. See *Kaogu* 5 (1986), 444, fig. 24, and 447, fig. 31.

75. Jiangsi sheng wenwu gongzuodui and Nanfeng xian bowuguan, "Jiangsi nanfeng xian sangtian song mu," *Kaogu* 4 (1988): 318-28.

Unless otherwise stated, illustrations are by author.

Tomb-Guardian Figurines:
Their Evolution and Iconography

Mary H. Fong
University of California, Davis

Among the clay tomb sculptures of the Tang dynasty the hybrid tomb-guardian creatures are the most intriguing. They have attracted the attention of art collectors, connoisseurs, and scholars and have been identified in various ways. These creatures have been named chimeras[1] for their resemblance to the fabulous monster of Greek mythology but also have been called *qitou*,[2] the Chinese cryptic name for a mask. In addition they have been classified as an apotropaic genie[3] or a hybrid animal that leads the soul to the Daoist Kunlun paradise.[4]

The term *qitou* was applied by the Chinese in their catalogue of Tang tomb figurines excavated in Shaanxi, *Shaanxi sheng chutu Tang yong xuanji* (1958);[5] the importance of this archaeological report accounts for the persistent use of the term among writers outside China. In China, after Xu Pingfang's 1963 study on Tang-Song tomb furnishings,[6] it was replaced with *zhenmushou* (tomb-guardian creature), a term that describes the function of the image.

More significantly, in recent decades archaeological activities in the People's Republic of China have amassed sufficient data from pre-Tang and Tang tombs to warrant a study of the origin of the hybrid guardian image. The archaeological evidence has also shown that a tomb is guarded by two different sets of clay figures, the pair of *zhenmushou* (or tomb-guardian creatures) and the pair of *zhenmuyong* (or tomb-guardian warriors). Their importance among the numerous figurines placed in the tomb is singled out by their larger size and the fact that they are products of the most advanced ceramic technology available at the time. This study, focusing on the emergence of these two sets of tomb-guardian figurines, will trace the origin and evolution of the iconography of each pair and demonstrate that they were intentionally created for the purpose of warding off evil attacks on the tomb occupant.

Tomb-guardian Creatures

In a survey of the corpus of pre-Tang and Tang tomb excavations during the last thirty or so years it has been found that a homogeneous mortuary culture existed in the *zhongyuan* (Central Plains) provinces of Shaanxi, Shanxi, and northern Henan. The tombs of the upper class in this area exhibit characteristics remarkably similar in plan, structure, and furnishings, undeniable proof of cultural continuity.[7]

One of the most persistent objects among the tomb furnishings is the set of tomb-guardian creatures in the form of a pair of fantastic beasts, one having a fearsome lion's head and the other that of a human. They have been found, for example, in the Northern Wei tomb of Yuan Shao (buried 528), excavated at Luoyang, Henan (figs. 1a-b),[8] the Eastern Wei tomb of a Ruru princess (buried 550), at Cixian, Hebei (figs. 2a-b),[9] the Northern Qi tomb of Yao Jun (buried 567), also at Cixian (figs. 3a-b),[10] the Sui tomb of Zhang Sheng (buried 594), at Anyang, Henan (figs. 4a-b),[11] and the early Tang tomb of Zheng Rentai

1a   1b   2a,b

3a,b   4a   4b

5a   5b

Figures

1a-b. A pair of tomb-guardian creatures. Earthenware with traces of slip colors, height 25.5 cm. Tomb of Yuan Shao, Northern Wei (528), Luoyang, Henan. From *Kaogu*, 1973, no. 4, pl. 12.2.

2a-b. Drawings: a pair of tomb-guardian creatures. Earthenware with traces of slip colors, height 32 and 35 cm. Tomb of a Ruru princess, Eastern Wei (550), Cixian, Hebei. From *Wenwu*, 1984, no. 4, p. 5, fig. 5.

3a-b. Drawings: a pair of tomb-guardian creatures. Earthenware with traces of slip colors, height 40 and 46 cm. Tomb of Yao Jun, Northern Qi (567), Cixian, Hebei. From *Wenwu*, 1984, no. 4, p. 18, fig. 9.

4a-b. A pair of tomb-guardian creatures. Grey-white stoneware with a greenish clear glaze, heights 48.5 and 50 cm. Tomb of Zhang Sheng, Sui (594), Anyang, Henan. From *Henan sheng bowuguan* (Beijing, Wenwu Press, 1985), pls. 106-7.

5a-b. A pair of tomb-guardian creatures. White *gaoling* clay with yellowish glaze, painted colors, and applied gold, height 63 cm. Tomb of Zheng Rentai, Tang (663), Liquan, Shaanxi. From *Wenwu*, 1972, no. 7, p. 35, figs. 6-7.

(buried 663), at Liquan, Shaanxi (figs. 5a-b).[12] Features common to all of these sets are their dorsal spikes and lionlike bodies. Also conspicuous are the evolutionary changes that manifested themselves over the course of time. In late Northern Qi (550-577), as if to match the pointed stub on the head of the human-faced image, a pair of horns sprouted on the lion's head, and an emblem resembling the two-pronged metal head of a lance was implanted immediately behind the heads of both figures. In the following Sui dynasty (581-618) the human-faced guardian was given a fleshy horn atop its head. By the Tang dynasty (618-906) both had taken on a strangely ominous appearance; a pair of wings had grown from the upper part of their forequarters, and their lion's paws were exchanged for cloven hoofs.

The perpetuation of their presence in the tombs of several successive dynasties in the Central Plains attests, on the one hand, to the traditional Chinese belief in afterlife and, on the other, to the genuine fear of evil attacks on the entombed deceased. Recent scholarship based on the spectacular finds of the Western Han (206 B.C.-A.D. 9) tombs at Mawangdui in Changsha, Hubei,[13] and at Fenghuangshan, in Jiangling, Hubei,[14] has confirmed the dualist Chinese view of the soul. Yu Ying-shih has written: "For the first time we have unmistakable and direct evidence that testifies fully as well as vividly to the indigenous Chinese imagination of death and afterlife in pre-Buddhist antiquity."[15] The Han Chinese firmly believed that every human individual possessed two souls, the *hun* and the *po*; separating at death, the *hun* returned to paradise, the source of its origin, and the *po* took up residence in the tomb, the underworld.[16] This belief explains the themes of Han funerary art, such as the painted banner from Han Tomb No. 1 at Mawangdui,[17] the murals of Bu Qianqiu's tomb in Luoyang, Henan,[18] and, of course, the tomb-guardian figurines.

When sixth-century B.C. textual evidence alluded to the currency of the idea of *hun*,[19] definite measures for the protection of the *po* began to emerge in the form of a tomb-guardian creature. As many as 155 tomb-guardian creatures were gathered from the excavations of more than 500 Chu State tombs in Jiangling, Hubei.[20] The 1986 comprehensive report on the two upper-class Chu tombs excavated at Xinyang, in northern Henan, has shown that a wooden tomb-guardian creature measuring over a meter tall was buried in each tomb.[21] The one from Tomb No. 1 (fig. 6.1) sits on its hindquarters like a man but bites a snake held to its mouth with the front paws. Having a pair of real antlers planted atop its head, enormous round eyes bulging from its forehead, and a long tongue protruding from its mouth, it assumes a uniquely grotesque configuration. Similarly strange-looking images had entered collections outside China and had been studied.[22] Describing

Figure

6. Drawings: tomb-guardian creatures. Wood with lacquer colors. Excavated from Warring States (480-221 B.C.) Chu tombs in Xinyang, Henan (1); and Changsha, Hunan (2, 3). From *Kaogu*, 1973, no. 4, p. 250, fig. 3.

them as horned wood figures, Alfred Salmony pointed out that they belong to a homogeneous group.[23] The one recovered in 1963 from a Chu tomb at Changsha, now in the Cox collection (fig. 6.2), is a smaller but somewhat simplified version of this type and stands on a square wooden plinth.[24] Another image, also discovered in Changsha (fig. 6.3), which has a close counterpart in the British Museum,[25] appears as an anthropomorphic creature that has a square pillar for its body and likewise stands on a plinth. Whether human- or animal-headed, each is given a pair of tall antlers and an extraordinarily long tongue descending from its mouth.

Sun Zuoyun, in his study of hybrid images, suggested that the Warring States (475-221 B.C.) tomb-guardian creatures are representations of Hou Tu (a spirit of the earth) or Sheji (god of the soil), also known as Tu Bo, who protected the dead from the attacks of snakes.[26] Basing his argument on the earliest known literary reference to Tu Bo in the Chu poem *Zhaohun* (The summons of the soul), which described him as the spirit dwelling in Youdu (a realm belonging to the spirit of the earth)[27] with sharp horns on its head, he contended that Tu Bo and Hou Tu were one and the same deity.[28] Sun also concluded that Yu, founder of the Xia dynasty, was deified after his death and became Hou Tu,[29] citing as evidence several ancient texts: *Zouzhuan* (Zuo commentary), which states that Hou Tu was the son of Gong Gong, the "first rebel" of the mythical age; *Liji* (Book of rites) which declares that Gong Gong's son was worshiped as a Spirit of the Earth for having controlled the great flood; and *Huainanzi*, a miscellany compilation sponsored by Liu An, King of Huainan (buried 122 B.C.), as well as *Shiji* (Records of the historian) that claim Yu, was also worshiped as Sheji for having controlled the floods of the Yellow River. Sun's theory explains the use of the human face on the Warring States tomb-guardian creature.

In Han pictorial art the hybrid image often appears as an auspicious omen.[30] One of the best-known examples is the representation of the legendary Chinese ancestors Fu Xi and Nu Wa, who were given serpentine bodies.[31] The combination of human and animal anatomies was a means for the Han artist to impart a semblance of transcendental quality to the representational image. However, so far as is known, the excavations of numerous Han tombs in the recent past have not uncovered specific examples of hybrid tomb-guardian sculptures. The ritual for burial in China, known from both literary texts and archaeological finds, had always been an undertaking of paramount importance since the beginning of civilization.[32] The Warring States practice of providing protection for the occupant of a tomb must have continued into the Han dynasty. Thus the pair of kneeling figures found in the tomb path of the Western Han Tomb No. 2 at Mawangdui, although described in the archaeological report as *ouren* (images of idols),[33] should be regarded as an early version of the tomb-guardian image. Made of wood strips, straw, and cords and finished with a layer of a mud and straw mixture shaped to resemble a man, each carries a pair of antlers atop its head. Moreover, measuring 1.18 and 1.05 meters in height, they correspond closely to the size of the Chu tomb-guardian figures. And, found facing each other in the tomb path that leads to the coffin chamber, they occupied the same places as that of the guardian creatures in later tombs.

Not unexpectedly, images of hybrid tomb-guardian creatures have been found in post-Han tombs. The 1965 excavation of a Wu Kingdom (222-280) tomb in Wuchang, Hubei, unearthed a creature that stands on all fours and has a human face; the Chinese archaeologists classified it as a *guaishou* (strange animal) but also suggested it might be a tomb-guardian creature.[34] The 1983 excavation of another Wu tomb in Ma'anshanshi, Anhui, yielded a second creature similar not only in form but also in size (fig. 7). The tomb at Ma'anshanshi, like the previous one, had been robbed, but fortunately most of the burial goods remained in their original positions. The human-faced creature was found standing near the doorway to the coffin chamber and facing the main entrance to the tomb.[35]

It would be a mistake to ascribe as fortuitous the fact that the hybrid form for the guardian creature should have surfaced in Hubei and Anhui, regions formerly belonging to the Chu State in the Warring States period. The Wu

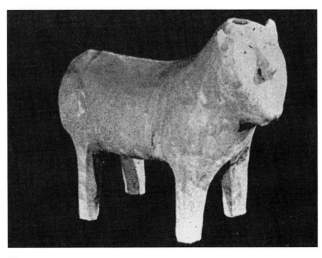

Figure
7.   Human-faced tomb-guardian creature. Stoneware with a green glaze, height 20.4 cm. Excavated from a tomb of the Wu Kingdom (222-80), Ma'anshanshi, Anhui. From *Kaogu*, 1986, no. 5, pl. 1.5.

tomb human-faced guardian creature, while embodying its mythical origin, had evolved into a new type, one that is a close prototype of the human-faced *zhenmushou* found in the *chungyuan* area (fig. 1a). The transformation suggests that the Wu Kingdom artist had turned to ancient literary texts for inspiration, just as his Han predecessors had done for their illustrative art.[36] Classical descriptions of such hybrid creatures abound in Han literature. For example, the *Shenyijing* (Classic of spirits and marvels), composed by the Western Han imaginative writer Dongfang Shuo, describes an animal known as *taowu*, which resembles a tiger but wears the coat of a dog, measures two feet (*chi*) long, and has a human face.[37] The Western Han *Shanhaijing* (Classic of mountains and seas), which contains descriptions of fantastic gods, demons, and animal deities, mentions several such anomalies. The passage on Kaiming, the animal that carried as many as nine human heads and was assigned to guard the nine entrances to Mount Kunlun, the home of Queen Mother of the West, identified succinctly the role of the hybrid animal.[38] But the text that describes the human-headed Shan Hui was probably the more exact source of inspiration: "Two hundred miles [li] further north is the Yufa Mountain....There dwells an animal which resembles a dog but has a human face, and is clever at hurling [things]. When it sees a man, it howls. Its name is Shan Hui."[39] Since a specific reference to this creature is contained in *Wudufu*, the famous rhapsody on the Wu Kingdom capital by the Jin scholar Zuo Si,[40] it seems more than likely that the Wu Kingdom artist was fully aware of the human-headed Shan Hui and had readily adopted it for his creation of the new iconography.

A possible direct descendant of the Wu Kingdom image is the human-faced guardian creature in the Schloss collection (fig. 8).[41] Believed to be a product of Northern Wei, this hybrid animal likewise stands on all fours. While the Wu figure has lost its horn and shows only a hole on the top of its head, the Wei image carries a single truncated horn on its head. The strikingly different position of its head, bending and looking downward, relates strongly to the human-faced guardian creature found in the tomb of the Northern Wei official Sima Jinlong (fig. 9), who died in 484 and was buried near Datong, the former Northern Wei capital.[42]

Sima Jinlong's guardian creature, the only one found in his tomb, appears to be one of the more immediate prototypes of the late Northern Wei example from Yuan Shao's tomb (fig. 1a); it sits on its haunches, and the underside of its body is hollowed out. Aside from these two distinctive features, which separate the image from the earlier Wu Kingdom image, it originally had a row of dorsal spikes; as will be shown, they are one of the most striking iconographic characteristics of the tomb-guardian creature. A row of five rectangular holes, evenly spaced along the spinal ridge from the top of the head to the rump of this figure, were prepared for the insertion of the dorsal spikes.[43] Other Northern Wei examples, excavated from tombs in China[44] as well as kept in museums outside China,[45] similarly carry a row of dorsal spikes. The one in the Asian Art Museum of San Francisco (fig. 10), a typical example, is also a prototype. Even though it raises its head to look upward in the same manner as Yuan Shao's image, it sits on its haunches in a half-crouching posture that is perceptibly midway between those of the Wu Kingdom and Sima Jinlong.

The other image of the pair, the lionlike tomb-guardian creature (fig. 1b), has analogous prototypes dating back to Eastern Han (25-221). The archaeological data indicate that prior to the establishment of the iconography in late Northern Wei three different types of animal creatures were assigned the role of a tomb-guardian. A frequently recurring Eastern Han example is the single-horned, rhinoceroslike creature; the pair of relief images on the stone door panels of the main entrance to the tomb of Yang Mengyuan (buried 96), at Suide, Shaanxi (fig. 11), are two of many examples found in northern Shaanxi.[46] Depicted in a combative posture with heads lowered and tails raised, they appear to be actively engaged in the battle of "warding off evil." A sculptural counterpart was discovered in 1978 in one of the several Eastern Han tombs excavated at Mianxian, Shaanxi.[47] Earlier, in the late 1950s, a total of seven wooden single-horned animals, whose bodies and legs resemble those of a deer, were recovered from the excavation of thirty-one Eastern Han tombs in Wuwei, Kansu.[48] Having found every one of them consistently placed near the entrance of a tomb, Chinese archaeologists considered them a type of tomb-guardian beast;[49] but the 1973 catalogue *An Exhibition of Archaeological Finds from*

8

9

Figures

8. Human-faced tomb-guardian creature. Grey earthenware, height 12 cm, length 30.5 cm. Northern Wei (early sixth century). Mr. and Mrs. Ezekiel Schloss collection, New York.

9. Human-faced tomb-guardian creature. Earthenware with slip colors, height 34.5 cm. Tomb of Sima Jinlong, Northern Wei (484), Datong, Shanxi. From *Cultural Relics Unearthed During the Cultural Revolution* (Beijing, Wenwu Press, 1972), pl. 142.

10. Human-faced tomb-guardian creature. Earthenware with traces of slip colors, height 23 cm. Northern Wei (early sixth century). Asian Art Museum of San Francisco.

11. Rubbing: stone reliefs of main entrance, height 1.74 cm, width 1.94 cm. Tomb of Yang Mengyuan, Eastern Han (96), Suide, Shaanxi. From *Wenwu*, 1983, no. 5, p. 29, fig. 2.

12. Lionlike tomb-guardian beast. Bronze, measurements unknown. Excavated from a tomb of Eastern Han (25-221), Zhucheng, Shandong. From *Wenwu*, 1981, no. 10, p. 14, fig. 2.

10

11

12

the People's Republic of China labeled the figures *qilin*, or Chinese unicorns.[50] In 1967 a bronze tomb-guardian beast was found in an Eastern Han tomb located west of Liangtaicun, in Zhucheng, Shandong (fig. 12).[51] Rendered with a slender body and in a striding posture with a raised tail, it resembles a lion; however, instead of a hairy mane, it has four bundles of hair matted into stiffly pointed locks arranged in a single row atop its head. This unusual feature was repeated in a later example, a type already known in museum collections outside China[52] and also recovered recently from Western Jin (265-316) tombs located in the Luoyang area (fig. 13).[53] In spite of its rhinoceroslike heavy body and short legs its lowered head with locks and striding posture with tail raised confirm its Han pedigree. The locks, only three in number and made to extend farther down the back of the head, anticipated the creation of a row of flamelike spikes spaced evenly along the length of the spinal ridge, such as that shown in the Eastern Jin (317-420) tomb-guardian beast (fig. 14).[54] Several similar Eastern Jin creatures were recovered from tombs in the Nanjing area but were variously designated a beast, a rhinoceros, or an oxlike animal.[55]

All of them, though somewhat different in form, are tomb-guardian creatures. The pair of dorsal-spiked tomb-guardian beasts recovered from the undisturbed Northern Wei tomb of Shao Zhen (buried 520), at Renjiakou in Xian, Shaanxi (fig. 15),[56] has confirmed this identification beyond doubt. Depicted in a crouching posture and found flanking the entrance to the tomb together with a pair of tomb-guardian warriors (fig. 27), this pair is key evidence, serving not only to verify their precedents but also providing the evolutionary linkage between the Eastern Han and late Northern Wei images. That they carry a row of dorsal spikes, a feature by then a well-established iconographic idiom, indicates the persistence of a burial tradition as well as the perpetuation of an iconographic formula.

Perhaps the varying types of tomb-guardian beasts that had emerged since Eastern Han are related to a textual precedent. The chapter "Records from the Western Regions" in the *Hanshu* (Han history) mentioned that three exotic animals, the *taoba* (which resembles a deer with a long tail), lion, and rhinoceros, were found in the Wuyishanli Kingdom.[57] The absence of a model for the tomb-guardian creature, which by its function should be different from the commonly known animals and also equipped with a measure of extraordinary power, must have prompted the artist to adopt these new and unfamiliar species for his creation.

Of the three exotic animals, the lion was ultimately chosen for the iconography. Viewing the pair of tomb-guardian creatures (figs. 1a-b) from the late Northern Wei tomb of Yuan Shao (buried 528), it is obvious that they were made to conform to the essential characteristics of a male lion. Aside from the human face on one of them, they were both given hairy manes, slender and graceful body proportions with narrow waists, large feline paws, and, above all, the regal posture of sitting on the haunches with head held high. This new configuration, so very different from that of the earlier pair (fig. 16) found in Shao Zhen's tomb (buried 520), compares remarkably with the pair of lions depicted in brick reliefs on the outermost ends of the side walls in the entrance corridor to a Southern Qi (479-502) tomb at Jinwangchen (or Jinjiacun) in Jianshan, Jiangsu (figs. 17a-b).[58]

Traditionally the lion was made a guardian of tombs in China. Since its introduction as a tribute gift from the Western kingdoms, such as Yueshi (Yuezhi), Anxi (Kucha), and Shulei (Kashgar), during Eastern Han,[59] pairs of stone lions have been placed in cemeteries containing important burial sites. The best-known pair are those found at the second-century Wu family cemetery in Jiaxiang, Shandong.[60] Others are those in Lushan, Sichuan,[61] and the recently unearthed pair from Xianyang, Shaanxi.[62] During the fifth century, when the lion, dictated by Indian Buddhist iconography, became an indispensable motif for the icon of the Buddha image,[63] a new surge of interest in the image of lion emerged in south China. The *Nan Qi shu* (Southern Qi history) recorded that the magician-general Wang Jingze saw himself riding on a five-colored lion in a dream;[64] and stone lions of monumental dimensions were made in pairs to stand guard on opposite sides of the Spirit Road leading to the imperial burial sites in the Nanjing area.[65] Furthermore several Southern Qi imperial tombs excavated in the 1960s, as mentioned above, have brick-relief depictions of the lion in the tomb entrance corridor.[66]

The use of the lion image for late Northern Wei guardian creatures is clearly an adoption of a tradition estab-

13

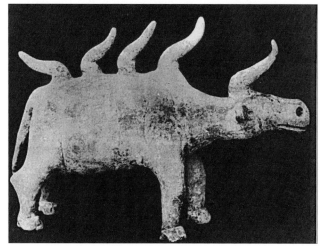

14

Figures

13. Rhinoceroslike tomb-guardian beast. Earthenware with slip colors, height 23.7 cm, length 34.5 cm. Excavated from a tomb of Western Jin (265-316), Xinyuancun, Yanshi, Henan. From *Kaogu*, 1985, no. 8,
    pl. 6.3.

14. Rhinoceroslike tomb-guardian beast. Earthenware, height 21.5 cm, length 29.7 cm. Excavated from a tomb of Eastern Jin (317-420), Shizigang, Nanjing (Zhonghuamen wai), Jiangsu. From *Nanjing Liu Chao chutu wenwu xuanji* (Shanghai, Renmin Meishu Chubanshe, 1959), pl. 23.

15. Longitudinal section and ground plan. Tomb of Shao Zhen, Northern Wei (520), Renjiakou, Xian, Shaanxi. From *Wenwu*, 1955, no. 12, p. 61

1 .... Pottery lamp	16 .... Metal belt hook	
2-7 .... Pottery tomb figurines	17-18 .... Tomb-guardian warriors	
8 .... Pottery tray	19-20 .... Tomb-guardian beasts	
9-13 .... Pottery bowls	21 .... Pottery rice grinder	
14 .... Pottery chicken	22 .... Pottery well-head	
15 .... Pottery bowl		

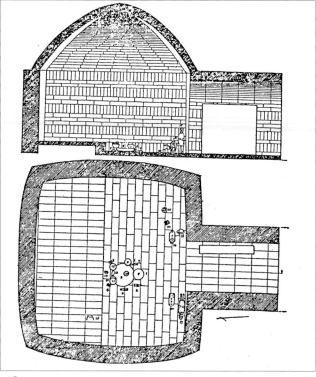

15

16a,b

17a

18

17b

Figures

16a-b. A pair of tomb-guardian beasts. Earthenware, height 15 cm, length 22 cm. Tomb of Shao Zhen, Northern Wei (520), Renjiakou, Xian, Shaanxi. From *Wenwu*, 1955, no. 12, p. 63, fig. 2.

17a-b. Rubbings of a pair of seated lions. Impressed brick reliefs, 77 x 113 cm, one on each side wall, entrance corridor to a tomb of Southern Qi (479-501), Jinwangchen, Jianshan, Jiangsu. From *Liu Chao yishu* (Beijing, Wenwu Press, 1981), pls. 201-2.

18. Stone relief of a seated lion, height 41 cm. Cave of the Six Lions, Northern Wei (c. 516-28), Longmen Cave Temples, Luoyang, Henan. From *Longmen shiku* (Beijing, Wenwu Press, 1981), pl. 102.

lished earlier in the tomb art of south China. Several studies on southern Chinese influences in the art of Northern Wei have been published.[67] The artistic achievements at the late Northern Wei Buddhist cave site Longmen, near Luoyang, Henan, provide the strongest evidence of influence from south China.[68] Specifically the relief carvings of lions in the so-called Cave of the Six Lions, opened during the reign of Emperor Xiao Ming (reigned 516-28), furnish the most pertinent visual documentation.[69] The comparison of one of the stone-relief lions (fig. 18)[70] with its south Chinese counterpart (fig. 17b)[71] reveals astonishing iconographic similarities in idioms such as the staring round eyes, protruding tongue in an open mouth, seated-on-the-haunches posture, raised right paw, and upswept tail. The late Northern Wei tomb-guardian creature (fig. 1b), which bears the very same features, is a virtual extension of the one in south China.

The decision of the Northern Wei artist to make the tomb-guardian creatures resemble the lion in its essential aspects may also have been stimulated by its prevalence in contemporary Buddhist art. In the late Northern Wei, pairs of lions sculpted in the round and given the seated-on-the-haunches posture already had proliferated as guards at the sides of the Buddha's throne in the cave temples of Yungang, Shanxi,[72] and Longmen, Henan,[73] that were constructed under imperial patronage. Yet what had ultimately contributed to the final iconographic choice was the lion's innate awesomeness as the king of beasts. Recorded in Yang Xuanzhi's *Luoyang jialanji* (A record of Buddhist temples in Luoyang) is an incident describing graphically the majestic aura of the lion: "The lion, a tribute gift from the King of Persia, was intercepted and retained by the treacherous Wanhou Chounu. Toward the end of the Yongan era (528), when the Chounu revolt was put down and the tribute finally reached the capital, Emperor [Xiao] Zhuang (reigned 528-30) turned to his court attendant Li Yu and said: 'I've heard that the tiger would prostrate at the sight of a lion. Let's find out.' So orders were issued to districts located near the mountainous regions to catch some tigers for the emperor. Gongxian and Shanyang presented two tigers and one leopard. The emperor made his observation in the Hualin Park. Both the tiger and leopard indeed closed their eyes and did not dare to look up [at the lion]."[74]

Likewise influenced by traditional precedence in south China is the pairing of a human-faced creature with an animal-faced one. Paired deities (human-headed and deer-headed birds) were found depicted in molded-tile reliefs on the wall of an Eastern Jin tomb excavated at Zhenjiang (near Nanjing), Jiangsu.[75] A similar wall decoration in a fifth-century Southern Dynasties tomb at Dengxian, Henan, identified the pair by inscription as auspicious symbols for longevity.[76] The pairing of a human-faced

being with a lion-faced one was a result of the desire to impart a felicitous connotation to the pair of tomb-guardian creatures.

Other features attesting to a traditional Chinese heritage are the horns and cloven hooves. The Wei Kingdom (220-65) scholar Meng Kang, who annotated the *Han History*, appended the following explanation to the section on the exotic *taoba* mentioned earlier: "*Taoba*, also known as *fuba*, resembles a deer with a long tail. If it has one horn, it may be a *tianlu* [heavenly deer]; if it has two horns, it may be a *bixie* [one who averts evil]."[77] This passage must have prompted the addition of a pair of horns on the Northern Qi lion-faced tomb-guardian creature (fig. 3a), a move already sanctioned by south Chinese precedents, the monumental stone images of *tianlu* and *bixie* that guarded the imperial tombs.[78] However, the incorporation of the idea of *bixie* was not fully realized until the early Tang, when the paws were replaced by cloven hooves (fig. 5), a distinctive characteristic of the deerlike *taoba*. Thus the Tang human-faced and cloven-hoofed creature (fig. 5a), also bearing a single horn on its head from the Sui Dynasty on (fig. 4a), matches its counterpart and functions as a *tianlu*, a symbol of heavenly blessings and a perfect compliment to the *bixie*, a symbol of evil averted.

What seems to be a mystery, as this writer has not found any literary references to the subject, is the Northern Qi insertion of a bannerlike lance head immediately behind the horns. Its identity is quite obvious; the same type of lance head is shown in a wall painting of an Eastern Wei tomb.[79] If the depiction of a warrior holding a lance signifies military protection, then the addition of the lance head should symbolize the same type of protective power accorded the tomb-guardian creatures. Since its appearance in late Northern Qi (fig. 3), it was subsequently incorporated in the images of the Sui and Tang (figs. 4 and 5).

Finally the Tang insertion of a pair of wings, a borrowing of the Han artistic device, which differentiates the representation of an immortal, whether man or beast, from that of a mortal, indicates that an image is endowed with supernatural power. The Han scholar Wang Chong (27-circa 100), author of *Lunheng* (Doctrines evaluated) wrote: "All those who can fly have wings; those who do not have wings and can[not] fly are [not] immortals, therefore depictions of immortals are given wings."[80] One of the most striking of the archaeological data is the ceiling painting in a Western Han tomb discovered at Luoyang. It illustrates clearly the use of the device; the souls of the deceased, Bu Qianqiu and his wife, are shown escorted to paradise by winged dragons and other winged beasts amid floating clouds.[81] Closer in time are the Six Dynasties monumental stone sculptures of beasts that guarded the Spirit Roads to the imperial cemeteries in the Nanjing area. All of them, whether *tianlu*, *bixie*, or lion, were given a pair of wings.[82]

The tomb-guardian creatures from the tomb of Zheng Rentai (fig. 5) illustrates clearly that it was in mid seventh-century Tang that the fully established iconography for the pair of tomb-guardian creatures emerged as composite beasts, one with the face of a man and body of a lion, the other the head and body of a lion, and both with the horns and feet of a deer and the wings of a supernatural being.

During the Tang, when the sculptural arts moved forward with the incorporation of new ideas and improved techniques, certain iconographic variations appeared, especially in the metropolitan region of Changan (Xian today), Shaanxi. By the early eighth century the guardian creatures were made to sit erect, like humans, with the right foreleg raised high to make a gesture and the left grasping the long tail, or else both remaining resting on the "knee."[83] Later in the mid eighth century they were made to stand upright, like humans, with right foreleg raised as if about to strike and the left hind leg stepping on the back of a dwarf monster,[84] in imitation of the threatening gesture of the Heavenly King Guardian, which will be discussed below.

Tomb-guardian Warriors

Pairs of warrior figurines found in the better-preserved mid sixth- to early seventh-century upper-class tombs in the *zhongyuan* provinces were inevitably the *zhenmuyong*, tomb-guardian warriors, designed specifically, along with the pair of tomb-guardian creatures, to protect the tomb occupant.

This pair of tomb-guardian warriors, designated by Chinese archaeologists as *andun wushiyong* (hand-resting-on-shield warrior figurine), are distinguished from other warrior figurines by the left hand that rests on a large rectangular shield, which is at least half the height of the image itself and placed vertically before the left leg. The persistence in type and form, as shown in the archaeological finds from the Northern Wei tomb of Yuan Shao (buried 528), excavated at Luoyang, Henan (fig. 19),[85] the Eastern Wei tomb of Zhao Huren (buried 547), at Dongchencun in Cixian, Hebei (fig. 20),[86] the Northern Qi tomb of Kudi Huiluo (buried 562), at Shouyang, Shanxi (fig. 21),[87] the Sui tomb of Li Jingxun (buried 608), at Xian, Shaanxi (fig. 22),[88] and the early Tang tomb of Dugu Kaiyuan (buried 642), at Xianyang, Shaanxi (fig. 23),[89] affirms that all through the successive Northern Dynasties into Sui and early Tang there existed a strong and conscientious adherence to a well-established burial tradition.

The outfit of this guardian warrior, to which Yang Hong in his study traces a Wei Kingdom (220-65) precedent, consists of the newly popularized *liangdang* or *mingguangkai* (bright and shining) armor with circular plaques on the breast, back plates held in place by straps, and shoulder

Figure

19. One of a pair of tomb-guardian warriors with a large shield. Earthenware with traces of slip colors, height 30.8 cm. Tomb of Yuan Shao, Northern Wei (528), Luoyang, Henan. From *Kaogu*, 1973, no. 4, pl. 8.1.

20   21   22

guards surmounted by a round collar.[90] Similarly clad warriors are seen in a mural in the tomb of the North Chinese minister Dong Shou (buried 357), buried in Anak, North Korea (fig. 24).[91] Shown positioned in the forefront, flanking the left and right sides of the parade formation, they represent a select group of specially trained warriors who were appointed guardsmen of high-ranking officials. It was certainly appropriate that the tomb-guardian warriors should be made in accordance with a contemporary model that symbolized military prowess to stand guard at the entrance to the tomb.

Although armed with shield and lance (the clasping fingers of the right hand make an aperture for the insertion of the handle of the weapon), this image is definitely not the exorcist *fangxiang* (or *fangxiangshi*) described in the *Zhouli* (Rites of Zhou) as being an officer assigned to the specific task of expelling the spirits of diseases: "*Fangxiangshi* wears over his head a bearskin with four golden eyes and is clad in a black upper garment and a red lower garment. Holding a lance and waving a shield, he leads his officials in the

performance of the seasonal exorcism; he searches through the houses and drives out pestilences. At a great funeral, he would march in front of the coffin. Upon arrival at the burial site, he would enter the tomb and strike the four corners [of the coffin chamber] with his lance to expel Fangliang."[92] Obviously neither the tomb-guardian warrior's contemporary armor nor his motionless stance at attention correspond in the least to the description of the exorcist.

The tomb-guardian warrior, like the tomb-guardian creatures, also had prototypes dating to the Han dynasty. The most significant examples are the shield- and lance-bearing warriors discovered in 1965 in several burial pits believed to belong to the Western Han minister Zhou Bo and his son Zhou Yafu, at Yangjiawan, in Xianyang, Shaanxi.[93] The more immediate prototypes are the post-Han warrior figurines from the tombs of Western Jin in north China (fig. 25)[94] and of Eastern Jin in south China (fig. 26).[95] The Western Jin warrior (shield not shown) differs from the latter in having a ferocious-looking face

23

24

25

Figures

20. One of a pair of tomb-guardian warriors with a large shield. Earthenware with traces of slip colors, height 47.5 cm. Tomb of Zhao Huren, Eastern Wei (547), Dongchencun, Cixian, Hebei. From *Kaogu*, 1977, no. 6, pl. 8.3.

21. One of a pair of tomb-guardian warriors with a large shield. Stoneware with slip colors and applied gold, height 58 cm. Tomb of Kudi Huiluo, Northern Qi (562), Shouyang, Shanxi. From *Kaogu xuebao*, 1979, no. 3, pl. 7.1.

22. One of a pair of tomb-guardian warriors with a large shield. Earthenware with slip colors, height 34 cm. Tomb of Li Jingxun, Sui (608), Xian, Shaanxi. From *Tang Changan Chengjiao Sui Tang mu* (Beijing, Wenwu Press, 1980), pl. 20.2.

23. One of a pair of tomb-guardian warriors with a large shield. Earthenware with slip colors, height 47.5 cm. Tomb of Dugu Kaiyuan, Tang (642), Xianyang, Shaanxi. From *Shaanxi sheng chutu Tang yong xuanji* (Beijing: Wenwu Press, 1958), pl. 1.

24. Drawing of wall painting: Dong Shou and his retinue. Tomb of Dong Shou, Six Dynasties (357), Anak, Korea. From *Kaogu*, 1959, no. 1, p. 32, fig. 11.

25. Tomb figurine of a warrior with a shield (not shown). Earthenware, height 59 cm. Excavated from a tomb of Western Jin (265-316), Xingyuancun, Yanshi, Henan. From *Kaogu*, 1985, no. 8, pl. 6.5.

26

27a,b

with thick-lidded large eyes, high cheekbones, and wide mouth with teeth showing as well as a threatening pose characterized by the right arm raised high in the gesture of throwing a spear and the legs spread apart in a lunging movement. Prior to the availability of archaeological data such images (several of which had entered museum collections outside China) had been assigned to the Han dynasty and identified as a representation of the exorcist *fangxiang*.[96] But recent Chinese studies, based on archaeological finds, have indicated otherwise, for the following reasons.

The 1984 excavation of the relatively undisturbed two-chambered Western Jin tomb, designated as Tomb M-34, at Xingyuancun, in Yanshi, Henan, has shown that the shield- and lance-bearing warrior figurine (fig. 25) as well as the tomb-guardian beast (fig. 13) were made larger in size than other tomb figurines and were placed near the entrance to the front chamber.[97] Both their size and allocation, therefore, have provided irrefutable confirmation of their roles as *zhenmuyong* and *zhenmushou* respectively. Zhang Xiaozhou's 1987 study of the tombs of the Wei and Jin Sixteen States period in north China suggests that Tomb M-34 dates to late Western Jin, the period of 270-300.[98] Hence the shield- and lance-bearing warrior figurine is undoubtedly a product of Western Jin. Its grotesque appearance, therefore, should be attributed to the stylistic preference and sculptural skill of the locale during a time when continual political upheavals had caused the best art-

Figures

26. Tomb figurine of a warrior holding a shield. Earthenware with slip colors, height 52.8 cm. Excavated from a tomb of Eastern Jin (317-420), Fuguishan, Nanjing, Jiangsu. From *Nanjing bowu guan* (Beijing, Wenwu Press, 1984), pl. 85.

27a-b. A pair of tomb-guardian warriors. Earthenware, height 43 cm. Tomb of Shao Zhen, Northern Wei (520), Renjiakou, Xian, Shaanxi. From *Wenwu*, 1955, no. 12, p. 63, fig. 1.

ists to die prematurely or migrate to the south. The Eastern Jin shield- and lance-bearing warrior figurine (fig. 26), as a product sculpted with significantly more refined modeling of the human face, bears testimony to the superior artistic heritage existing in south China. In north China the continuation of the Western Jin model into Northern Wei can be seen in the pair of warrior figures excavated from the tomb of Shao Zhen (buried 520), at Renjaikou, in Xian, Shaanxi (fig. 27), which are characterized by the same type of facial features.[99] Although not equipped with shield and lance, they were found, together with the pair of tomb-guardian beasts (fig. 16), at the entrance to the tomb chamber (fig. 15). They must therefore be tomb-guardian warriors and, like the Western Jin image, are also prototypes of the later Northern Wei pair from Yuan Shao's tomb (fig. 19).

In addition, Xu Pingfang, who disagreed with the *fangxiang* identification, pointed out in her study of Tang-Song burial practices that the *fangxiang* image was traditionally made of perishable materials such as straw or bamboo, which accounted for the total absence of *fangxiang* figures in the excavated tombs. She cited the passage from *Bizangjing* (the Tang-Song handbook on burial practices) that mentions *fangxiang* figures were "woven in five colors, had four eyes, and held tree branches in their hands."[100] It seems likely, then, that the *fangxiang* image was never made in clay nor in the semblance of a warrior figurine. For visual evidence Xu referred to the wooden images found in the perfectly preserved Western Han tombs at Mawangdui and Fenghuangshan. They are totally different from clay tomb figurines, and Chinese archaeologists classified them as a type of *bixie* figure.[101] Those from Mawangdui consist of split peach-tree branches,[102] and those from Fenghuangshan of wooden slips.[103] Both were simply notched at one end to indicate the human head, and the facial features were summarily rendered in ink. What confirms beyond doubt that even later in the Tang dynasty a clear distinction between the *fangxiang* and the tomb-guardian warrior images was maintained is the section in the book on Tang institutions, *Da Tang liudian*, which states that if a person were to perform the task of *fangxiangshi*, he would "put on a mask with four golden eyes and wear a bearskin outfit."[104] Another section in the same work, which gives the number and size of tomb figurines allowed in accordance with the court rank of the deceased, mentions two sets of tomb-guardian figurines by their special names, *dangkuang* and *dangye* for the pair of tomb-guardian warriors and *zuming* and *dizhou* for the pair of tomb-guardian creatures,[105] a terminology that persisted into Northern Song.[106]

There is no question, then, that in the Tang dynasty neither the tomb-guardian warrior nor the tomb-guardian creature was ever confused with the *fangxiang* image. William Watson's statements that the Tang Heavenly King Guardian is a "transformation of the ancient genie Fang-hsiang [*fangxiang*]" and that the Tang tomb-guardian creature is "another apotropaic genie, Ch'i-tou [*Qitou*]... [who] took on a new guise and assumed the function of the earlier Fang-hsiang"[107] are inaccurate. The confusion apparently stemmed from a misinterpretation of the term *qitou* which the Han scholar Zheng Xuan had used to annotate the passage on "*fangxiangshi*" in the *Zhouli*. Zheng Xuan clearly began his annotation with the explanation that the character *meng* means *mao*, in other words, "to wear over one's head," and hence what follows, "mao xionpi zhe, yi jinggu yili zhi qui, ru jin qitou ya,"[108] means "the bear skin worn over one's head to expel the demon of pestilences resembles today's *qitou*" and not "the one who wears the bear skin to expel the demon of pestilences is today's *qitou*." That in Han times the term *qitou* signifies a mask, not a mythological creature, is corroborated in a passage in the Eastern Han text *Fengsu tongyi* (Comprehensive meaning of customs), wherein the author Ying Shao mentioned explicitly, "It is said that the *hun*-spirit of the dead would float away, so a *qitou* was made to keep it in place, that is, the head was made to appear frighteningly larger."[109]

Recent archaeological finds have revealed another aspect of influence on the iconographic formulation of the tomb-guardian figurines produced in the central plains of north China. More than one Southern Qi tomb of imperial dimensions in south China have a pair of armor-clad warriors depicted in brick relief, one on each side wall, next to the lion, in the entrance corridor to the tomb chamber. The best preserved example (fig. 28),[110] together with the earlier mentioned pair of lions (fig. 17), could very well have been the models for the late Northern Wei artist. The frequent diplomatic relations with Southern Qi, made possible by the move of the Northern Wei capital from Pingcheng (Datong today), in Shanxi, southward to Luoyang, in Henan, during 495, had enhanced contacts with south China. When Southern Qi collapsed under the stronger military forces of Liang, the great exodus of Southern Qi leaders in 499-500 to Northern Wei, where they offered their services, must have intensified the northward flow of artistic diffusions.[111] For example, the refugee Wang You, a scholar and an expert copyist of painting who found favor in the court of Northern Wei at Luoyang, could have been responsible for making known the burial customs prevalent in Southern Qi.[112] According to archaeological data known to this date of writing, it was in late Northern Wei, some time after the influx of Southern Qi refugees, that the two sets of tomb-guardian figurines emerged with the fully established iconography that continued into early Tang.[113] The significance of Southern Qi influences is manifestly apparent in the comparison of the two sets of tomb-guardian figurines from the 520 tomb of

28a

28b

Shao Zhen located in Renjiakou, Xian (figs. 16 and 27), with those from the 528 tomb of Yuan Shao at Luoyang (figs. 1 and 19). Whereas the figures of Shao Zhen's tomb, as products of Renjiakou, a region far away from the artistic developments taking place at Luoyang, adhered to the old Han-Jin formula, those of Yuan Shao, being made by better informed artists at Luoyang, are late Northern Wei counterparts of the seated lions and military guards depicted in the Southern Qi tomb.

Of significance to the evolution of the tomb-guardian figurine is the fact that during Sui and early Tang, when the country was unified under one rule after centuries of political upheaval and the people enjoyed greater peace and prosperity, the developing arts, including the making of tomb figurines, incorporated newer ideas that engendered certain iconographic changes.

The fully armed Northern Wei tomb-guardian warrior was soon supplanted by one without the shield, known generally as *wushiyong* (warrior tomb figurine). The change, initiated in the Sui, as found in the image from Zhang Sheng's tomb (buried 595), excavated in Anyang, Henan (fig. 29),[114] appeared in early Tang in Cheng Rentai's tomb (buried 663), at Liquan, Shanxi (fig. 30).[115] Both their left hands make a clenched fist, while the right is still modeled to hold a long-handled weapon. The Sui image, in fact, still carries iconographic features of the tomb-guardian warrior of previous ages, such as trousers tied at the knees (fig. 19), elbow-length shoulder guards

29
30
31a

(figs. 20 and 21), and a helmet with two-layered, shoulder-length ear flaps (figs. 19-21). The Tang image, although obviously derived from the Sui model, had been adapted to wear the armor of the new dynasty. Basically an elaborate version of the Six Dynasties "bright and shining" type, it is now distinguished by tiger-headed shoulder guards and colorful trimmings around the edges of the helmet, collar, breast plaques, and thigh guards. In addition, the breast plaques are stylized into confronting "D shapes" with scalloped edges on the straight side, the midriff guard has become a distinctly form-fitting corsetlike piece, and the split-front thigh guard wraps tightly around the hip like a skirt. The row of pleats around the lower edge of the thigh guard and the cascade of drapery folds over the legs suggest the presence of knee-length as well as ankle-length garments worn under the armor. The flaring sleeve cuffs pushed up to the elbows by what seems to be forearm guards must belong to one of the long robes.[116] Such an ornate outfit, impractical for combat, must have been modeled on the costume of the Tang palace guards, especially as the tomb of the Tang aristocratic class was designed to resemble the residence of the deceased in real life.[117]

Figures

28a-b. Rubbings of a pair of tomb-guardian warriors. Impressed brick reliefs, height 77 cm, one on each side wall, entrance corridor to a tomb of Southern Qi (497-501), Jinwangchen, Jianshan, Jiangsu. From *Liu Chao yishu* (Beijing: Wenwu Press, 1981), pls. 203-4.

29. One of a pair of tomb-guardian warriors. Gray-white stoneware with clear glaze, height 73 cm. Tomb of Zhang Sheng, Sui (594), Anyang, Henan. From *Henan bowu guan* (Beijing: Wenwu Press, 1985), pl. 109.

30. One of a pair of tomb-guardian warriors. White *gaoling* clay with yellowish glaze, painted colors, and applied gold, height 71.5 cm. Tomb of Zheng Rentai, Tang (663), Liquan, Shaanxi. From *Shaanxi bowuguan* (Beijing: Wenwu Press, 1983), pl. 44.

31a-b. A pair of Heavenly King tomb guardian. Earthenware with slip colors, height 98.5 cm. Tomb of Li Shuang, Tang (668), Yangtouzhen, Xian, Shaanxi. From *Shaanxi sheng chutu Tang yong xuanji* (Beijing:Wenwu Press, 1958), pls. 20-21.

Yet this new image of the tomb-guardian warrior did not last through the fast-developing seventh century Tang. The popularity of the Buddhist cult images of the Four Lokapalas or Sidatianwang (Four Great Heavenly Kings), which had been gathering momentum since the Sui dynasty, came to prominence during early Tang. The ico-

31b

581-605).[118] This strikingly novel addition to the Sui repertoire of funerary art no doubt was derived from Buddhist art; the Northern Zhou Emperor Ming (reigned 559-60) is known to have ordered a temple dedicated to the Four Great Heavenly Kings built in his capital, Changan,[119] which later became the Sui dynasty capital. The Sui devotion to the Heavenly Kings continued into Tang in the form of guardian images of Buddhist temples[120] as well as tomb chambers.

At this writing the earliest known dated pair of *tianwangyong* (Heavenly King tomb figurines) is from the tomb of Li Shuang (buried 668) excavated at Yangtouzhen, near Xian, Shanxi (fig. 31).[121] The image wears the same type of outfit as Cheng Rentai's tomb-guardian warrior; the only difference is the shortening of the thigh guards as well as the ankle-length robe, thus revealing the greaves on a pair of stiff legs. Shown standing on a buffalo, it probably represents the Heavenly King Guardian of the South, Zengchang (Virudhaka), the only one of the four that stands on an animal instead of a monster.[122] The choice may have been governed by the fact that the entrance to the Tang tomb was located on the south side.[123] Later, as evidenced in the pair from the tomb of Li Mengjiang (buried 682), excavated at Liquan, Shaanxi, the Heavenly King Guardian, like those depicted on Li He's stone coffin, stands atop a demonlike dwarf.[124] This version was carried into the eighth century, as exemplified in the pair found in the tomb of Dugu Sijing (buried 709) in Xian, Shaanxi.[125] The substitution of the set of tomb-guardian warriors for that of the Heavenly King guardians is well documented by archaeological data; Tang tombs in which the former are present do not contain the latter.[126]

Conclusion

It was within the norms of the Chinese artistic convention of representational art that the iconography for the two sets of tomb-guardian figurines developed during Han, Wei, and Jin became fully established by late Northern Wei and continued into Sui and early Tang. As demonstrated in this paper, the human-headed tomb-guardian creature was made neither to wear a mask nor to usurp the role of *fangxiangshi*, but was intentionally created as a hybrid image to be paired with a lionlike counterpart for the protection of the tomb occupant. Similarly the Heavenly King Guardian was not a transformation of *fangxiangshi* but a late seventh-century replacement of the tomb-guardian warrior that was created in pre-Tang times as a distinctive type of tomb-guardian figurine. In the Tang dynasty the pair of tomb-guardian warriors, whether *wushiyong* or *tianwangyong*, were known as *dangguang* and *dangye*, and the pair of tomb-guardian creatures as *zuming* and *dizhou*, the usage of which was lost through the inevitable changes wrought by time.

nography of the Heavenly King, a warrior standing on a demonlike dwarf, carried such a powerful connotation of *bixie*, or "evil successfully averted," that it was readily adopted to replace the tomb-guardian warrior. This new image appeared first in the Sui dynasty and later in mid seventh-century Tang. A rare Sui example is the relief representation on the stone coffin of Li He (buried 582), a highly placed Northern Zhou (557-581) general who was equally honored by the first Sui emperor, Wen (reigned

100

Notes

1. Rene-Yvon Lefebvre d'Argence, *Chinese Ceramics in the Avery Brundage Collection* (San Francisco: The de Young Museum Society, 1967), 58.

2. Margaret Medley, *T'ang Pottery and Porcelain* (London: Faber and Faber, 1981), 59.

3. William Watson, *The Genius of China: An Exhibition of Archaeological Finds of the People's Republic of China* (London: Times Newspapers, 1973), 144. Later he changed it to "apotropaic man-lion"; see his *Tang and Liao Ceramics* (London: Thames and Hudson, 1984), 205.

4. Anthony Christie, *Chinese Mythology* (New York: Peter Bedrick, 1983), 77.

5. Shaanxi Provincial Cultural Relics Commission, *Shaanxi sheng chutu Tang yong xuanji* (A catalogue of Tang tomb figurines excavated in Shaanxi Province) (Beijing: Wenwu Press, 1958), 5, and pls. 12-13.

6. Xu Pingfang, "Tang Song muzang zhong di 'mingqi shensha' yu 'muyi' zhidu—du *Da Han yuanling Bizangqing* zhaji" (The exorcistic burial objects and burial practices of Tang-Song funeral rituals—notes from reading the *Da Han yuanling Bizangqing*), *Kaogu*, 1963, no. 1: 87-106.

7. See my article "Antecedents of Sui-Tang Burial Practices in Shaanxi," which will be published in *Artibus Asiae*.

8. Luoyang Museum, "Luoyang Bei Wei Yuan Shao mu" (The Northern Wei tomb of Yuan Shao in Luoyang), *Kaogu*, 1973, no. 4: 222, and pls. 12.1-2. Yuan Shao, as identified by his epitaph inscription, was a grandson of Emperor Xiao Wen (reigned 471-77) and was killed by the rebel Er-zhu Rong in the 528 massacre of the Northern Wei ruling family. Yet he was buried with full honors, posthumously awarded the titles of Courtier-in-Attendance, Grand General of Cavalry, Governor of Dingzhou, and Cultured and Reverential Prince of Changshan; this accounts for the high quality of furnishings in his tomb.

9. Cixian Cultural Center, "Hebei Cixian Dong Wei Ruru gongzhumu fajue jianbao" (A brief report on the excavation of the tomb of the Eastern Wei Ruru Princess at Cixian, Hebei), *Wenwu*, 1984, no. 4: 4-5, 8-9, and fig. 5. In the middle of the sixth- century the nomadic Ruru people, after having invaded the northern frontiers of the Wei empire for many generations, were themselves threatened by the rising Turks and sought a defensive alliance with the Eastern Wei regime. In 541, to solemnize the treaty that followed, the kingmaker Gao Huan sent one of his daughters to be married to the heir of the Ruru chief. A few months later he had his ninth son, Gao Zhan, marry the chief's granddaughter, Princess Lin He (538-50). At the time the boy was eight years old and the girl was five. Gao Zhan grew up and eventually became the fourth Northern Qi emperor, Wu Cheng (reigned 561-64). When the ex-barbarian princess died at twelve in 550, Gao Zhan was still a junior with the rank of duke. Thus the girl's burial, though rich, was presumably well below the imperial level. She has a brief note among the Northern Qi empresses in *Bei shi* (History of the Northern Dynasties) (Beijing: Zhonghua shuju, 1974), 14.517-18; and the marriage is recorded in the annals, ibid., 8.281; *Bei Qi shu* (History of Northern Qi) (Beijing: Zhonghua shuju, 1972), 7.89; and biography of the Ruru tribe, *Bei shi*, 98.3265. (As of this writing, no Western Wei tomb dated by epitaph inscription has been found.)

10. Cixian Cultural Center, "Hebei Cixian Dongchencun Bei Qi Yao Jun mu" (Excavation of the Northern Qi tomb of Yao Jun in Dongchencun at Cixian, Hebei), *Wenwu*, 1984, no. 4: 18-22, and fig. 9. Yao Jun (505-66), a grandson of Yao Xuan, was buried with his two wives. His epitaph stone, inscribed with thirty-one by thirty-one lines of text, mentions the familiar official posts—Provincial Governor, Generalissimo of Cavalry, and so on. The Yao clan, as recorded in *Bei shi*, 27.998-1000, and *Bei Qi shu*, 20.267-70, owed its prominence in the northeast during the mid sixth-century to its early support of the kingmaker Gao Huan against the briefly troublesome Er-zhu clan.

11. Institute of Archaeology, Anyang Excavation Team, "Anyang Sui Zhang Sheng mu fajue ji" (Notes on the excavation of the Sui tomb of Zhang Sheng at Anyang), *Kaogu*, 1959, no. 10: 541, 545, and pls. 9.5 and 9.8. Zhang Sheng (502-94) is not recorded in the dynastic history, but his epitaph inscription addresses him as "The Late Enemy-defeating Sui General and Zhangsan Dafu (honorary court title)."

12. Shaanxi Provincial Museum et al., "Tang Cheng Rentai mu fajue jianbao" (A brief report on the excavation of the Tang tomb of Cheng Rentai), *Wenwu*, 1972, no. 7: 35, 39-41, and figs. 6-7. Cheng Rentai (buried 663) has no biographies in the two Tang dynastic histories. His epitaph inscription mentions that he fought many battles for Emperor Tai Zong (reigned 618-27) and was commander in chief of six districts in the northwest, Governor of Liangzhou, and honored as "Pillar of the State." His epitaph stone cover accords him the title "Right Guard Great General of Great Tang."

13. Hunan Provincial Museum et al., *Changsha Mawangdui yihao Han mu* (Han Tomb Number One at Mawangdui, Changsha) (Beijing: Wenwu Press, 1973); and "Changsha Mawangdui erhao, sanhao Han mu fajue jianbao" (A brief report on the excavation of Han Tombs Number Two and Three at Mawangdui, Changsha), *Wenwu*, 1974, no. 7: 39-48 and 63.

14. Jinancheng Fenghuangshan Han Tomb Number 168 Excavation and Reporting Team, "Hubei Jiangling Fenghuangshan 168 hao Han mu fajue jianbao" (A brief report on the excavation of Han Tomb Number 168 at Fenghuangshan in Jiangling, Hubei), *Wenwu*, 1975, no. 9: 1-7; and Fenghuangshan Han Tomb Number 167 Excavation and Reporting Team, "Jiangling Fenghuangshan 167 hao Han mu fajue jianbao" (A brief report on the excavation of Han Tomb Number 167 at Fenghuangshan in Jiangling), *Wenwu*, 1976, no. 10: 31-37 and 50.

15. Yu Ying-shih, "New Evidence on the Early Chinese Conception of Afterlife—A Review Article," *Journal of Asian Studies* 41, no. 1 (November 1981): 82.

16. Michael Loewe, *Chinese Ideas of Life and Death: Faith, Myth and Reason in the Han Period (202 B.C-A.D. 220)* (London: Allen & Unwin, 1982), 26-27; and Michael Loewe, *Ways to Paradise* (London: Allen & Unwin, 1979), 9-10.

17. Loewe, *Ways to Paradise*, 30-59.

18. Luoyang Museum, "Luoyang Xi Han Bu Qianqiu bihuamu fajue jianbao" (A brief report on the excavation of the Western Han tomb with wall paintings of Bu Qianqiu in Luoyang), *Wenwu*, 1977, no. 6: 1-12, figs. 33-34, and pls. 2-3.

19. Yu Ying-shih, "New Evidence," 83.

20. Wang Ruiming, "'Zhenmu shou' kao" (A study of the tomb- guardian creature), *Wenwu*, 1979, no. 6: 87.

21. Henan Provincial Cultural Relics Research Institute, *Xinyang Chu Mu* (Chu tombs at Xinyang) (Beijing: Wenwu Press, 1986), 60-61, and pls. 58-59; and 114, and pl. 109. Carved from a single piece of wood and painted in black lacquer with definitions in red and yellow, both are first-rate sculptures.

22. Mizuno Seiichi, "Some Wooden Figures from Changsha, Hunan," *Toho Gakuho* 8 (1937): 238-39.

23. Alfred Salmony, *Antler and Tongue: An Essay on Ancient Chinese Symbolism and Its Implication* (Ascona: Artibus Asiae Publishers, 1954), 7.

24. Ibid., 8-9, and fig. 11.

25. Ibid., 7-8, figs. 5-6.

26. Sun Zuoyun, "Mawangdui yihao Han mu qiquan hua kaoshi" (A study on the paintings found on the lacquer coffin of Han Tomb

Number One from Mawangdui), *Kaogu*, 1973, no. 4: 247-48.

27. *Ch'utz'u* (Ch'u poems) (Taipei, Shih-chieh shu-chu, 1972), 9.121; and David Hawkes, *Ch'u tz'u: The Songs of the South* (Boston: Beacon Press, 1962), 105.

28. Sun Zuoyun, "Mawangdui yihao," 248.

29. Ibid., 248-50. For the references to the texts, see respectively: *Chunqiu Zuozhuan zhengyi* in *Sibu beiyao* (hereafter SBBY) (see Zhao Gong 29th year), 53.6a; *Liji zhengzhu* in SBBY (see Jifa), 14.4b; *Huainanzi* in SBBY (see Fanlunpian), 13.22a; and *Shiji* (Beijing, Chunghua shuju, 1959), 28.1357.

30. Michael Loewe, "Man and Beast, the Hybrid in Early Chinese Art and Literature," *Numen* 25, no. 2 (1978): 97-117; and Martin J. Powers, "Hybrid Omens and Public Issues in Early Imperial China," *Bulletin of the Museum of Far Eastern Antiquities* (Stockholm), no. 55 (1983): 1-55.

31. Edouard Chavannes, *Mission archeologique dans la Chine septentrionale* (Paris: Ernest Leroux, 1909-15), pl. XLIV, no. 75; Richard C. Rudolph, *Han Tomb Art of West China* (Berkeley: University of California Press, 1951), pls. 58-59 and 99; Zeng Zhaoyu et al., *Yinan Guhuaxiang shimu fajue baogao* (A report on the excavation of an ancient stone tomb with pictorial representations at Yinan) (Beijing: Wenwu Press, 1956), pl. 25; and Jiangsu Provincial Cultural Relics Commission, *Jiangsu Xuzhou Hanmu xiangshi* (Pictorial stone reliefs from Han tombs at Xuzhou, Jiangsu) (Beijing: Kexue Press, 1959), pl. 66.85.

32. The solemnity of burials, which reflects a seriousness of intention dating from prehistoric times, can be observed in the innumerable scientific excavations of ancient tombs in China. See Chang Kwang-chih, *The Archaeology of Ancient China* (New Haven: Yale University Press, 1986, 4th ed., rev. and enlarged); Li Xueqin, *Eastern Zhou and Qin Civilizations*, trans. by K. C. Chang (New Haven: Yale University Press, 1985); and Wang Zhongshu, *Han Civilization*, trans. K. C. Chang and collaborators (New Haven: Yale University Press, 1982).

33. Hunan Provincial Museum, "Changsha Mawangdui erhao," 40.

34. Hubei Provincial Cultural Relics Commission, "Wuchang Lianxisi Dong Wu mu qingli jianbao" (A brief report on the excavation of a Wu Kingdom tomb at Lianxisi in Wuchang), *Kaogu*, 1959, no. 6: 189, and pl. 5.1.

35. Anhui Provincial Institute of Cultural Relics and Archaeology, "Anhui Ma'anshanshi Jiashan Dong Wu mu qingli jianbao" (A brief report on the excavation of a Wu Kingdom tomb at Ma'anshanshi in Jiashan, Anhui), *Kaogu*, 1986, no. 5: 408, fig. 3, and pls. 1.1 and 1.5.

36. F. S. Drake, "Sculpture Stones of the Han Dynasty," *Monumenta Serica* 8 (1943): 286-93.

37. *Shenyijing* in *Shuo ku*, 1 (*Sibu zayao*: Zi bu), 4a (16).

38. *Shanhaijing* in SBBY, 2.17a-b and 2.19a-b (Kunlun Mountains, home of Xi Wang Mu), and 11.3a-4a (Kaiming). For stone-relief examples in Han art, see Li Falin, "Han huaxiang zhong di jiutou renmianshou" (The representation of the nine-human-headed creature in Han stone relief), *Wenwu*, 1974, no. 12: 82-86; and "Luetan Han huaxiangshi di diaoke jifa ji qi fenqi" (A brief discussion on the carving techniques of Han pictorial stone reliefs and their periods), *Kaogu*, 1965, no. 4: 200, and fig. 2.

39. *Shanhaijing* in SBBY, 3.6a-b.

40. *Wenxuan* (Anthology of poetry and prose), annotated by Li Shan (Hong Kong: Commercial Press, 1974), 99. Zuo Si, alias Taichong, spent ten years writing his famous "Sandufu" (Rhapsody of three capitals), one of which is "Wudufu"; see his biography in *Jin shu* (History of Jin) (Beijing: Zhonghua shuju, 1974), 92.2375-77.

41. Ezekiel Schloss, *Ancient Chinese Ceramic Sculpture from Han through Tang* (Stamford: Castle Publishing, 1977), pl. 25.

42. Shanxi Datong Municipal Museum, "Shanxi Datong Shijiazhai Bei Wei Sima Jinlong mu" (Northern Wei tomb of Sima Jinlong, at Shijiazhai, in Datong, Shanxi), *Wenwu*, 1972, no. 3: 22, 24, 27, and fig. 14.4. Sima Jinlong (buried 484), the son of a celebrated refugee from the South, had claimed to be a member of the imperial Sima clan and so had been treated very generously. Also, Jinlong's mother had been a Wei princess. His tomb, located outside modern Datong in northern Shanxi, is the earliest of the high-ranking Wei burials.

43. I have examined the piece in the exhibition "The Quest for Eternity" and have found the five rectangular holes, as stated in the archaeological report, along the spinal ridge.

44. Hebei Provincial Museum and Cultural Relics Commission, "Hebei Quyang faxian Bei Wei mu" (The discovery of a Northern Wei tomb at Quyang, Hebei), *Kaogu*, 1972, no. 5: 33, and pl. 11.

45. Lefebvre d'Argence, *Chinese Ceramics*, pl. XVI, fig. c, and Schloss, *Ancient Chinese*, pl. 28a.

46. Suide County Museum of Art, "Shaanxi Suide Han huaxiang shimu" (A Han stone tomb with relief representations at Suide, Shaanxi), *Wenwu*, 1983, no. 5: 29, and fig. 2. For additional examples, see Shaanxi Provincial Museum and Shaanxi Provincial Cultural Relics Commission, *Shaanxi Dong Han huaxiang shike xuanji* (A catalogue of Eastern Han pictorial stone reliefs from Shaanxi) (Beijing: Wenwu Press, 1958), figs. 4-5, 29-30, 40-41, 43-44, 68-69, and 106-7

47. Guo Qinghua, "Shaanxi Mianxian Laodaosi sihao Han mu fajue jianbao" (A brief report on the excavation of Han Tomb No. 4 at Laodaosi, in Mianxian, Shaanxi), *Kaogu yu Wenwu*, 1982, no. 2: 26. For an illustration, see Los Angeles County Museum of Art, *The Quest for Eternity: Chinese Ceramic Sculptures from the People's Republic of China*, exh. cat. (San Francisco: Chronicle Books, 1987), 27, bottom (cat. no. 37).

48. Gansu Provincial Museum, "Gansu Wuwei Mojuji Han mu fajue" (The excavation of Han tombs at Mojuji, in Wuwei, Gansu), *Kaogu*, 1960, no. 9: 19.

49. Ibid., 18.

50. Watson, *The Genius*, 120 (cat. no. 225).

51. Ren Rixin, Zhucheng County Museum, "Shandong Zhucheng Han mu huaxiangshi" (Pictorial stone reliefs from a Han tomb in Zhucheng, Shandong), *Wenwu*, 1981, no. 10: 14, and fig. 2.

52. C. Hentz, *Chinese Tomb Figurines* (London: Edward Goldston, 1928), pl. 37a; Suzanne G. Valenstein, *A Handbook of Chinese Ceramics* (New York: The Metropolitan Museum of Art, 1975), pl. 15; and Schloss, *Ancient Chinese*, pl. 18a.

53. Chinese Academy of Social Sciences et al., "Henan Yanshi Xingyuancun di liangzuo Wei Jin mu" (The excavation of two Wei and Jin tombs at Xingyuancun in Yanshi, Henan), *Kaogu*, 1985, no. 5: 733-34, fig. 17.6, and pl. 6.3. For the dating of this tomb to late Western Jin, see Zhang Xiaozhou, "Bei fang diqu Wei Jin shiliu guo muzang di fenqu yu fenqi" (A study on the periodization and regionalization of the tombs of the Wei and Jin of the Sixteen States period in north China), *Kaogu xuebao*, 1987, no. 1: 24-27. For additional excavated examples, see Henan Provincial Bureau of Culture Second Excavation Team, "Luoyang Jin mu di fajue" (The excavation of Jin tombs at Luoyang), *Kaogu xuebao*, 1957, no. 1, pl. 3.8; Henan Provincial Bureau of Culture First Excavation Team, "Henan Zhengzhou Jin mu fajue ji" (A record of the excavation of a Jin tomb at Zhengzhou, Henan), *Kaogu*, 1957, no. 1, pl. 14.4; and Institute of Archaeology Luoyang Excavation Team, "Luoyang Xijiao Jin mu di fajue" (The excavation of Jin tombs at the western suburbs of Luoyang), *Kaogu*, 1959, no. 11, pl. 4.6.

54. Wang Deqing, "Nanjing Shashishan faxian Nanchao mu" (The discovery of a Southern Dynasty tomb at Shashishan in Nanjing), *Kaogu*, 1956, 4: 40-41, and fig. 2; and Jiangsu Provincial Cultural Relics Commission, *Nanjing Liu Chao mu chutu wenwu xuanji* (A catalogue of cultural relics excavated from the Six Dynasties tombs in Nanjing) (Shanghai, 1957), pl. 23.

55. Li Weiran, "Nanjing Liuchao muzang" (Six Dynasties tombs at Nanjing), *Wenwu*, 1959, no. 4: 22, and fig. 15; and Terukazu Akiyama et al., *Arts of Ancient China: Neolithic Cultures to the T'ang Dynasty—Recent Discoveries* (Tokyo: Kodansha, 1968), pl. 362. See also Nanjing Municipal Cultural Relics Commission, "Nanjing Banqiaozhen Shizhahu Jin mu qingli jianbao" (A brief report on the excavation of a Jin tomb at Shizhahu in Banqiaozhen, Nanjing), *Wenwu*, 1965, no. 6: 43, and pl. 4.1.

56. Shaanxi Provincial Cultural Relics Commission, "Xian Renjiakou M229 hao Bei Wei mu qingli jianbao" (A brief report on the excavation of Tomb M229 at Renjiakou, in Xian), *Wenwu*, 1955, no. 12: 62, and fig. 2. See also Akiyama et al., *Arts of Ancient China*, pl. 361.

57. *Han shu* (History of Han) (Beijing: Zhonghua shuju, 1962), 96A.3889.

58. Nanjing Museum of Art, "Jiangsu Danyangxian Huqiao, Jianshan liangzuo Nanchao muzang" (Two Southern Dynasties tombs at Huqiao and Jianshan, in Danyangxian, Jiangsu), *Wenwu*, 1980, no. 2: 4, and fig. 5. There is no doubt that the tomb containing the depiction of the lion belongs to Southern Qi; see ibid., 8-10. The tomb structure as well as the brick wall reliefs are closely similar to the one identified as belonging to Xiao Daosheng (buried circa 478 or after 479); see Nanjing Museum of Art, "Jiangsu Danyang Huqiao Nanchao damu ji zhuanke bihua" (The large Southern Dynasties tomb with pictorial brick reliefs at Danyang, Jiangsu), *Wenwu*, 1974, no. 2: 44-54; and Susan Bush, "Floral Motifs and Vine Scrolls in Chinese Art of Late Fifth to Early Sixth Centuries, A.D.," *Artibus Asiae*, 38, no. 1 (1976): 49-50. For good-quality illustrations, see Yao Qian and Gu Bing, *Liuchao yishu* (Six Dynasties art) (Beijing: Wenwu Press, 1981), pls. 201-2.

59. For tributes from Yueshi, see *Hou Han shu* (History of Later Han) (Beijing: Zhonghua shuju, 1965), 3.158 and 47.1580; from Anxi, see ibid., 4.168 and 4.189; and from Shule, see ibid., 6.263. See also He Zhenghuang, "Shike shuangshi he xiniu" (Stone sculptures of a pair of lions and a rhinoceros), *Wenwu*, 1961, no. 12: 48; Berthold Laufer, *Chinese Pottery of the Han Dynasty* (Leiden: E. J. Brill, 1909), 236-38; and Barry Till, "Some Observations on Stone Winged Chimeras at Ancient Chinese Tomb Sites," *Artibus Asiae* 42, no. 4 (1980), 262, n. 6.

60. Ibid., 262, and fig. 4. See also Osvald Siren, "Indian and Other Influences in Chinese Sculpture," in J. Hackin et al., *Studies in Chinese Art and Some Indian Influences* (London: The India Society, 1938), fig. 2. A similar stone lion is in the former Gualino Collection, Turin; see Till, "Some Observations," fig. 6.

61. Tao Mingkuan and Cao Hengjun, "Lushanxian di Dong Han shike" (The Eastern Han stone sculptures from Lushanxian), *Wenwu*, 1957, no. 10: 41-44, and figs. 2 and 5; and Till, "Some Observations," 262-63, and fig. 7.

62. He Zhenghuang, "Shike shuangshi," 48-49; and Till, "Some Observations," 263, and figs. 8a-b. This pair resembles more the lioness than its counterpart and thus is stylistically different from the Wu Liang lion. He Zhenghuang has some reservations in assigning it to Eastern Han and believes it was probably produced during the early part of the Six Dynasties period.

63. Matsubara Saburo, *Chinese Buddhist Sculpture* (Tokyo, Yoshikawa Kobunkan, 1966), pl. 6.

64. *Nan Qi shu* (History of Southern Qi) (Beijing: Zhonghua shuju, 1972), 26.479.

65. Yao Qian and Gu Bing, *Liuchao yishu*, pls. 50, 64-68, 72-73,

78-79, and 86-87.

66. Nanjing Museum of Art, "Jiangsu Danyang Huqiao Nanchao damu ji zhuanke bihua" (Excavation of a large Southern Dynasties tomb with brick relief murals at Huqiao in Danyang, Jiangsu), *Wenwu*, 1974, no. 2: 48-50; and Lin Shuzhong, "Jiangsu Danyang Nan Qi lingmu Zhuanyin bihua tantao" (A study on the brick relief murals in the Southern Qi imperial tombs at Danyang, Jiangsu), *Wenwu*, 1977, no. 1: 64-73.

67. The theory that the development of Northern Wei art was indebted to influences from the Southern Dynasties was first pointed out by Professor Alexander C. Soper; see his "South Chinese Influence on the Buddhist Art of the Six Dynasties Period," *Bulletin of the Museum of Far Eastern Antiquities* (Stockholm) no. 32 (1960): 47-112. For subsequent affirmation of the theory, see Susan Bush, "Thunder Monsters, Auspicious Animals, and Floral Ornament in Early Sixth-century China," *Ars Orientalis*, no. 10 (1975): 19-33; and "Thunder Monsters and Wind Spirits in Early Sixth Century China and the Epitaph Tablet of Lady Yuan," *Bulletin of the Museum of Fine Arts, Boston* 72, no. 367 (1974): 25-55.

68. Soper, "South Chinese," 56-81.

69. The Cave of the Six Lions is located north of Kuyang Cave; it contains a triad of Buddhas, each of which is flanked by a pair of relief lions (height: 41 cm) seated in the regal posture; see Lungmen Institute of Cultural Preservation, *Longmen Shiku* (Longmen cave temples) (Beijing: Wenwu Press, 1981), note for pl. 101.

70. Ibid., pl. 102. The same iconography appeared in one of the Northern Qi Buddhist cave temples at Xiangtangshan; see Mizuno Seiichi and Nagahiro Toshio, *The Buddhist Cave Temples of Hsiang-t'ang-ssu* (Kyoto: Academy of Oriental Culture, 1937), pls. 10b and 11b. It also appeared in the early Tang Thousand Buddha Cave (Wanfosi) at Longmen; see Edouard Chavannes, pl. clxxxii. This pair of lions was removed from the tomb site and are now kept separately, one in the Nelson-Atkins Museum Art, Kansas City, and the other in the Boston Museum of Fine Arts; see David B. Little, "A Chinese stone lion from Lung-men datable to A.D. 680-1," *Bulletin of the Museum of Fine Arts, Boston* 38, no. 228 (August 1940): 52-53.

71. Yao Qian and Gu Bing, *Liuchao yishu*, pl. 202. As the lions depicted on the brick walls of the Southern Qi tombs are identical in iconography, it is evident that all of them were derived from one and the same source, probably a painting; see Luo Zongzhen, "Nanjing Xishanqiao Youfangcun Nan Chao damu di fajue" (Excavation of a large Southern Dynasties tomb at Youfangcun, in Xishanqiao, Nanjing), *Kaogu*, 1963, no. 6: 300.

72. Mizuno Seiichi and Nagahiro Toshio, *Unko Sekkutsu* (Yun-kang: The Buddhist Cave Temples of the Fifth Century A.D. in North China), vol. 2 (Kyoto: Kyoto University, 1951-56), pls. 21 and 48 (Cave 5); vol. 4, pls. 33, 39, and 40 (Cave 7); and vol. 5, pls. 34 and 37 (Cave 8). For the suggested dates of Cave 5 and Caves 7-8, see Alexander C. Soper, "Imperial Cave-chapels of the Northern Dynasties: Donors, Beneficiaries, Dates," *Artibus Asiae* 28, no. 4 (1966): 244 and 243 respectively.

73. Longmen Institute of Cultural Preservation, *Longmen shiku*, pls. 25 (Guyang Cave, constructed circa 488-528), 58 (Central Binyang Cave, circa 505-23); and 71-72 (Lotus Cave, circa 527).

74. Yang Xuanzhi, *Luoyang jialan ji* (A record of the Buddhist temples in Luoyang), annotated by Fan Xiangyong (Shanghai: Gudian Wenxue Press, 1958), 161-62.

75. Zhenjiang City Museum, "Zhenjiang Dong Jin Huaxiang zhuanmu" (The mold-impressed brick-relief representations of an Eastern Jin tomb in Zhenjiang, Jiangsu), *Wenwu*, 1973, no. 4: 51-55, and figs. 10-11; and Yao Qian and Gu Bing, *Liuchao yishu*, pls. 150-53.

76. Henan Provincial Cultural Relics Commission, *Dengxian caise huaxiang zhuanmu* (The colorful mold-impressed representations from a brick tomb in Dengxian, Henan) (Beijing: Wenwu Press, 1959), color pl. on 9; and Akiyama et al., *Arts of Ancient China*,

color pl. 190. For a study on the mythology of this pair of hybrid birds, see Susan Bush, "Thunder Monsters," 30-51.

77.   *Han shu*, 96A.3889.

78.   Till, "Some Observations," 261 mentions that these monumental sculptures were known by several terms *fuba, taoba, tianlu, bixie,* and *qilin* and that even the Chinese scholars are not sure which term or terms are correct. Chu Hsi-tsu, "T'ien-lu p'i-hsieh k'ao" (A study on *tianlu* and *bixie*), *Monumenta Sinica* 1 (1935): 183-99, pointed out that besides the lion there was the *taoba,* the tribute animal that was introduced to China along with the lion in Western Han. He further mentioned that in the Han dynasty the *tianlu* was placed on the left and the *bixie* on the right side of the tomb (but their positions were reversed in the Six Dynasties), and that the use of the term *qilin* for identifying *tianlu* and *bixie* was a misnomer that occurred during Southern Qi or Liang and persisted into Tang-Song times.

79.   Tang Chi, "Dong Wei Ruru gongzhumu bihua shitan" (A study on the murals in the tomb of the Eastern Wei Ruru princess), *Wenwu,* 1984, no. 4: 14, fig. 3.

80.   *Lunheng* in SBBY, vol 6, 18a.

81.   See note 18.

82.   Yao Qian and Gu Bing, pls. 2 (Song); 4 (Southern Qi); 43, 85 and 87 (Liang); and 111 (Chen).

83.   Shaanxi Provincial Cultural Relics Commission, *Shaanxi sheng,* pls. 28-29.

84.   Ibid., pls. 86-87.

85.   Luoyang Museum, "Luoyang Bei Wei," 219, and pl. 8.1.

86.   Cixian Cultural Center, "Hebei Cixian Dongchencun Dong Wei mu" (An Eastern Wei tomb at Dongchencun in Cixian, Hebei), *Kaogu,* 1977, no. 6: 392, 399-400, fig. 3.8, and pl. 8.3. The epitaph inscription identifies the deceased as Zhao Huren (469-547), a daughter of Prefect Zhao Shang of Nanyang, who was married to Yao Rong, the third son of Yao Xuan (*Bei shi,* 27.998), and who had three sons, Yao Xiong (*Bei Qi shu,* 20.267-69; *Bei shi,* 27.999-1000), Yao Fen (*Bei Qi shu,* 20.269-70), and Yao Jun (no biographies, but see note 10, the report on the excavation of his tomb). Her epitaph cover addresses her as "Wei, the Late Yao shi, Zhao Jun Jun (wife of a fourth-rank official)," as she had been honored as Lady Zhao, Jun Jun of Nanyang.

87.   Wang Kelin, "Bei Qi Kudi Huiluo mu" (The Northern Qi tomb Kudi Huiluo), *Kaogu xuebao,* 1979, no. 3: 391, 399-400, and pl. 7.1. Kudi Huiluo (506-62) has biographies in *Bei Qi shu,* 19.254-55; and *Bei shi,* 53.1908. His epitaph, thirty-one by thirty-one lines of text, has a cover that reads: "Qi, the Late Governor of Dingzhou, Grand Chief of Armies, Prince Kudi of Shunyang." A warrior from the far north whose career began in the service of the Er-zhu family, he fortunately shifted allegiance to Gao Huan in time to share the generous benefits. His first wife, a Lady Hu-lu, given a fifteen by fifteen lines epitaph, died in 545 at age thirty-three and was reburied with him in 562; another wife, Lady Wei, given an eighteen by twenty-one lines epitaph, died in 559 and was also reburied with him.

88.   Chinese Academy of Social Sciences and Institute of Archaeology, *Tang Changan chengjiao Sui Tang mu* (Sui and Tang tombs excavated in the suburbs of Changan [ancient capital] of Tang) (Beijing: Wenwu Press, 1980), 10, 25-28, and pl. XX. Li Jingxun (599-608), who died at the age of nine, has a twenty by twenty lines epitaph with a three by three lines cover that reads: "Sui, Left Guanglu Dafu's daughter." She was the fourth daughter of Li Min, Governor of Qizhou, and great granddaughter of Li Xian (503-69), who during the late Northern Wei upheavals chose to support the future Northern Zhou founder. In appreciation the ruler paid him two personal visits at his home and made him a member of the ruling Yu-wen clan. Later he was honored as "Pillar of the State," Generalissimo and commander-in-chief of the armies of ten provinces, and Governor of Yuanzhou, in western Gansu. His biographies are in *Zhou shu*

(History of Northern Zhou) (Beijing, 1971), 25.413-18; and *Bei shi,* 59.2105-107.

89.   Shaanxi Provincial Cultural Relics Commission, *Shaanxi sheng,* pl. 1. The excavation of his tomb was never published.

90.   Yang Hong, "Zhongguo gudai di jiazhou, xiapian" (Studies on the ancient Chinese armor, part 2), *Kaogu xuebao,* 1976, no. 2: 68-72, and figs. 28-29 and 32-33. They are called *mingguangkai* because the circular plaques fastened to the front and sometimes also to the back plates reflect sunlight. See also Albert E. Dien, "A Study of Early Chinese Armor," *Artibus Asiae* 43, nos. 1-2 (1981-82): 31-32, and figs. 33-34.

91.   Hong Qingyu, "Guanyu Dong Shou mu di faxian he yanjiu" (Concerning the discovery and research on the tomb of Dong Shou), *Kaogu,* 1959, no. 1: 31-35, and fig. 11; and Alexander C. Soper, *Textual Evidence for the Secular Arts of China in the Period from Liu Sung through Sui (A.D. 420-618)* (Ascona: Artibus Asiae Publishers, 1967), 54, and fig. 1. Dong Shou (288-357) had his brief epitaph written in ink on a wall of his tomb. He served one of the barbarian regimes in northeast China, fled to the north Korean kingdom Kokuli as a refugee, and finished his career there. He helped to keep the Korean king in contact by seas with the Eastern Jin regime in the south. Upon his death he was granted middle-rank military, provincial, and court titles by the Jin dynasty.

92.   *Zhouli* in SBBY, 31.6b-7a. For a study of *fangxiangshi,* see Kobayashi Taichiro, "A Study of the Fang-hsiang Expelling Pestilences" (in Japanese) *Shinagaku* 11, no. 4 (1946): 401-47. See also Derk Bodde, *Festivals in Classical China: New Year and Other Annual Observances during the Han Dynasty 206 B.C.-A.D. 220* (Princeton: Princeton University Press, 1975), 77-117.

93.   Shaanxi Provincial Cultural Relics Commission and Xianyang Municipal Museum, "Shaanxi sheng Xianyangshi Yangjiawan chutu dapi Xi Han caihui taoyong" (A large quantity of Western Han painted clay funerary sculptures excavated at Yangjiawan in Xianyang, Shaanxi), *Wenwu,* 1966, no. 3: 1-5; and Shaanxi Provincial Cultural Relics Commission et al., "Xianyang Yangjiawan Han mu fajue jianbao" (The excavation of Han tombs at Xianyang in Yangjiawan), *Wenwu,* 1977, no. 10: 10, 16, and fig. 11.

94.   Chinese Academy of Social Sciences, "Henan Yanshi Xingyuancun di liangzuo Wei Jin mu," 733, figs. 17.1-2, and pl. 6.5.

95.   Nanjing Museum of Art, "Nanjing Fuguaishan Dong Jin mu fajue baogao" (A report on the excavation of an Eastern Jin tomb at Fuguaishan, Nanjing), *Kaogu,* 1966, no. 4: 202, and pl. 6.7.

96.   Berthold Laufer, *Chinese Clay Figures,* pt. 1, in *Field Museum of Natural History* (Chicago), publication 177, anthropological series, 13, no. 2 (1914): 198-99, and pls. XV-XVII; W. A. Thorpe, "Fang Hsiang Shih," *Pantheon* (Munich), 5 (May 1930): 234-38; Hentze, *Chinese Tomb,* 72, and pl. 22; Bodde, *Festivals,* 118, and fig. 1; and Schloss, *Ancient Chinese,* 79-81, and pl. 10. This particular type of warrior figurine has been found in excavated Western Jin tombs and identified simply as *wushiyong* (warrior tomb figurines); see Henan Provincial Bureau, "Luoyang Jin mu," 177, and pl. 3.6; and "Henan Zhengzhou Jin mu," 39, and pl. 14.3; and Chinese Academy of Social Sciences, "Henan Yanshi," 733, figs. 17.1-2, and pl. 6.5.

97.   Chinese Academy, "Henan Yanshi," 726-27, 733-35, and fig. 10.

98.   Zhang Xiaozhou, "Bei fang," 24-27.

99.   All of the Western Jin warriors are characterized by the same type of facial features; see note 96.

100. Xu Pingfang, "Tang Song muzang," 91.

101. Zhang Guangli, "Manhua Xi Han muyong di zaoxing tedian" (A preliminary discussion on the structural characteristics of the Western Han wooden tomb figurines), *Wenwu* 1982, no. 6: 80, and fig. 9.

102. Hunan Provincial Museum, *Changsha Mawangdui,* 100-101, fig. 93,

and pl. 200.

103. Jinancheng Fenghuangshan, "Hubei Jiangling," 5, and fig. 11.

104. *Da Tang liudian*, reprint (Taipei: Wen-hai Publishers, 1962), 14.62b; and Xu Pingfang, "Tang Song muzang," 90. Wang Qufei, "Sishen, jinzi, gaoji" (Four spirits, head kerchiefs, and tall coiffures), *Kaogu*, 1956, no. 5: 50-52, points out that the two sets of tomb-guardian figurines were known as *sishen* (four spirits) during the Kaiyuan era (713-42).

105. *Da Tang liudian*, 23.18b.

106. *Song shi* (History of Song) (Beijing, 1977), 124.2910; and Xu Pingfang, "Tang Song muzang," 90-91.

107. Watson, *The Genius*, 143-44 (cat. nos. 297-98).

108. *Zhouli* in SBBY, 31.7b.

109. Ying Shao, *Fengsu Tongyi xiaoshi* (Tianjin: Renming Press, 1980), 428.

110. Yao Qian and Gu Bing, *Liuchao yishu*, pl. 203.

111. Emperor Xiao Wen (reigned 471-500) became a successor to the Northern Wei throne at the age of nine. The regent, his foster grandmother the Dowager Empress Wen Ming, was a Chinese. A daughter of Fang Lang, who was governor of two important western provinces but was executed for some unspecified offense, she entered the imperial palace. In 454 she became a consort and soon afterwards empress of Emperor Wen Cheng (reigned 452-65) and thus was the first Northern Wei empress of Chinese descent. In 465, when she was twenty-three, she was widowed. Capable and intelligent, she plotted and succeeded in ruling Northern Wei as regent during 476-90, and thus Emperor Xiao Wen was educated and brought up as a Chinese. He was instrumental in bringing more Chinese officials into the Northern Wei court, promulgating the adoption of Chinese models in government administration and style of living, moving the nation's capital from Pencheng (Datong), in northern Shanxi, southward to the ancient Chinese capital site, Luoyang, in Henan, and even changing the imperial family name to the Chinese surname Yuan; see *Wei shu*, 7B.173-79 and 13.328-30; and Soper, "South Chinese Influence," 67-68 and 72-81.

112. Ibid., 78. Wang You's accomplishments are recorded in *Wei shu*, 71.1588-89.

113. See my forthcoming article, "Antecedents of Sui-Tang Burial Practices in Shaanxi" in *Artibus Asiae*.

114. Institute of Archaeology, "Anyang Zhang Sheng," 541, and pl. 9.4.

115. Shaanxi Provincial Museum, "Tang Zheng Rentai," 35, and pl. 4.1. For a similar example kept in the Royal Ontario Museum, Canada, see Medley, *T'ang Pottery*, pl. 43.

116. Yang Hong, "Zhongguo gudai," 76-79 and Table 3.

117. *Tang dazhaoling ji* (Tang imperial edicts) (Taipei: Hua-wen Press,

1968, reprint), 80.12a. The phrase *mu wei zhenshai*, or "[construct] the tomb as a genuine residence" is most explicit.

118. Shaanxi Provincial Cultural Relics Commission, "Shaanxi sheng Sanyuanxian Shuangshengcun Sui Le He mu qingli jianbao" (A brief report on the excavation of the Sui tomb of Li He at Shuangshengcun in Sanyuanxian, Shaanxi), *Wenwu*, 1966, no. 1: 31-33, and fig. 41 (left). The ancestors of Li He (505-82) came from Ditao (Lanzhou today) in Gansu. As a gifted strategist whose rise in an age of constant warfare was already noteworthy at the beginning of Western Wei (535-556), he was awarded the non-Chinese surname Yu-wen, as a special mark of gratitude. Having been invested with military and court titles of honor, he was enfeoffed as a high-ranking duke and a provincial governor. In his old age he was given the highest honor, "Pillar of State." He died a year after the Sui founder overthrew the disintegrating Northern Zhou (557-80) regime. His biographies are in *Zhou shu*, 29.497-98 and *Bei shi*, 66.2323-24.

119. Alexander Coburn Soper, *Literary Evidence for Early Buddhist Art in China* (Ascona: Artibus Asiae Publishers, 1959), 234-35.

120. Perhaps the most striking example is the pair of colossal Heavenly King Guardians in the Fengxian Cave Temple at Longmen; see Longmen Institute of Cultural Preservation, *Longmen shiku*, pls. 154 and 159. For the origin and evolution of the Four Heavenly King Guardians, see Soper, *Literary Evidence*, 231-35.

121. Shaanxi Provincial Cultural Relics Commission, *Shaanxi sheng*, pls. 20-21.

122. According to the surviving images of the Four Heavenly King Guardians in Japan, there does not seem to be a formula for the allocation of the demon-buffalo to a specific Heavenly King Guardian. In the group at Horyu-ji, Nara, Chiguo (Dhrtarastra) of the East stands on a buffalo, but in the group at Daishogun-ji, Osaka, Guangmu ((Virupaksa) of the West stands on it; see Ishida Mosaku, *Bukkyo Bijutsu no Kihon* (Fundamentals of Buddhist Art) (Tokyo: Tokyo Bijutsu, 1967), 125.

123. Shaanxi Provincial Cultural Relics Commission, "Xian Yangtouzhen Tang Li Shuang mu di fajue" (The excavation of the Tang tomb of Li Shuang at Yangtouzhen in Xian), *Wenwu*, 1959, no. 3: 43.

124. Shaanxi Provincial Cultural Relics Commission, "Tang Lin Chuan gongzhu mu chutu di muzhi he zhaoshu" (The excavation of the epitaph and imperial edict tablets of the Tang Princess Lin Chuan), *Wenwu*, 1977, no. 10: 50-52, and figs. 9-10. Princess Lin Chuan (623-82), a daughter of Emperor Tai Zong (reigned 627-50), died at age fifty-nine and was buried in his mausoleum precincts. She is mentioned in *Xin Tang shu* (New history of Tang) (Beijing, Zhonghua shuju, 1975), 83.3646.

125. Chinese Academy of Social Sciences, *Tang Changan chengjiao*, 44-46, and pl. 63.

126. See Table C in my forthcoming article, "Antecedents of Sui-Tang Burial Practices in Shaanxi" in *Artibus Asiae*.

Ancient Mortuary Traditions of China

Designed by Michelle Gauthe´

Electronically composed using the Macintosh IIci
and PageMaker 4.01, text set in Goudy

Printed and bound by Delta Lithograph Company